Praise for
AMONG THE EARLY EVANGELICALS

"It's not every day that a historian upsets the historiographical applecart with new perspectives that essentially transform the way we understand a given subject, but that is exactly what Gorman has done with this book. For decades, scholars of the Stone-Campbell Movement—myself included—have assumed it was quintessentially American in its inception, framework, and ideology. But Gorman, picking up on the work of the late Hiram Lester, has demonstrated that the transatlantic evangelical missions movement of the late eighteenth century shaped the Campbells' thinking on virtually all the key issues that defined the Stone-Campbell tradition—restoration of a simple gospel, missions, the unity of all Christians, and the coming millennial age. Kudos to Gorman for such a trailblazing book!

—**Richard T. Hughes**, author, *Reviving the Ancient Faith: The Story of Churches of Christ in America*

"Readers of James Gorman's illuminating *Among the Early Evangelicals* will learn a great deal not only about the origins of the Stone-Campbell Movement, but also about the shaping of early evangelical Christianity in Britain, Ireland, and America. I recommend Gorman's book enthusiastically."

—**Thomas S. Kidd**, Distinguished Professor of History, Baylor University

"The work of Thomas and Alexander Campbell in creating a new religious tradition that developed into the various branches of the Churches of Christ and Disciples has been seen as a specifically American phenomenon. James Gorman shows that such an estimate is a mistake. On the contrary, their program was rooted in the missions movement of the eighteenth century, culminating in the 1790s, that marked the whole Evangelical world. By the 1790s, there was enthusiasm for discarding denominational obstacles to the spread of the gospel in England, Ireland, and Scotland, and the Campbells imbibed that spirit. This book is a major reinterpretation of the Campbell movement, but it is also more: a case-study that forms a powerful critique of American religious exceptionalism."

—**David Bebbington**, Professor of History, University of Stirling

"Thoroughly informed by transatlantic studies and meticulous in his original research, James Gorman has provided the most comprehensive account to date of the Campbells' crucial interconnectedness with their British evangelical precursors. Moving beyond previous studies, Gorman sets the Campbells squarely in their context, giving new and valuable insights into their passion for unity and restoration. Gorman's work is an important contribution to Stone-Campbell studies and to the new global historiography of the church."

—**Douglas A. Foster**, Professor of Church History, Director of The Center for Restoration Studies, Abilene Christian University

AMONG *the* EARLY
EVANGELICALS

AMONG *the* EARLY EVANGELICALS

THE TRANSATLANTIC ORIGINS OF THE STONE-CAMPBELL MOVEMENT

JAMES L. GORMAN

AMONG THE EARLY EVANGELICALS
The Transatlantic Origins of the Stone-Campbell Movement

Copyright © 2017 by James L. Gorman

ISBN 978-0-89112-582-2

Printed in the United States of America

ALL RIGHTS RESERVED
No part of this publication may be reproduced, stored in a retrieval system, or transmitted in any form by any means—electronic, mechanical, photocopying, recording, or otherwise—without prior written consent.

Library of Congress Cataloguing in Publication Data is on file at the Library of Congress, Washington, DC.

Cover design by Thinkpen Design, LLC
Interior text design by Sandy Armstrong, Strong Design

For information contact:
Abilene Christian University Press
ACU Box 29138
Abilene, Texas 79699

1-877-816-4455
www.acupressbooks.com

17 18 19 20 21 22 / 7 6 5 4 3 2 1

Dedicated to Doug Foster, who got me started on this project, and Richard Hughes, whose insight helped me finish it well.

Acknowledgments

A HOST OF INDIVIDUALS AND INSTITUTIONS HAVE SHAPED THIS book. Doug Foster drew me into Stone-Campbell Movement studies and helped form the basic research question that became this book project. Nearly a decade ago, he suggested I study the Evangelical Society of Ulster for a research project at Abilene Christian University. Researching that question for many years brought me to the conclusions in this book. I am grateful for my colleagues and professors at Baylor University for intellectual challenge and creativity that enlivened this research project. Finally, my thanks to my colleagues and students at Johnson University who encouraged me throughout the research and writing process.

This book is a revision of my dissertation at Baylor University, and I am grateful to my dissertation committee—Bill Pitts, Doug Weaver, Thomas Kidd, and Richard Hughes. I am especially grateful to Richard, who, although not at Baylor, freely offered extensive comments that made this book better and provided much encouragement throughout the writing and researching process. I am grateful for the willingness and ability of Abilene Christian University Press to guide this project from a dissertation into a monograph. Jason Fikes and other readers for ACU Press have shaped this book in positive ways.

My deepest source of encouragement has been my family. My Mom and Dad have always supported academic endeavors, and my Dad, Charles

Gorman, read and commented on early versions of these chapters. Thank you to my wife, Heather Gorman, for loving me and our daughters so well. To my daughters, Anna Marie and Elisabeth Lee, who were born while I worked on this book: I love you more than words can say.

Contents

Chapter One 13
    Reframing the Religious and Historical Context of the
    Campbell Movement

Chapter Two 25
    The Rise of Transatlantic Evangelical Missions in the
    Eighteenth Century

Chapter Three 55
    The Explosion of Transatlantic Evangelical Missions in the 1790s

Chapter Four 95
    Thomas Campbell's Formative Background in Irish
    Evangelical Missions

Chapter Five 125
    The Influence of Scottish Evangelical Missions on
    Alexander Campbell

Chapter Six 153
    From the British Isles to the United States:
    The Christian Association of Washington, 1809–1812

Chapter Seven 189
    A Baptist and Anti-Missionary Viewpoint, 1812–1830

Chapter Eight 209
    Conclusion: The Campbell Movement's Roots in Transatlantic
    Evangelical Missions

Postscript 215
    Viewing Campbell Movement Churches through a New Lens

Bibliography 219

CHAPTER ONE

Reframing the Religious and Historical Context of the Campbell Movement

When Alexander Campbell became the first president of the American Christian Missionary Society in 1849, his supporters and opponents asked legitimate questions about the consistency of his position on missionary societies. Twenty-five years prior to this appointment, Campbell vehemently rejected the legitimacy of missionary and other parachurch societies in his iconoclastic religious periodical, *The Christian Baptist*. Campbell critiqued these societies throughout the 1820s for numerous reasons—lack of New Testament commands or examples for parachurch societies, the proclivity of missionary societies to perpetuate (instead of destroy) denominationalism, the large sums of money missionaries made, the perceived disproportionate expense of the missionary enterprise to the number of converts, and the seeming opposition of missionary societies to Jesus's plan for the conversion of the world (John 17:20–23 suggests that Christian unity would lead to conversion of the world).

However, as Campbell warmed to the practice of congregations' cooperating for missions and other ministries, he wrote a series of articles in the 1830s and 1840s to defend parachurch cooperation. He argued that missionary societies were expedient means to accomplish missions, and he appealed to New Testament examples of congregations' cooperating. Therefore, although by 1849 Campbell had justified the propriety of his presidency of the American Christian Missionary Society, many within the Stone-Campbell Movement[1] who preferred his 1820s writings had trouble accepting missionary societies. Indeed, the American Christian Missionary Society, along with parachurch societies, became one of the key issues of contention leading to the first major division of the Stone-Campbell Movement.[2]

The central place and contentious nature of missionary societies in the first century of the Stone-Campbell Movement ensured the prominence of missions in its historiography, but these and other factors also led, ironically, to the omission of missions in its historiographical origins. That is, Campbell's anti-societies rhetoric in the 1820s has detracted the attention of historians from Campbell's missions ideas before 1823—the year that Campbell began the *Christian Baptist*—to critique all the denominations for not following the New Testament pattern of worship, government, and discipline. Nearly all the scholarly work on the history of missions in the Stone-Campbell Movement begins with Campbell's anti-missionary society arguments recorded in *The Christian Baptist*, or focuses on the subsequent missionary-society controversy that was a determinative issue for the first major division of the Movement.[3] Consequently, historians have almost

---

[1] The Stone-Campbell Movement (a.k.a. Restoration Movement) took definitive shape in early nineteenth-century America under the leadership of reformers Thomas Campbell, Alexander Campbell, Barton Stone, and Walter Scott. As the Stone and Campbell Movements grew separately in the 1820s, many noticed the similarities of the two and sought to unify them. Beginning in 1832, Campbell and Stone congregations began uniting, marking the beginning of the merged "Stone-Campbell Movement." In this study, I focus only on the Campbell tradition, as that in itself has more than enough to fill the pages of this book. Even so, a fruitful area of future research will be examining the leaders of the "Christians" (e.g., Abner Jones, Elias Smith, Barton Stone, Rice Haggard, and James O'Kelly) with the same questions about religious and historical context that I have put to the Campbell tradition in this volume.

[2] Doug Priest, "Missionary Societies, Controversy Over," ed. Douglas A. Foster et al., *The Encyclopedia of the Stone-Campbell Movement* (Grand Rapids: Eerdmans, 2004), 534–36.

[3] For example, see David. S. Burnet, *The Jerusalem Mission Under the Direction of the American Christian Missionary Society* (New York: Arno Press, 1977); Martin Bailey Clark, "The Missionary Position of the Movement of Disciples of Christ in the Early Years of the Nineteenth Century Reformation" (master's thesis, Butler University, 1949); Morrison Meade Davis, *How the Disciples Began and Grew: A Short History of the Christian Church* (Cincinnati: Standard Publishing Company, 1915); Anthony L. Dunnavant, *Restructure: Four Historical Ideals in the Campbell-Stone Movement and the Development of the Polity of the Christian Church (Disciples of Christ)* (New York: P. Lang, 1993); David Filbeck, *The First Fifty Years: A Brief History of the Direct-Support Missionary Movement* (Joplin: College Press, 1980); Phillip Wayne Elkins, *Church-Sponsored Missions: An Evaluation of Churches of Christ* (Austin: Firm Foundation Publishing House, 1974); Francis Marion Green, *Christian Missions, and Historical Sketches of Missionary Societies Among the Disciples of Christ: With Historical and Statistical Tables* (St. Louis: J. Burns Pub. Co., 1884); Bill J. Humble, "The Missionary Society Controversy in the Restoration Movement (1823–1875)"

completely neglected Campbell's substantial connection to the missionary movement prior to 1823.[4] Historians have seen a "first Campbell" in the 1820s who opposed missionary societies, and a "second Campbell" who eventually embraced them. But there was a "third," or chronologically "first," Campbell who was drastically different from the Campbell of the 1820s. For more than twenty years before the 1820s, Alexander Campbell and his father, Thomas Campbell, received their most influential religious formation in the evangelical missionary movement. The influences of the evangelical missionary movement that emerged throughout the transatlantic region in the 1790s was the clearest and most comprehensive context that produced the earliest manifestation of the Campbell Movement in 1809.

The findings in this book expand the historical understanding of Stone-Campbell Movement origins, and they propose a historiographical revision. If this study is correct in locating Campbell's roots in earlier evangelical missions, why have historians previously missed this connection? Not all of them have. Robert Richardson's *Memoirs of Alexander Campbell* tangentially notes the influence of the Irish and Scottish missions milieu on both Campbells, but Richardson simply did not have the primary or secondary sources to construct the larger religious context.[5] Although subsequent historians have relied on Richardson's account, scholars quickly lost sight of Richardson's claims about the importance of the new missionary movement in the formation of the Campbells. Instead, later historians sought to identify

---

(PhD diss., University of Iowa, 1964); Walter Wilson Jennings, *Origin and Early History of the Disciples of Christ: With Special Reference to the Period Between 1809 and 1835* (Cincinnati: The Standard Publishing Company, 1919); George Kresel, "Alexander Campbell's Theology of Missions" (PhD diss., Boston University, 1961); Thomas H. Olbricht, "Missions and Evangelization Prior to 1848," *Discipliana* 58, no. 3 (Fall 1998): 67-79; Doug Priest, *Unto the Uttermost: Missions in the Christian Churches/Churches of Christ* (Pasadena: William Carey Library, 1984); Priest, "Missionary Societies, Controversy Over"; Henry Webb, "A History of the Independent Mission Movement of the Disciples of Christ" (PhD diss., Southern Baptist Theological Seminary, 1954); Paul Allen Williams, "Missions, Missiology," ed. Douglas A. Foster et al., *The Encyclopedia of the Stone-Campbell Movement* (Grand Rapids: Eerdmans, 2004).

[4] One of the few exceptions is Anthony Dunnavant's 1984 dissertation, published in 1993. He argued that four ideals—restoration, unity, liberty, and missions—constituted the main thrust of the founders and followers of the Movement, though later generations stressed one or several ideals over others. He was primarily interested to note the connection between the Christian Association of Washington and extra-congregational organization, but he does hint at the missionary-society backgrounds of the Association. Anthony Leroy Dunnavant, "Restructure: Four Historical Ideals in the Campbell-Stone Movement and the Development of the Polity of the Christian Church (Disciples of Christ)" (PhD diss., Vanderbilt University, 1984).

[5] Robert Richardson, *Memoirs of Alexander Campbell: Embracing A View of the Origin, Progress and Principles of the Religious Reformation Which He Advocated*, vol. 1 (Cincinnati: Standard Publishing Company, 1890), 59-60, 71-75, 149-63, 233-42.

a number of important backgrounds to the Campbell tradition that made it seem uniquely American.[6] Nathan Hatch's focus on democratization led him to interpret the Stone-Campbell Movement as "that most American of denominations,"[7] while W. E. Garrison utilized Frederick Jackson Turner's thesis to suggest that the frontier created the Campbells.[8] Others have looked to Great Britain for early influences, but they typically focused on Lockean origins of unity or Scottish origins of restorationism.[9] Richard Hughes and Leonard Allen argued for Protestant Reformation, Christian Humanist, and Puritan origins.[10] But it was not until the work of David Thompson and the discoveries of Hiram Lester in the 1980s that some of the earlier connections between these various influences became clearer.[11] This book picks up where Lester left off.[12]

Religious and Historical Context

The Campbells were formed in the religious and historical context of transatlantic evangelical missions, so each of these three terms is important and deserves brief definition.

---

[6] For example, see Paul Keith Conkin, *American Originals: Homemade Varieties of Christianity* (Chapel Hill: University of North Carolina Press, 1997), 1–56.

[7] Nathan O. Hatch, *The Democratization of American Christianity* (New Haven: Yale University Press, 1989), 220.

[8] Winfred Ernest Garrison, *Religion Follows the Frontier: A History of the Disciples of Christ* (New York: Harper & Brothers Publishers, 1931).

[9] After analyzing accounts of denominational and U.S. religious historians, I have explained elsewhere how historians omitted the influence of transatlantic evangelical missions culture in favor of origins that seemed more useful or obvious based on later historical developments, personal agendas, and frameworks for historical interpretation. See my forthcoming article and/or chapter of my dissertation: James L. Gorman, "The Omission of Missions: Transatlantic Evangelicalism and the Historiography of Stone-Campbell Movement Origins" *Stone-Campbell Journal, forthcoming*; James L. Gorman, "Transatlantic Evangelical Missions Culture and the Rise of the Campbell Movement" (PhD diss., Baylor University, 2015), chap. 2.

[10] Richard T. Hughes and C. Leonard Allen, *Illusions of Innocence: Protestant Primitivism in America, 1630-1875* (Abilene, TX: Abilene Christian University Press, 2008), 4.

[11] David M. Thompson, *Let Sects and Parties Fall: A Short History of the Association of Churches of Christ in Great Britain and Ireland* (Birmingham: Berean Press, 1980), 9; David M. Thompson, "The Irish Background to Thomas Campbell's *Declaration and Address*," *Journal of the United Reformed Church History Society* 3, no. 6 (1985): 215–25; David M. Thompson, "The Irish Background to Thomas Campbell's *Declaration and Address*," *Discipliana* 46 (1986): 23–27; Hiram J. Lester, "The Form and Function of the *Declaration and Address*," in *The Quest for Christian Unity, Peace, and Purity in Thomas Campbell's* Declaration and Address: *Text and Studies*, eds. Thomas H. Olbricht and Hans Rollmann, ATLA Monograph Series 46 (Lanham: Scarecrow Press, 2000), 173–92; Hiram J. Lester, "Alexander Campbell's Early Baptism in Ecumenicity and Sectarianism," *Restoration Quarterly* 30 (1988): 85–101; Hiram J. Lester, "An Irish Precursor for Thomas Campbell's Declaration and Address," *Encounter* 50, no. 3 (1989): 247–67; Hiram J. Lester, "The Case Against Sectarianism," *The Disciple* 17, no. 3 (1990): 10–12.

[12] For a thorough historiography, see James L. Gorman, "The Omission of Missions."

"Transatlantic" signifies both the geographical areas around the transatlantic basin and also the historical perspective utilized in this book, which seeks to move the boundary of historical inquiry from national to transnational.[13] Central to transnational history is the attempt to deprovincialize U.S. history in order to highlight the ways in which various nations and cultures have shaped each other, assuming that history is richer when viewed from a wider vantage point.[14] A transatlantic perspective of history is especially useful in the study of evangelicalism, which has been a transatlantic movement from its beginnings.

"Evangelical"[15] has had many meanings throughout history, which has made it a term of controversy among scholars.[16] Nonetheless, two converging descriptions (one historical and one theological) of "evangelical" restrict it enough to form a historically coherent subject, while not denying the immense diversity within the category.[17] In a historical sense, a discrete network of Protestant Christian movements arose during the eighteenth century in Great Britain and its colonies, and in Germany. Four major

---

[13] Nicholas Canny and Phillip Morgan, "Introduction: The Making and Unmaking of an Atlantic World," in *The Oxford Handbook of the Atlantic World: 1450–1850*, eds. Nicholas Canny and Phillip Morgan, (Oxford: Oxford University Press, 2012); Philip D. Morgan and Jack P. Greene, *Atlantic History: A Critical Appraisal*, Reinterpreting History (Oxford: Oxford University Press, 2009); Ian Tyrrell, "Reflections on the Transnational Turn in United States History: Theory and Practice," *Journal of Global History* 4, no. 3 (2009): 453–74; Ian Tyrrell, *Transnational Nation: United States History in Global Perspective since 1789* (New York: Palgrave Macmillan, 2007); Thomas Bender, ed., *Rethinking American History in a Global Age* (Berkeley: University of California Press, 2002).

[14] Will Kaufman and Heidi Slettedahl Macpherson, "Introduction," in *New Perspectives in Transatlantic Studies* (Lanham: University Press of America, 2002), xi–xxv.

[15] It should be noted that late eighteenth and early nineteenth-century Christians used the term "evangelical" to describe themselves, their theologies, and their voluntary societies. In my use of "evangelical," I follow David Bebbington's *Evangelicalism in Modern Britain* and Mark Hutchinson's and John Wolffe's *A Short History of Global Evangelicalism*. On evangelicals, see David W. Bebbington, *Evangelicalism in Modern Britain: A History from the 1730s to the 1980s* (London: Routledge, 1989), 1–19; Mark Hutchinson and John Wolffe, *A Short History of Global Evangelicalism* (Cambridge: Cambridge University Press, 2012), 1–25; Mark A. Noll, D. W. Bebbington, and George A. Rawlyk, "Introduction," in *Evangelicalism: Comparative Studies of Popular Protestantism in North America, the British Isles, and Beyond 1700–1990*, eds. Mark A. Noll, D. W. Bebbington, and George A. Rawlyk (New York: Oxford University Press, 1994), 3–15; Timothy Larsen, "Defining and Locating Evangelicalism," in *The Cambridge Companion to Evangelical Theology*, eds. Timothy Larsen and Daniel J. Treier (Cambridge: Cambridge University Press, 2007), 1–14; Mark A. Noll, *The Rise of Evangelicalism: The Age of Edwards, Whitefield, and the Wesleys*, A History of Evangelicalism 1 (Downers Grove: InterVarsity Press, 2003), 15–21; W. R. Ward, "Evangelical Awakenings in the North Atlantic World," in *The Cambridge History of Christianity: Volume VII, Enlightenment, Reawakening and Revolution 1660–1815*, eds. Stewart J. Brown and Timothy Tackett (Cambridge: Cambridge University Press, 2006), 329–47.

[16] For these meanings, see *The Oxford English Dictionary*, 2nd ed. (Oxford: Clarendon, 1989), 5:447–50. A current analysis of the debate is found in Hutchinson and Wolffe, *Short History of Global Evangelicalism*, 1–25.

[17] This two-prong description relies on Noll, Bebbington, and Rawlyk, "Introduction," 1–6.

tributaries fed into the river of evangelicalism.[18] First and most influential was English Puritanism, which included Baptists, Independents, and English Presbyterians. Second, Scottish Presbyterianism was a transatlantic evangelical force, as the Scottish diaspora from the early seventeenth century created evangelical hubs in places such as Ireland and Pennsylvania.[19] Third, high-church Anglicanism provided the form of voluntary religious societies that became the key structure through which evangelicals influenced Christianity. Also, devotional societies like the Holy Club were prominent especially in Bristol and London, and most famously contributed to the development of leading evangelical personalities George Whitefield and John Wesley. Fourth, continental Pietism contributed to the beginnings of new-birth experiential theology, small gatherings for Bible reading and lay participation, social activism through August Hermann Francke's institutional ingenuity at the University of Halle, and the vision of the Moravian community for missions. By the middle of the eighteenth century, the confluence of these tributaries had created a distinctive transatlantic evangelical community that grew to dominate the social life of some areas.[20] This historical sense of "evangelical" is complemented by a theological description based on a pattern of convictions and attitudes, which include, according to David Bebbington, "biblicism (a reliance on the Bible as ultimate religious authority), conversionism (a stress on new birth), activism (an energetic, individualistic approach to religious duties and social involvement), and crucicentrism (a focus on Christ's redeeming work as the heart of essential Christianity)."[21]

---

[18] I borrow the tributaries metaphor from Hutchinson and Wolffe, *A Short History of Global Evangelicalism*, 1–25.

[19] The Campbells lived in both Ulster and Pennsylvania, following the enormous Scotch-Irish migrations to Pennsylvania in the colonial and early national periods. See Peter Gilmore, "Rebels and Revivals: Ulster Immigrants, Western Pennsylvania Presbyterianism and the Formation of Scotch-Irish Identity, 1780–1830" (PhD diss., Carnegie Mellon University, 2009).

[20] This discrete network of Protestants throughout England, Scotland, Wales, Ireland, Germany, and North America experienced a series of intense religious "awakenings," often associated with revivals and experiential conversion. The confluence of Protestant tributaries does not necessitate continuity with those tributaries. In fact, discontinuity was an important factor in the intensity of the religious awakenings and crucial for evangelical identity. See Hutchinson and Wolffe, *A Short History of Global Evangelicalism*, 26–32; Thomas S. Kidd, *The Great Awakening: The Roots of Evangelical Christianity in Colonial America* (New Haven: Yale University Press, 2007), xiv.

[21] Bebbington, *Evangelicalism in Modern Britain*, 1–19; Noll, Bebbington, and Rawlyk, "Introduction," 6.

"**Missions**" in this book is shorthand for the Protestant missionary movement that arose throughout the eighteenth century and reached fever pitch in the 1790s. Historian Ruth Rouse claims, "No outburst of missionary zeal, unless it be the Jesuit Mission of the 16th century, has ever paralleled the missionary developments resulting from the Evangelical Awakening between 1790 and 1820."[22] Historians agree that the Protestant missionary movement was an evangelical undertaking. And although there were a handful of missionary efforts prior, the 1790s witnessed the rise of the leaders and missionary societies that shaped the subsequent history of world Christianity. Some of the missionary societies were voluntary interdenominational groups, and others were governed by single denominations. Nearly all missions advocates believed that the missionary errand at that moment in time was eschatologically charged—they were participating in carrying the gospel to the "heathen" in anticipation of the return of Christ. The Campbells' major religious influences in Ireland, England, and Scotland were all leaders of the interdenominational missionary movement which, in the 1790s, had distinctive features that the Campbells adopted.

In the 1790s, advocates of interdenominational missions across the transatlantic basin constructed what anthropologist Clifford Geertz calls a religious "culture."[23] For Geertz, culture denotes a "historically transmitted pattern of meanings embodied in symbols, a system of inherited conceptions expressed in symbolic forms by means of which [people] communicate, perpetuate, and develop their knowledge about and attitudes toward life."[24] Evangelicals concerned with interdenominational missions created a

---

[22] Ruth Rouse, "Voluntary Movement and the Changing Ecumenical Climate," in *A History of the Ecumenical Movement, 1517–1948*, ed. Ruth Rouse and Stephen Charles Neill, 3rd ed. (Geneva: World Council of Churches, 1986), 310.

[23] Geertz's analytical categories have been and continue to be useful to historians for a number of reasons, especially for his view of cultures as particular (i.e., they are all different) and his argument that scholars should describe other cultures based on their own perspectives and ideas. Clifford Geertz, "Thick Description: Toward an Interpretive Theory of Culture," in *The Interpretation of Cultures: Selected Essays* (New York: Basic Books, 2000), 3–30; Clifford Geertz, "Religion as a Cultural System," in *The Interpretation of Cultures: Selected Essays* (New York: Basic Books, 2000), 87–125; Rosalind I. J. Hackett, "Anthropology of Religion," in *The Routledge Companion to the Study of Religion*, ed. John Hinnells, 2nd ed. (New York: Routledge, 2010), 165–68; Daniel L. Pals, *Seven Theories of Religion* (New York: Oxford University Press, 1996), 233–67; Brian M. Howell and Jenell Williams Paris, *Introducing Cultural Anthropology: A Christian Perspective* (Grand Rapids: Baker Academic, 2011), 175–99. Most of the essays in *The Interpretation of Cultures* were written in the 1960s, and Basic Books published the first edition of this volume of essays in 1973. Geertz wrote "Thick Description" in 1973 as an introduction to these essays.

[24] Geertz, "Religion as a Cultural System," 89.

conceptual world with their magazines, sermons, prayers, societies, missionary errands, interactions with the "heathen" world, and public gatherings, which dramatically influenced the way an entire generation of religious leaders viewed Christianity, the world, and the role of the Christian in both. Consistent use of symbols, especially embodied ritual actions of itinerant preaching, missionary meetings, and periodicals, solidified the culture. It was in these ritual or ceremonial actions that people became convinced of the veracity of their religious conceptions.

For example, among the most pervasive motivations for evangelical missions was a desire to cooperate with other Christians to spread a simple evangelical gospel to otherwise damned "heathens" around the world. Missions leaders argued that Christians of different denominations could unite in prayer and missions because, despite different denominational affiliation, they shared a commitment to the "primitive," "apostolic," or "simple" gospel that preceded and superseded their denominational identities. Furthermore, the challenges of converting the "heathen" world required a united effort among evangelicals. The manifestation of Christian unity for missions in the voluntary societies and the actual missionaries they sent both suggested to these evangelicals that God blessed their work, and that they did this work in the last days. These ideas and practices about unity, a simple gospel, evangelizing the world, and the end-times became inextricably linked in the evangelical conception of and attitude toward daily Christian life. The evangelical missions culture brought unity, restoration, missions, and millennialism together into a persuasive religious package.

By the end of the eighteenth century, transatlantic evangelicals who were devoted to missions constituted an identifiable religious culture that centered on transatlantic evangelical missions. This culture immensely influenced Thomas and Alexander Campbell. Motivated by millennial anticipation, pity for the "heathen," and a belief that converted Christians in all denominations could unite for prayer and missions based upon a primitive gospel devoid of party and sect, many missions advocates utilized voluntary societies as a means for interdenominational cooperation to accomplish their worldwide errand. The Campbells came onto the scene in the midst of this religious and historical context. Both men imbibed this evangelical missions culture, which motivated their early religious movement in the United States.

Telling a Transatlantic, Evangelical, and Restorationist Story

From its inception in the early eighteenth century, the Protestant missionary movement was a transatlantic project of evangelicals, which is the story presented in Chapter Two. Evangelicals who constructed and shaped the missionary movement combined ideals and practices that became distinct to this religious culture, though different advocates naturally emphasized some parts more than others. Constructing transatlantic evangelical missions from its beginning provides a foundation for examining the solidification of this effort in the 1790s.

Transatlantic evangelical missions reached its apex in 1795 with the founding of the London Missionary Society. Protestant Christians of different denominations gathered together in London for four days in September 1795 to organize the London Missionary Society, which was the most influential interdenominational missionary society of the era. Excitement at this interdenominational cooperation for missionary efforts burst like rhetorical fireworks, as evidenced from missionary sermons and reports of the founding meetings. For example, leading missions advocate David Bogue optimistically proclaimed in his sermon at the London Missionary Society foundational meetings, "Behold us here assembled with one accord to attend the funeral of *bigotry*."[25] For Bogue and his contemporaries, interdenominational cooperation for missionary action harbingered, on the one hand, the death of "bigotry" or "partyism," and on the other, the imminent, latter-day, millennial reign of Christ.

The London Missionary Society became the hub of evangelical networking for missions and the model for dozens of smaller societies created in the transatlantic region over the next two decades. In 1805, ten years after the founding of the London Missionary Society, Edward Dorr Griffin in his missionary sermon, "The Kingdom of Christ," said to the General

---

[25] David Bogue, "Objections Against A Mission to the Heathen, Stated and Considered," in *Sermons, Preached in London, at the Formation of the Missionary Society, September 22, 23, 24, 1795; To Which Are Prefixed, Memorials, Respecting the Establishment and First Attempts of That Society* (London: printed and sold by T. Chapman, 1795), 130.

Assembly in Pennsylvania that some believed they already saw the "light purpling the east" as the "dawn of a better day" approached in the wake of the founding of "numerous missionary societies . . . on both sides of the Atlantic."[26] In 1809, Samuel Worcester proclaimed to a meeting of the Massachusetts Missionary Society that the day of the founding of the London Missionary Society "will long be held in grateful remembrance, as a distinguished epoch in the annals of Christendom." Worcester believed the institution of the London Missionary Society produced "an influence more grateful than the dew of Hermon, than the dew that descended on the mountains of Zion. The holy flame there lighted from the altar of heaven, spread with rapidity in all directions."[27] Worcester lauded the work because of its influence in prompting so many more likeminded societies. Chapter Three describes the solidification of the evangelical missionary culture in the 1790s and devotes significant space to the central institution of the London Missionary Society.

Chapters Four and Five cover the major evangelical influences on Thomas and Alexander Campbell in Great Britain. The Evangelical Society of Ulster in Ireland constituted a sister society of the London Missionary Society. Thomas Campbell (1763–1854) cofounded the Evangelical Society of Ulster, and argued for its legitimacy to his Presbyterian Synod when it came under attack. Both Campbells heard some of the leading architects of the interdenominational missionary movement through their connection to the Evangelical Society of Ulster. In Scotland, few leaders of the early missionary movement were more influential than Greville Ewing and brothers James and Robert Haldane. Not only did the Haldanes' Society for Propagating the Gospel at Home cooperate with Thomas Campbell's Evangelical Society of Ulster, but Ewing became a major influence and mentor of Alexander Campbell during Campbell's time in Scotland. Chapters Four and Five

---

[26] Edward Dorr Griffin, *The Kingdom of Christ: A Missionary Sermon Preached before the General Assembly of the Presbyterian Church in Philadelphia, May 23, 1805* (Philadelphia: printed by Jane Aitken, 1805), 25; William R. Hutchinson, *Errand to the World: American Protestant Thought and Foreign Missions* (Chicago: University of Chicago Press, 1987), 55.

[27] Samuel Worcester, "Sermon to the Massachusetts Missionary Society, May 1809," in *The Life and Labors of Rev. Samuel Worcester, D.D.*, ed. Samuel Melancthon Worcester (Boston: Crocker and Brewster, 1852), 2:72–73; Charles Maxfield, "The 'Reflex Influence' of Missions: The Domestic Operations of the American Board of Commissioners for Foreign Missions, 1810–1850" (PhD diss., Union Theological Seminary, 1995), 58–59.

devote substantial space to describing the evangelical missions work in Ireland and Scotland in the 1790s and 1800s, because it comprised the context that most powerfully shaped the earliest writings and actions of the Campbell Movement in the United States. In Ireland and Scotland, as in other parts of the transatlantic, interdenominational missionary societies emphasized Christian unity for the purpose of evangelizing the world with a simple evangelical gospel, and were often driven by millennial rhetoric. It's no coincidence that the early Campbell Movement shared all of these emphases, nor that Thomas Campbell's first organization in the United States was an interdenominational evangelical missionary society (the Christian Association of Washington), in form and function similar to the ones he knew in Great Britain.

Chapter Six examines the Christian Association of Washington, founded in Pennsylvania by Thomas Campbell in 1809, and compares and contrasts it to the evangelical missions environment from whence it came. Chapter Seven recounts the Campbells' support of missionary societies until 1821 and Alexander Campbell's anti-missionary society campaign which began in 1823, and explains reasons for that drastic change.

The Conclusion summarizes the overarching argument of the book, which is that the Campbell Movement in the United States emerged from transatlantic evangelical missions of the late eighteenth and early nineteenth centuries. The earliest Campbell tradition, as articulated in the Christian Association of Washington and its 1809 *Declaration and Address*, was more indebted to the evangelical missionary movement than it was to the fertile frontier and democratic soil in the United States. The latter inextricably influenced the development and trajectory of the Movement, but the Christian Association of Washington and its *Declaration and Address* emerged from transatlantic evangelical missions, and not from anything uniquely American.

Chapter Two

THE RISE OF TRANSATLANTIC EVANGELICAL MISSIONS IN THE EIGHTEENTH CENTURY

BORN-AGAIN CHRISTIANS IN THE EIGHTEENTH CENTURY CREated a robust missions infrastructure that provided ample raw materials for later interdenominational missions and Bible and tract societies of the 1790s and beyond. Thomas and Alexander Campbell were greatly influenced by these transatlantic evangelical missions societies, which shared several core characteristics:[1]

---

[1] Many scholars have traced the origins of the missionary movement to earlier evangelical awakenings. Andrew F. Walls, "The Evangelical Revival, the Missionary Movement, and Africa," in *The Missionary Movement in Christian History: Studies in the Transmission of Faith* (Maryknoll: Orbis Books, 1996), 79-80; Ruth Rouse, "Voluntary Movement and the Changing Ecumenical Climate," in *A History of the Ecumenical Movement, 1517-1948*, eds. Ruth Rouse and Stephen Charles Neill, 3rd ed. (Geneva: World Council of Churches, 1986), 309-10; Martin Schmidt, "Ecumenical Activity on the Continent of Europe in the Seventeenth and Eighteenth Centuries," in *A History of the Ecumenical Movement, 1517-1948*, eds. Ruth Rouse and Stephen Charles Neill, 3rd ed. (Geneva: World Council of Churches, 1986), 84; Charles L. Chaney, *The Birth of Missions in America* (Pasadena: William Carey Library, 1976); Wilbert R. Shenk, *Changing Frontiers of Mission*, American Society of Missiology Series 28 (Maryknoll: Orbis Books, 1999), 143; Douglas A. Sweeney, *The American Evangelical Story: A History of the Movement* (Grand Rapids: Baker Academic, 2005), 79; W. R. Ward, "Evangelical Awakenings in the North Atlantic World," in *The Cambridge History of Christianity: Volume VII, Enlightenment, Reawakening and Revolution 1660-1815*, eds. Stewart J. Brown and Timothy Tackett (Cambridge: Cambridge University Press, 2006), 329-32; Mark A. Noll, *The Rise of Evangelicalism: The Age of Edwards, Whitefield, and the Wesleys*, A History of Evangelicalism 1 (Downers Grove: InterVarsity Press, 2003), 223-32; Thomas S. Kidd, *The Great Awakening: The Roots of Evangelical Christianity in Colonial America* (New Haven: Yale University Press, 2007), chap. 13; Mark Hutchinson and John Wolffe, *A Short History of Global Evangelicalism* (Cambridge:

- Interdenominational cooperation for prayer and missions
  - Interdenominational cooperation was bolstered by Enlightenment ideals of toleration.
  - "Partyism" precluded the unity and cooperation required for the enormous task at hand (i.e., convert the "heathen").
  - Cooperation signaled the death of "bigotry" and "partyism."
  - Cooperation and the end of "partyism" harbingered the imminent return of Christ.
- A means of cooperation for missions (e.g. voluntary societies that allowed individuals from different denominations to cooperate)
- A basis of cooperation (e.g. a "primitive," "simple," "apostolic," or "evangelical" gospel that preceded the historical denominations)
- Interdenominational cooperation, subsequent missions to the "heathen," and the Atlantic revolutions, which suggested the imminence of the last days (unity and missions-fueled millennialism)
- Millennialism as a motive for a united missions effort (millennialism fueled cooperative missions).

This chapter describes the development of transatlantic evangelical missions from their evangelical roots in the early eighteenth century, and covers the most influential proponents of Protestant missions before the 1790s.

The Rise of Evangelical Missions: Pietists, Puritans, and Moravians

Continental Pietism was one of the major tributaries feeding into the evangelical missionary movement.[2] Lutheran minister Philip Jacob Spener's (1635–1705) *Pia Desideria* (1675) laid the foundations of Pietism. Spener's thought was indebted to mystical theologians such as Johann Arndt

---

Cambridge University Press, 2012), 26–36; James A. De Jong, *As the Waters Cover the Sea: Millennial Expectations in the Rise of Anglo-American Missions, 1640–1810*, 2006 reprint (Kampen: J. H. Kok, 1970); Andrew Porter, "Church History, History of Christianity, Religious History: Some Reflections on British Missionary Enterprise since the Late Eighteenth Century," *Church History* 71, no. 3 (2002): 567–76; Dana Lee Robert, "Introduction," in *Converting Colonialism: Visions and Realities in Mission History, 1706–1914*, ed. Dana Lee Robert, Studies in the History of Christian Missions (Grand Rapids: Eerdmans, 2008), 1–20.

[2] Hutchinson and Wolffe, *Short History of Global Evangelicalism*, 30–32.

(1555–1621), who taught an experiential, inward piety.[3] Historian Peter Erb explains, "Unlike his Orthodox opponents, Spener focused more on the subjective appropriation of the believer's redemption than on God's objective saving act in history in the incarnation."[4] Spener sought to revitalize the Lutheran church after the Thirty Years' War, teaching that the concept of priesthood of believers meant all Christians should mimic the love of Christ and lead lives of intense devotion and study. Spener's Pietism proposed small gatherings (*collegias pietas*) devoted to Bible study and discussion, the practice of love in conjunction with knowledge, the practice of charity in religious controversy, and heartfelt preaching that emphasized holy living rather than doctrinal polemics.[5] Pietism increased its organization under the patronage of Frederick III, Elector of Brandenburg and Duke of Prussia, who founded the University of Halle in 1694. Under the leadership of August Hermann Francke, Halle became the central hub of Pietist activity and a major influence on the early Protestant missionary movement.[6]

The major contributions of Pietism to evangelical missions included a proto-ecumenical ecclesiology centered on experiential new birth and an emphasis on cooperative missions.[7] For example, Frederick III promoted Pietism in an explicit effort to popularize a type of Christianity, one focused on inward piety and practice, that could build bridges between Reformed and Lutheran groups in his realm.[8] The focus on new birth, especially as Francke taught it, represented a radical breakthrough into establishing the kingdom of God.[9] This new-birth experience shaped Pietist and evangelical ecclesiology in the sense that it became a basis of fellowship for Christians in various denominations. As scholar Martin Schmidt describes, the new birth "brings into being an invisible, 'spiritual' Church, which, as the true Church, reaches far beyond all the limits of all the historical and concrete

---

[3] Peter C. Erb, "Introduction," in *Pietism: Selected Writings*, ed. Peter C. Erb, The Classics of Western Spirituality (New York: Paulist Press, 1983), 3–4.

[4] Ibid., 6.

[5] Philip Jacob Spener, *Pia Desideria*, trans. Theodore G. Tappert (Eugene: Wipf and Stock, 2002).

[6] Hutchinson and Wolffe, *Short History of Global Evangelicalism*, 30.

[7] Ward, "Evangelical Awakenings in the North Atlantic World," 329–32; Schmidt, "Ecumenical Activity on the Continent of Europe in the Seventeenth and Eighteenth Centuries," 84.

[8] James E. Bradley, "Toleration and Movements of Christian Reunion, 1660–1789," in *The Cambridge History of Christianity: Volume VII, Enlightenment, Reawakening and Revolution 1660–1815*, eds. Stewart J. Brown and Timothy Tackett (Cambridge: Cambridge University Press, 2006), 361–62.

[9] Erb, "Introduction," 9.

Churches."[10] Thus, the new birth became a common ground for cooperation with born-again Christians across denominational lines, though it also became the basis for acrimonious divisions (e.g., claims of the converted vs. the unconverted) during the later awakenings.

Protestant missions were almost nonexistent at the turn of the eighteenth century when Pietists organized the Danish-Halle Mission in 1706. The work of John Eliot (1604–1690) resulted in one of the few substantial Protestant missions to non-Christians before 1706.[11] The Protestant movement was initially preoccupied with refuting other Christians and establishing confessional identities in the sixteenth and seventeenth centuries, rather than with converting non-Christians. Furthermore, some Protestants believed that Christ's command to preach the gospel to the ends of the earth (Matt. 28:18–20) was meant only for the apostles.[12] The established churches in England and Scotland did create several societies that had evangelization as a goal—the Society for Propagation of the Gospel in New England (1649), the first Protestant missionary society; the Society for the Propagation of Christian Knowledge (1698); the Society for Propagation of the Gospel (1701), which had conversion of "heathens and infidels" as its purported principal aim; and the Society in Scotland for Propagating Christian Knowledge (1709). Royal charters for several British colonies in the United States also expressed evangelization of "heathens" as a motive for colonization.[13] Among these earliest stirrings of missionary effort, a decisive moment for early Protestant missions unfolded in 1706 when Lutheran King Frederick IV of Denmark sent two Pietist Lutherans from the University of Halle to his small colony, Tranquebar, on the coast of

---

[10] Schmidt, "Ecumenical Activity on the Continent of Europe in the Seventeenth and Eighteenth Centuries," 83.

[11] William R. Hutchinson, *Errand to the World: American Protestant Thought and Foreign Missions* (Chicago: University of Chicago Press, 1987), 24; Stephen Neill, *A History of Christian Missions*, 2nd ed., The Penguin History of the Church 6 (London: Penguin Books, 1986), 193; De Jong, *As the Waters Cover the Sea*, 122–24; Douglas H. Shantz, *An Introduction to German Pietism: Protestant Renewal at the Dawn of Modern Europe* (Baltimore: Johns Hopkins University Press, 2013), 237–38.

[12] Neill, *A History of Christian Missions*, 189.

[13] For the rise of missions thought and institutions covered in this paragraph, see Ibid., 179–204; Dana Lee Robert, *Christian Mission: How Christianity Became a World Religion* (Chichester: Wiley-Blackwell, 2009), 31–52; De Jong, *As the Waters Cover the Sea*, 5–115; R. Pierce Beaver, *Pioneers in Mission: The Early Missionary Ordination Sermons, Charges, and Instructions* (Grand Rapids: Eerdmans, 1966); Frederick V. Mills, Sr., "The Society in Scotland for Propagating Christian Knowledge in British North America, 1730–1775," *Church History* 63, no. 1 (1994): 15–30; Chaney, *The Birth of Missions in America*.

India, which became legendary in missions memory.[14] Halle and its Pietist networks supplied many Protestant missionaries in the early years of the missionary movement.[15]

A common feature of this earliest stage of Protestant missions was international cooperation and connection among Christian traditions. Frederick V. Mills, Sr., demonstrates that there was a "cooperative or ecumenical quality about the Society in Scotland for Propagating Christian Knowledge that characterized its relations with the Society for Propagation of the Gospel in New England and the Society for Propagating of the Gospel."[16] The Society for the Propagation of Christian Knowledge maintained close connections and cooperated throughout the eighteenth century with continental churches and their clergy.[17] The Society for Propagation of the Gospel followed similar patterns, even if managers of these societies relegated their efforts to work the church had always done (e.g., ordain and equip clergy).[18] From its earliest years, the Danish-Halle Mission cooperated with the Society for the Propagation of Christian Knowledge and Congregationalists. Missions historian Stephen Neill notes that English Christians followed the work in Tranquebar more closely than Christians anywhere else; they had the *Annual Letters* of the missionaries translated into English and read at Society for the Propagation of Christian Knowledge meetings.[19] Thus, the earliest Protestant missions were intimately connected, and the participants themselves deliberately fostered transnational and interdenominational connections. As Ernst Benz has made clear, Cotton Mather in Boston, August Francke in Halle, and Society for the Propagation

---

[14] On the Danish-Halle mission to Tranquebar, see Shantz, *An Introduction to German Pietism*, 240–53.

[15] Robert, *Christian Mission*, 41–44; Brij Raj Singh, *The First Protestant Missionary to India: Bartholomaeus Ziegenbalg, 1683–1719* (New Delhi: Oxford University Press, 1999).

[16] Mills, Sr., "The Society in Scotland for Propagating Christian Knowledge in British North America, 1730–1775," 160–61.

[17] The Society for the Propagation of Christian Knowledge supported German Lutheran missionaries in South India. From 1710 to 1728, the Society for the Propagation of Christian Knowledge contributed financial help to the missionaries sent out by the Danish-Halle Mission to Tranquebar. Between 1728 and 1825, the Society for the Propagation of Christian Knowledge employed or supported in part about sixty missionaries who had received Lutheran ordination. See Norman Sykes, "Ecumenical Movements in Great Britain in the Seventeenth and Eighteenth Centuries," in *A History of the Ecumenical Movement, 1517–1948*, eds. Ruth Rouse and Stephen Charles Neill, 3rd ed. (Geneva: World Council of Churches, 1986), 160–61.

[18] Andrew F. Walls, "Missionary Societies and the Fortunate Subversion of the Church," *Evangelical Quarterly* 88, no. 2 (1988): 143.

[19] Neill, *A History of Christian Missions*, 197; Ernst Benz, "Pietist and Puritan Sources of Early Protestant World Missions (Cotton Mather and A. H. Francke)," *Church History* 20, no. 2 (1951): 31–32.

of Christian Knowledge secretaries in London were connected through correspondence and a common commitment to ecumenical concerns and the mission work in Tranquebar.[20]

American Congregational Pietist Cotton Mather (1663–1728), whose thought directly connected Christian unity, world missions, and the eschaton, was particularly important for subsequent evangelical missions.[21] Mather's biography of John Eliot, his correspondence with Francke and the Tranquebar missionaries, and other writings revealed in the early eighteenth century the interrelated themes of unity, missions, and eschatology that eventually dominated evangelical missions.[22] Mather praised John Eliot's plan to unite Presbyterians and Congregationalists for missions, and he rejoiced at a merger of English Presbyterians and Independents.[23]

Mather's mature thought on Christian unity owed much to Pietism.[24] Mather praised Francke and other Pietists and identified his own ideas in accord with Pietism. For example, he said one of his essays could be titled "American Pietism."[25] In at least seven books, Mather argued for a Christian unity based on the "uniting Maxims" of the gospel.[26] Mather argued, "These Divine, Ancient, Eternal MAXIMS of the Gospel, which are laid up in the *Mines* of Sacred Scriptures, are to be dug from thence,"

---

[20] Benz, "Pietist and Puritan Sources," 28–55; Ernst Benz, "Ecumenical Relations between Boston Puritanism and German Pietism: Cotton Mather and August Hermann Francke," *Harvard Theological Review* 54, no. 3 (July 1961): 159–93; Brijraj Singh, "'One Soul, Tho' Not One Soyl'? International Protestantism and Ecumenism at the Beginning of the Eighteenth Century," *Studies in Eighteenth Century Culture* 31 (January 2002): 61–84.

[21] Chaney describes Mather as the quintessential figure who tied together the periods from Eliot to Edwards. See Chaney, *The Birth of Missions in America*, 49–56; Don Herbert Yoder, "Christian Unity in Nineteenth-Century America," in *A History of the Ecumenical Movement, 1517–1948*, eds. Ruth Rouse and Stephen Charles Neill, 3rd ed. (Geneva: World Council of Churches, 1986), 226–32; Richard F. Lovelace, *The American Pietism of Cotton Mather: Origins of American Evangelicalism* (Grand Rapids: Christian University Press, 1979); De Jong, *As the Waters Cover the Sea*, 79–115.

[22] Chaney, *The Birth of Missions in America*, 49–56; Benz, "Pietist and Puritan Sources," 28–55; Cotton Mather, *The Triumphs of the Reformed Religion, in America: The Life of the Renowned John Eliot* (Boston: printed by Benjamin Harris and John Allen for Joseph Brunning, 1691). A number of editions of *Life* followed, many of which are accessible from Early English Books Online.

[23] He recorded this in a sermon on Christian union. See Cotton Mather, *Blessed Unions. An Union with the Son of God by Faith. And, An Union in the Church of God by Love, Importunately Pressed; In A Discourse Which Makes Divers Offers, for Those Unions; Together with a Copy of Those Articles, Where-upon A Most Happy Union, Has Been Lately Made between Those Two Eminent Parties in England, Which Have Now Changed the Names of Presbyterians, and Congregationals, for that of United Brethren* (Boston: printed by B. Green, 1692).

[24] Chaney, *The Birth of Missions in America*, 54–56.

[25] Cotton Mather, *The Heavenly Conversation* (Boston: Printed by Barth Green, for Eleazar Phillips, 1710), Preface.

[26] Listed in Chaney, *The Birth of Missions in America*, 88, n58.

so in 1716 he excavated fourteen primitive and eternal maxims from the Bible.[27] The first three maxims were about God, Christ, and Scripture; the rest concerned individual conversion[28] and pious living.[29] Mather believed that Christians who agreed on these basic maxims of Scripture "ought with a *Christian affection* to embrace one another, and with *United Endeavors*, and an heavenly Harmony, and Agreement, prosecute *Good Purposes* to advance *Piety*, and the *Kingdom of God*." He chided Christians who went beyond the basic maxims to create unnecessary "*Terms of Communion*" by which they justified excluding from the Eucharist and ecclesiastical privileges those whom Christ had received. Christians with diverse opinion could unite on the basis of piety: "In this *Diversity* let *Charity* be kept in its Vigour. . . . Their diversity in *Lesser Matters* will but render the more Amiable their *Unity* in the *Greatest Matters*; in the Love of God, and our Neighbour; in a Lively Faith on our Saviour, and in *Pure, & Undefiled Religion*." The people who had these "*Evangelical* and *Everlasting Maxims* written on their Hearts" were the true people of God. Mather highlighted a central distinction between the united people of God, who embraced the inclusive maxims, and those who adhered to an exclusive "Party" spirit.[30]

Mather created his unity maxims with the missionary enterprise and subsequent eschaton in mind. He explained that the maxims not only served to unite Christians, but also formed a basis for the missionary's message: "This Pure, Genuine, and Primitive Christianity makes that Invitation of Christ unto the Nations . . . ; *Come to me, ye that labour, and are heavy-laden, and I will give you Rest: Take my Yoke upon you; An easy Yoke, a*

---

[27] Cotton Mather, *The Stone Cut Out of the Mountain, And the Kingdom of God, in Those Maxims of It, That Cannot Be Shaken* (Boston: n.p., 1716), 1–5.

[28] Mather explained conversion as a new birth that become central to evangelicalism: "I must, by a Rectifying, and Purifying *Change*, Produced by the SPIRIT of GOD upon me, become a *New Creature*." Ibid., 5.

[29] Mather later reduced these fourteen to three maxims ([1] one God in three persons who created the world and whom we should obey; [2] Christ the eternal Son of God who became incarnate and reconciles us to God and on whom our faith is based; [3] love of God means it is our duty to love our neighbor and live after the golden rule) in a short pamphlet titled "The Religion Which All Good Men Are United In" and in his December 31, 1717 letter to Tranquebar missionary Bartholomew Ziegenbalgh. Both documents are printed in Cotton Mather, *India Christiana: A Discourse, Delivered unto the Commissioners, for the Propagation of the Gospel among the American Indians Which Is Accompanied with Several Instruments Relating to the Glorious Design of Propagating Our Holy Religion, in the Eastern as Well as the Western, Indies, An Entertainment Which They That Are Waiting for the Kingdom of God Will Receive as Good News from A Far Country* (Boston: printed by B. Green, 1721), 52–55, 62–74.

[30] Mather, *The Stone Cut Out of the Mountain*, 6, 10.

golden one, and one that will never be repented of."[31] The maxims of piety would make known the "*Way of God*" to all the nations, a prerequisite to the coming of God's new Pentecost—when God would pour out the Holy Spirit upon the nations in the latter days (he cited Joel 2:38). "The Day is at Hand," Mather declared, "when these *Maxims of the Everlasting Gospel* shall be a *Stone Cut out of the Mountain*" (he referenced Daniel 2:45). The stone would smite the "Papacy" and God would shake the nations. "Arise now, *O ye Ministers of God* . . . and consider, *What shall now be done, that the Kingdom of God may appear by the most Explicit Union of all Good Men, on the Eternal Maxims of it!*" Mather taught that subscription to, observation of, and propagation of these maxims would lead to Christian unity, strengthen missions, and herald the eschaton.[32] Just as Christian unity upon maxims or essentials of Christian faith became central to the missionary enterprise, so did millennial motivation.

As Mather represented the early Pietist missionary-impulse in North America, Scottish Presbyterian minister Robert Millar (1672–1752) represented the evangelical inclination in Scotland.[33] Millar's historical and apologetic work, *The History of the Propagation of Christianity* (1723), was quite popular, seeing at least three editions and a Dutch translation. Two scholars have compared him with the twentieth-century missions historian Kenneth Scott Latourette,[34] and missions historian Johannes van den Berg has suggested that Millar's work was "perhaps the most important example of Scottish missionary interest" in the period between Puritanism and Methodism.[35] Millar was part of the transatlantic correspondence by which early evangelicalism networked and constructed identity (e.g., Mather wrote Millar in 1725 to extol Millar's book, mentioning that he had shown it to several friends).[36]

---

[31] Ibid., 8.

[32] Ibid., 8–13.

[33] See Sweeney, *The American Evangelical Story*, 85–86; Richard B. Sher, "Millar, Robert (1672–1752)," *Oxford Dictionary of National Biography* (Oxford: Oxford University Press, 2004), http://www.oxforddnb.com/view/article/67754.

[34] John Foster, "A Scottish Contributor to the Missionary Awakening: Robert Millar of Paisley," *International Review of Missions* 37 (1948), 139; Ronald E. Davies, "Robert Millar: An Eighteenth-Century Scottish Latourette," *Evangelical Quarterly* 62 (1990), 143–56.

[35] Johannes van den Berg, *Constrained by Jesus' Love: An Inquiry into the Motives of the Missionary Awakening in Great Britain in the Period between 1698 and 1815* (Kampen: J. H. Kok, 1956), 58.

[36] Mather to Robert Millar, May 28, 1725, in Cotton Mather, *Selected Letters of Cotton Mather*, ed. Kenneth Silverman (Baton Rouge: Louisiana State University Press, 1971), 405–06.

Millar's *History* supports the idea that the most important evangelical missions advocates in the transatlantic during the early eighteenth century had similar motives for missions.[37] First, Millar invoked pity as motivation for missions. Like most contemporary evangelicals, Millar believed non-Christian religions were evil. His interpretation of Romans 1:21–32, Ephesians 2:1–3, and other passages led him to see paganism as Satan's tyrannical trick.[38] Therefore, Millar admitted that he hoped "*to move our Bowels of Pity for that Slavery and Thraldom to which the* Heathens, *who make up so great a Part of the World, are yet chained by the Enemy of Mankind.*"[39] He believed Christians would be moved to pity when they learned the extent and character of paganism in the world. Christians who properly viewed reality would envision the helpless "heathen" under the influence of darkness and destined for eternal torment; the "heathens" only hope was in Christians who would fulfill Jesus's command to preach the gospel to the ends of the earth.[40] Throughout his book, Millar beseeched Christians to construct and execute proper means for the conversion of the "heathen," particularly by imitating John Eliot and the Danish missionaries.[41] Moving from pity for the doomed "heathen" to motivation for mission became a pattern in the evangelical construction of religious meaning which undergirded early evangelical motivation for missionary action.

Second, Millar proposed the same sort of cooperative method as Mather and Francke, whose works he had read. The cooperative motif was limited to Protestants and related to Catholicism. Millar argued:

> The zeal of the Church of *Rome*, in their College for propagating the Faith, ought to excite Protestants to the like endeavors; not to propagate their own opinions, to make proselytes to a party, and subject foreigners to a *Roman Pontiff*, but to *turn sinners from darkness to light, and from the power of Satan unto God;*

---

[37] For treatment of a number of motives for missions in the eighteenth century, see van den Berg, *Constrained by Jesus' Love*; De Jong, *As the Waters Cover the Sea*, 79–115.

[38] Robert Millar, *The History of the Propagation of Christianity and Overthrow of Paganism*, 3rd ed. (London: printed for A. Miller, 1731), 2:389–90; Andrew F. Walls, "Romans One and the Modern Missionary Movement," in *The Missionary Movement in Christian History: Studies in the Transmission of Faith* (Maryknoll: Orbis Books, 1996), 55–67.

[39] Millar, *The History of the Propagation of Christianity and Overthrow of Paganism*, 1:iii.

[40] Ibid., 2:394–95.

[41] Ibid., 2:354ff.

that they may receive the forgiveness of sins, and an inheritance among them that are sanctified; to promote true Christianity over the world, and to use all proper means for attaining so good an end.[42]

Millar proceeded to praise Francke's piety, his orphanage, his university, and his missions endeavors. Citing Mather's account of the University of Halle, Millar declared it would be good if "all our schools were managed by such rules as the *Pietas Hallensis* has exemplified." Millar also praised William Stevenson, chaplain of the East India Company at St. George, and quoted at length his December 27, 1716, letter to the Society for the Propagation of Christian Knowledge. In that letter, Stevenson asked the Society to be wary of impediments to mission work among pagans, particularly "*the mixing of disputable opinions with the plain and necessary doctrines of the Gospel.*" Instead of propagating opinion, "Nothing ought to be taught among [the natives] but the plain and unquestionable truths of the *Christian Faith.*" Thus, Stevenson's first proposed method of prosecuting the missionary work was to

> unite the hearts and endeavours of the several Societies in *England, Denmark* and *Germany*, that have engaged to support the Protestant Mission, that laying aside all distrust and jealousy of one another, concerning the point of national honour, in carrying on this design, and all partiality and prejudices in favour of their several schemes and opinions, they may agree to promote the glory of God, and the conversion of the Heathen, by all proper methods and persons, without disputing about rights, precedence or superior direction.... When one common Society for promoting the Protestant Mission is happily formed, one of the first things that can fall under their consideration, is, how to raise a sufficient fund for carrying on so great a work, toward which 'tis but reasonable, that all charitable Christians will readily contribute.[43]

---

[42] Ibid., 2:370.
[43] Letter from William Stevenson to the Secretary of the Society for the Propagation of Christian Knowledge on December 27, 1716, printed in Ibid., 2:380–89, quoted from 386.

Millar and Stevenson both presupposed a belief similar to one expressed in Mather's maxims: there was a simple or core gospel message in Scripture, and then there were historical traditions added onto that core through time; missionaries should take only the plain gospel to pagans and leave the added traditions at home. That is why Millar could believe that a movement of prayer and action for missions to convert the "heathen" would "silence the clamour of parties, would confirm the truth of our holy Religion."[44] "If *Christians* would serve God in *Spirit* and *Truth* at home; if they would lay aside their *Divisions*, *Parties*, and unchristian *Humours*...," Millar wrote, "what a glorious addition to the *Church* of Christ might we justly expect?"[45]

Third, Millar proposed prayer as the foundation of a successful Protestant missionary effort, and such prayer proposals became a common feature of eighteenth-century evangelical missionary culture. Millar wrote:

> The promises of the enlargement of the New Testament Church are many, and the time is near when they shall be fully accomplished: We ought then every one of us, in our station, to throw in our mite for the conversion of the heathen world, not only by frequent prayers to the throne of grace upon ordinary occasions, but also by joining in solemn days of humiliation and prayer for that end.[46]

John Foster noted the extraordinary impact that this idea, which was already represented in 1723, had on the missionary movement. The Scottish concert-of-prayer movement, which began in 1744, prepared the way for the ecumenical missionary awakening. The prayer movement is discussed below, but suffice it say for now, this movement directly impacted many of the leaders of the missionary explosion in the 1790s. Prayer was not only the first means of propagating the gospel; it was instrumental in creating an interdenominational evangelical movement for missions.[47]

Fourth, a united and prayerful missionary effort would also lead to the fulfillment of God's eschatological promises. Millar's missionary eschatology

---

[44] Ibid., 2:371, 380, 394.
[45] Ibid., 1:x.
[46] Ibid., 2:355.
[47] Foster, "A Scottish Contributor to the Missionary Awakening," 142.

was similar to Mather's. Millar believed that although God had already fulfilled many promises found in Scripture, "there is a fuller performance of them to be expected before the end of the world; for our Lord himself foretold, *This Gospel of the Kingdom shall be preached in all the world for a witness unto all nations, and then shall the end come.*"[48] Furthermore, Millar argued that Christians should propagate the gospel in Asia, Africa, and America, because he understood Romans 11:25 to be a prophecy meaning the Jews would convert to Christianity only after the "fulness of the Gentiles be come in" (KJV). The whole eschaton therefore relied on Christians' obedience to preach the gospel to the Gentiles. Millar reasoned, "Since we are encouraged by these precious promises, to expect a more glorious day of the conversion of the nations . . . , and the time I hope is near; ought not every *Christian* to pray, long and wait for that time, and contribute his best endeavours to promote so great a work."[49]

Millar was for Scotland what Mather was for colonial America and Francke was for Germany: an astute and persuasive missions advocate. Millar's work on missions reveals his desire for a Protestant cooperative effort to take the plain gospel to "heathen" lands and rescue them from Satan's grasp. He exhibited an optimistic spirit and emphasis on morality as the design of the gospel that was not too far from the latitudinarians, yet his belief that a revival in piety and prayer at home were prerequisites to a widespread conversion of pagans, along with his praise of Francke's missionary endeavors, placed him directly in line with Pietism. As Johannes van den Berg noted, "So we find also with him that seeming *coincidentia oppositorum*, that blend of Rationalism and Pietism, which again and again has proved to be one of the main characteristics of the British missionary enterprise."[50] How much Millar influenced the 1740s prayer movement in Scotland is uncertain, but Millar's successors in Paisley, including John Witherspoon and John Snodgrass, supported the Society in Scotland for Propagating Christian Knowledge, and Snodgrass also supported the London Missionary

---

[48] Millar, *The History of the Propagation of Christianity and Overthrow of Paganism*, 2:393. He quoted Matthew 24:14.
[49] Ibid., 2:394.
[50] van den Berg, *Constrained by Jesus' Love*, 59. That same blend manifested in the thought of Thomas Campbell.

Society.⁵¹ In these connections and through his writings, Millar contributed much to evangelical missions.

Pietism entered evangelical missionary culture not only through Mather, Millar, and the Danish-Halle Tranquebar mission, but also through the Moravian church (*Unitas Fratrum*) and its leaders' influence on transatlantic evangelicals.⁵² Indeed, J. C. S. Mason's recent study demonstrates the enormous influence of Moravian missions upon the leaders of the most influential missionary societies of the 1790s.⁵³

Under the patronage of Count Nicholas Ludwig von Zinzendorf (1700–1760), Bohemian Brethren refugees settled in Saxony at Herrnhut from 1722, establishing in 1727 a "Brotherly Union and Agreement" which described the rules and ecumenical theology of the Moravian community:

> Hernnhut, and its original old inhabitants must remain in a constant bond of love with all children of God belonging to the different religious persuasions—they must judge none, enter into no disputes with any, nor behave themselves unseemly toward any, but rather seek to maintain among themselves the pure evangelical doctrine, simplicity, and grace.⁵⁴

Zinzendorf's de-emphasis on denominationalism was founded on his view of inward experiential conversion as the chief criterion of Christian identity. "Religion," he declared, "must be a matter which is able to be grasped through experience alone without any concepts."⁵⁵ He vehemently opposed the idea that intellectual knowledge or formularies determined one's Christian identity. Only *fiducia implicita*, "the undisclosed but affecting believing within the heart," constituted saving faith.⁵⁶ Therefore, the genuine character of a Christian had nothing to do with one's religious denomination: "It is a rule belonging absolutely to the character of the

---

⁵¹ Davies, "Robert Millar," 144–47.

⁵² Erb, "Introduction," 20–21; Shantz, *An Introduction to German Pietism*, chap. 9.

⁵³ J. C. S. Mason, *The Moravian Church and the Missionary Awakening in England, 1760–1800* (Woodbridge: Royal Historical Society/Boydell Press, 2001).

⁵⁴ Count Nicholas Ludwig von Zinzendorf, "Brotherly Union and Agreement at Herrnhut (1727)," in *Pietism: Selected Writings*, ed. Peter C. Erb, The Classics of Western Spirituality (New York: Paulist Press, 1983), 325.

⁵⁵ Count Nicholas Ludwig von Zinzendorf, "Thoughts for the Learned and Yet Good-Willed Students of Truth (1732)," in ibid., 291.

⁵⁶ Count Nicholas Ludwig von Zinzendorf, "Concerning Saving Faith (1746)," in ibid., 305.

true Christian that, properly speaking, he is neither Lutheran nor Calvinist, neither of this nor the other religious denomination."[57] By making new birth the most important criterion for Christian identity, Zinzendorf's ecumenism surpassed that of the earlier Pietists. He broadened Spener's concept of *ecclesiolae in ecclesia* to suggest the various denominations were divinely instituted schools that were directing believers toward the eventual renewed form of the true church.[58] "Now thus far it is good that we have many religious denominations," Zinzendorf declared, "so much so that I despise anyone who, without the deepest and most thoroughly examined reason, changes over from one denomination to another."[59] He believed the differences between denominations were important, but they were only fluid outward expressions of the more important commonality of Christian identity: Christians were those whose hearts Christ had changed through experiential conversion, and they were found in all denominations.[60] Pietist thought on new birth—transmitted through Zinzendorf, Mather, the Moravians, and others—undergirded the evangelical view of inward experiential conversion as a more important marker of Christian identity than denominational affiliation. Evangelicals used essentials of the gospel—whether new birth or some other essential maxim—as justification for interdenominational cooperation, which culminated in the interdenominational societies of the 1790s.

Zinzendorf's emphasis on ecumenism and experiential conversion greatly influenced the development of evangelical missions. Moved by the petitions of Anton Ulrich, a native of the Caribbean island of St. Thomas, the Moravian community became convinced of their missionary purpose.[61] Their first missionaries went to the Caribbean in 1732, and within that same decade, they had missions in Africa, India, South America, and North America. The Moravians had more missionaries in foreign lands by the end of the 1730s than all Protestants had in the prior two hundred

---

[57] Count Nicholas Ludwig von Zinzendorf, "On the Essential Character and Circumstances of the Life of a Christian (1746)," in ibid., 311.
[58] Erb, "Introduction," 20–21.
[59] Zinzendorf, "On the Essential Character," 312.
[60] Ibid., 312–24.
[61] Jon F. Sensbach, *Rebecca's Revival: Creating Black Christianity in the Atlantic World* (Cambridge: Harvard University Press, 2005), 49.

years.[62] Emphasis on missions led to the centrality of the Moravian practice of *Gemeintag* by 1728. *Gemeintag* was a community gathering for the reading of various news, but it focused on missionary reports and letters. This practice influenced British societies' public readings of international news on what became known as "Letter Days." Furthermore, missionary letters and reports quickly took a place alongside revival reports in the transatlantic evangelical magazines of the 1740s and beyond.[63]

These missionary endeavors placed the Moravians at the center of the transatlantic evangelical religious exchange during the evangelical awakening of the 1730s and 1740s. This was notably present in John Wesley's encounter with Moravians on the voyage to the American colonies and in Moravian missions in Georgia and Pennsylvania.[64] In missionary William Carey's opinion, the Moravians surpassed all previous efforts for mission. Similarly, to the advocates of interdenominational societies in the 1790s, Zinzendorf was a religious symbol of what they perceived to be the best kind of Christian unity (unity without uniformity), coupled with a zeal for cooperative missions.[65] All the ideas noted above led Zinzendorf to argue that missionaries should not impose doctrinal and cultural provincialisms upon their converts. Instead, each society should apply the gospel to its own language and customs.[66] Herein lies the seed and substance for late eighteenth-century theorists of interdenominational missions—Christians cooperating to carry out a simple evangelical gospel devoid of the denominations' particular packaging of that gospel.

Jonathan Edwards: Eschatology, Prayer, and Brainerd

A contemporary of Zinzendorf named Jonathan Edwards was the most important theologian for evangelical missionary thought in the American colonies; his ideas guided transatlantic evangelical missions for decades

---

[62] Robert, *Christian Mission*, 44–45.

[63] Susan O'Brien, "A Transatlantic Community of Saints: The Great Awakening and the First Evangelical Network, 1735-1755," *The American Historical Review* 91, no. 4 (1986): 825–26; Noll, *The Rise of Evangelicalism*, 115–19.

[64] John Wesley, *The Journal of the Reverend John Wesley, A.M., Sometime Fellow of Lincoln College, Oxford* (New York: Carlton & Phillips, 1855), 1:18, 62–80; Richard P. Heitzenrater, *Wesley and the People Called Methodists* (Nashville: Abingdon Press, 1995), 58–96.

[65] Roger H. Martin, *Evangelicals United: Ecumenical Stirrings in Pre-Victorian Britain, 1795-1830* (Metuchen: Scarecrow Press, 1983), 4, 31–33.

[66] Hutchinson, *Errand to the World*, 26.

after his death. Missions historian Charles Chaney claims that Edwards's "thought is the great intellectual and spiritual vein from which missionary theology in the period is mined. His theology is the most profound expression of the fresh and vigorous impulse that flavored missionary thought and activity through the next seventy-five years."[67] Edwards received a tradition of missionary involvement from Solomon Stoddard, who, with Cotton Mather and Benjamin Coleman, ensured the continuation of American Indian missions after King Phillip's War.[68] Edwards gave seven years to missionary service at Stockbridge, and he became the spiritual father of colonial American missionaries.[69] Ronald Davies argues that if William Carey and Samuel Hopkins are the "fathers" of modern missions on their respective sides of the Atlantic, then Jonathan Edwards is the "grandfather of modern Protestant missions" on both sides of the Atlantic.[70] Stuart Piggin's recent chapter documents Edwards's extraordinary influence on the leaders of the major missionary societies of the 1790s.[71]

Chaney describes four of Edwards's contributions to the missionary movement—a theology of evangelism, eschatological motivation, movement of united prayer for revival and missions, and a new missionary image. First, in the wake of the 1734–35 Northampton Awakening, Edwards was filled with optimism concerning these exciting times, so he preached with urgency.[72] The Awakening convinced him that he lived during one of the special times when God poured out his spirit in extraordinarily powerful ways. Edwards encouraged people to use all the means of moving toward conversion, because God had opened wide the doors of mercy. In his famous 1741 Enfield sermon, Edwards pleaded with his hearers:

> Now you have an extraordinary opportunity, a day wherein
> Christ has flung the door of mercy wide open, and stands in the

---

[67] Chaney, *The Birth of Missions in America*, 57.
[68] Ibid., 58.
[69] George M. Marsden, *Jonathan Edwards: A Life* (New Haven: Yale University Press, 2004), chap. 23.
[70] Ronald E. Davies, "Jonathan Edwards: Missionary Biographer, Theologian, Strategist, Administrator, Advocate—and Missionary," *International Bulletin of Missionary Research* 21, no. 2 (April 1997): 60.
[71] Stuart Piggin, "The Expanding Knowledge of God: Jonathan Edwards's Influence on Missionary Thinking and Promotion," in *Jonathan Edwards at Home and Abroad: Historical Memories, Cultural Movements, Global Horizons*, eds. David William Kling and Douglas A. Sweeney (Columbia: University of South Carolina Press, 2003), 266–96.
[72] On the revival and its background, see Kidd, *The Great Awakening*, chap. 2.

door calling and crying with a loud voice to poor sinners; a day wherein many are flocking to him, and pressing into the kingdom of God.... Will you neglect this precious season? ... Let everyone that is out of Christ, now awake and fly from the wrath to come.[73]

Edwards's understanding of conversion in an extraordinary time of the Spirit's outpouring undergirded most Calvinist evangelistic and missionary enterprises undertaken in the eighteenth century.[74]

Second, Edwards's theology of evangelism was intricately bound to his eschatology.[75] In a series of thirty-nine sermons Edwards delivered to his congregation in 1739, Edwards described history in three epochs. The third epoch stretched from Christ's resurrection to the end of the world. Edwards assigned missionary activity an important place in this last epoch, when Antichrist would fall and the church would enter an age of prosperity. In fact, Edwards identified revivals and missions as signs of the latter days, when outpourings of the Spirit would renew the church and increase conversions as the gospel was preached to the entire world. Edwards cited Revelation 14:6 and Isaiah 66:7–9 to contend that "The gospel shall be preached to every tongue, and kindred, and nation, and people, before the fall of Antichrist; so we may suppose, that it will soon be gloriously successful to bring in multitudes from every nation."[76]

Edwards saw the beginnings of this evangelistic age in recent successes of the gospel accompanying the discovery of the Americas (e.g., Christian proselytization of American Indians) and Pietist missions in India. He thought America—New England, in particular—would be the place for the rise of the glorious latter days, and the awakenings of the 1730s and

---

[73] Jonathan Edwards, "Sinners in the Hands of an Angry God," in *Jonathan Edwards's Sinners in the Hands of an Angry God: A Casebook*, eds. Wilson H. Kimnach, Caleb J. D. Maskell, and Kenneth P. Minkema (New Haven: Yale University Press, 2010), 49–50.

[74] Chaney, *The Birth of Missions in America*, 63; Noll, *The Rise of Evangelicalism*, 207–10; Peter Johannes Thuesen, *Predestination: The American Career of a Contentious Doctrine* (Oxford: Oxford University Press, 2009), 114–15; N. L. Geisler, "Predestination," *Dictionary of Christianity in America* (Downers Grove: InterVarsity Press, 1990), 927–28.

[75] De Jong, *As the Waters Cover the Sea*, 124–37.

[76] Jonathan Edwards Jr. and John Erskine cooperated to publish these sermons in 1774: Jonathan Edwards, *A History of the Work of Redemption: Containing the Outlines of a Body of Divinity in a Method Entirely New* (Boston: reprinted by Draper and Folsom, 1782), 230–37, quoted at 251; De Jong, *As the Waters Cover the Sea*, 126.

beyond surely seemed like possible beginnings.[77] He interpreted recent technological advances in printing and sea navigation by way of the mariner's compass, as well as increased learning, to be divine preparations for the coming conversion of people throughout the world. As the church eventually gained victory over the "heathen," Christians would have a "wonderful spirit of pity towards them, and zeal for their instruction and conversion . . . , and many shall go forth and carry the gospel unto them."[78] Missionary action was an essential obligation of the church in Edwards's eschatological schema. Worldwide missionary endeavors were the instrument of God's final redemptive work in history—both to win converts and to destroy Antichrist.[79] As missions historian Pierce Beaver concluded, "Edwards brought the Church, in popular expectation, to the dawn of the millennium, and made it possible for that millennial expectation to become a motive for mission at the end of that century."[80]

Third, Edwards's support of the burgeoning prayer movement made a lasting impact on the missionary movement's foci of unity and prayer. In 1744, a group of Scottish ministers beseeched Christians to join them for a portion of time on Saturdays, Sundays, and the first Tuesdays of each quarter in "united extraordinary" prayer to God to "appear in his Glory" and "manifest his Compassion to the World . . . by an abundant Effusion of his *Holy Spirit* on all Churches, and the whole habitable Earth, to revive True religion in all Parts of Christendom, and to deliver *all Nations* from their great and manifold spiritual Calamities and Miseries."[81] The response in Scotland to this movement, which linked prayer with unity, revival, and missions, was so positive that, after the two years of proposed prayer, the ministers issued a similar call to transatlantic Protestants in *A Concert for Prayer, To Be Continued for Seven Years* (1746).[82] Because Edwards

---

[77] De Jong, *As the Waters Cover the Sea*, 130.

[78] Edwards, *Work of Redemption*, 257.

[79] Chaney, *The Birth of Missions in America*, 68.

[80] Millennialism had been a motive for Anglo-American missions from their very inception, as demonstrated by De Jong. See R. Pierce Beaver, "The Concert for Prayer for Missions: An Early Venture in Ecumenical Action," *Ecumenical Review* 10, no. 4 (1958): 424; De Jong, *As the Waters Cover the Sea*, 1–158.

[81] The story is recounted in Jonathan Edwards, *An Humble Attempt to Promote Explicit Agreement and Visible Union of God's People in Extraordinary Prayer for the Revival of Religion and the Advancement of Christ's Kingdom on Earth, Pursuant to Scripture—Promises and Prophecies Concerning the Last Time* (Boston: printed for D. Henchman in Cornhill, 1747), 14–20; Beaver, "The Concert for Prayer for Missions," 420–27.

[82] Reprinted in Edwards, *An Humble Attempt*, 20–25.

corresponded with the signers of the *Concert*, he received one of the copies.[83] He subsequently promoted the concert of prayer in his congregations and throughout the world by publishing *An Humble Attempt to Promote Explicit Agreement and Visible Union Among God's People in Extraordinary Prayer for the Revival of Religion and the Advancement of Christ's Kingdom on Earth* (1747).

An Humble Attempt constituted Edwards's clearest articulation of how eschatology should motivate Christians to unite in prayer and missions. Edwards based his appeal for united prayer on an exposition of Zechariah 8:20–22, which contained a prophecy of a "future glorious Advancement of the Church" that would constitute the greatest time of increase in the last days.[84] This triumph of the church was imminent, but Edwards, like Mather, believed the church's triumph in the last days was directly related to Christian unity in prayer. Edwards concluded his exposition of the text:

> From the Whole we may infer, That it is a very *suitable* Thing, and *well-pleasing to God*, for many People, in different Parts of the World, by express *Agreement*, to come into a *visible Union*, in extraordinary, speedy, fervent and constant *Prayer*, for those great Effusions of the *Holy Spirit*, which shall bring on that *Advancement* of Christ's Church and Kingdom, that God has so often promised shall be in the *latter Ages* of the World.[85]

The concert of prayer wielded extraordinary influence on missions.[86] The prayer movement continued in the 1780s and 1790s, during which time *An Humble Attempt* saw several printings in the transatlantic world, and wielded great influence on William Carey and the founders of the London Missionary Society in 1795.[87]

---

[83] On the Edwards, Scottish correspondence, see Christopher W. Mitchell, "Jonathan Edwards's Scottish Connection," in *Jonathan Edwards at Home and Abroad: Historical Memories, Cultural Movements, Global Horizons*, eds. David William Kling and Douglas A. Sweeney (Columbia: University of South Carolina Press, 2003), 222–47.

[84] Edwards, *An Humble Attempt*, 1–15.

[85] Ibid., 13.

[86] De Jong, *As the Waters Cover the Sea*, 133.

[87] "The United Prayers of the Churches, for the Universal Spread of the Knowledge and Glory of Christ," *The Evangelical Magazine* 3 (May 1795): 198–202; Stephen Orchard, "Evangelical Eschatology and the Missionary Awakening," *Journal of Religious History* 22, no. 2 (1998): 138; Davies, "Robert Millar," 154; Beaver, "The Concert for Prayer for Missions," 422–26; Neill, *A History of Christian Missions*, 280.

Fourth, Edwards constructed a Protestant missionary image through his most popular written work, *The Life of David Brainerd*.[88] Brainerd became a missionary saint after Edwards's biography of him became a best seller in the eighteenth and nineteenth centuries around the transatlantic.[89] Brainerd went to work for the Society in Scotland for Propagating Christian Knowledge in the Middle Colonies in 1742, shortly after Yale expelled him for purportedly claiming one of the unconverted Yale tutors had "no more grace than a chair."[90] Brainerd's work with American Indians only had small signs of success, such as the awakening among the Delawares in 1745. He eventually succumbed to tuberculosis and died in the Edwards's Northampton parsonage in 1747.

Before he died, Brainerd agreed to publish his diary. Edwards inherited the uncompleted manuscript and published *The Life of David Brainerd* in 1749. It was an edited version of Brainerd's intimate spiritual diary presenting Brainerd as a Christian hero and the archetypal evangelical missionary. The distinctive marks of the Brainerd missionary image included a concern to glorify God, show compassion for lost souls and pity for pagans, and embrace self-denial and self-sacrifice in the tradition of the apostle Paul.[91] Brainerd's Society in Scotland for Propagating Christian Knowledge sponsors, whose correspondents wrote a preface to *The Life of David Brainerd*, saw eschatology as a primary motivation for mission. As James De Jong notes, Edwards's edition of *Life of David Brainerd* also "consciously linked the work of revival, regarded as the first victories in the church's latter-day glory, with mission efforts."[92] Edwards's *Life of David Brainerd* exerted an

---

[88] Chaney argues that, "until 1748, there was, with the possible exception of John Eliot, and perhaps, among some in Northern Europe, Bartholomaus Zigenbalg, no great Protestant missionary saint." Chaney, *The Birth of Missions in America*, 71.

[89] Joseph Conforti, "Jonathan Edwards's Most Popular Work: 'The Life of David Brainerd' and 19th-Century Evangelical Culture," *Church History* 54, no. 2 (1985): 188–201; Andrew F. Walls, "Missions and Historical Memory: Jonathan Edwards and David Brainerd," in *Jonathan Edwards at Home and Abroad: Historical Memories, Cultural Movements, Global Horizons*, eds. David William Kling and Douglas A. Sweeney (Columbia: University of South Carolina Press, 2003), 248–65.

[90] Kidd, *The Great Awakening*, 196.

[91] Ibid., 195–201; Conforti, "Jonathan Edwards's Most Popular Work," 189; Hutchinson and Wolffe, *A Short History of Global Evangelicalism*, 44–45.

[92] De Jong, *As the Waters Cover the Sea*, 148–49.

enormous influence on leaders of the transatlantic evangelical missionary movement.[93]

Edwards provided the evangelical missionary movement with a theology of evangelism, millennial motives for missions, a movement of united prayer for revival and missions, and a new missionary image in Brainerd. As De Jong puts it:

> The circumstances in Edwards' life co-operated to forge a coalition of millennial thought and missionary enterprise that was a major force in the origin of the modern missionary movement in the 1790's.... If the two major forces behind the nineteenth century Anglo-American missions could be isolated, a convincing case could be constructed for their being the theology of Jonathan Edwards and the example of David Brainerd.[94]

"In Anglo-American eschatology," De Jong averred, "the latter days had always been associated with the universal knowledge of Christ. When the revivals of this period [1735 to 1776] were linked with the latter days, therefore, every prayer for the revival or for the kingdom assumed an immediate missionary dimension."[95] After Edwards's work, evangelical missions in the eighteenth and early nineteenth centuries were almost always tied to united prayer movements, revivals, and eschatology.

---

[93] The book went through more editions and reprints than any other popular Edwardsian work. In the second half of the eighteenth century, the *Life* was reprinted in the United States, England, Scotland, and Holland, and it was the first U.S. biography to reach a large European audience. During the first half of the nineteenth century, when evangelicals looked for inspirational models for missionary work and millennialism, the *Life* attained its widest popularity in the United States and abroad. The *Life* was one of the most successful publications of the American Tract Society in the nineteenth century. It influenced leading transatlantic evangelicals, such as John Wesley, William Carey, Andrew Fuller, John Ryland, Henry Martyn, Francis Asbury, and Francis Wayland. Joseph Conforti explained, "To Carey, one of the first Baptist missionaries to India, the *Life* was 'almost a second bible.' Martyn claimed that he was drawn into missionary work through reading the *Life*. . . . In America evangelicals from Francis Asbury in the late eighteenth century to Francis Wayland in the middle of the nineteenth testified to the importance of Brainerd's example." Brainerd was not just a missionary model, but a model of evangelical piety and experimental Christianity. The *Life* also became the archetype for the missionary memoir. Like Edwards's goal for the *Life*, later evangelical missionary biography aimed to excite and encourage Christians to pray and work for the advancement of Christianity in the world. See Conforti, "Jonathan Edwards's Most Popular Work," 192.
[94] De Jong, *As the Waters Cover the Sea*, 137.
[95] Ibid., 157.

George Whitefield and John Wesley

George Whitefield (1714–1770) and John Wesley (1703–1791) were also influential on early evangelical missions. Key contributions of Whitefield, Wesley, and their traditions included an ecumenism based on new birth conversion, de-emphasis on denominational identity rooted in Methodist connexions, and organization of itinerant preaching.[96]

Whitefield acquired evangelical fame as a gifted orator and was the central international celebrity in the transatlantic awakenings of the mid-eighteenth century.[97] Like other prominent evangelicals (e.g., Zinzendorf and John and Charles Wesley), Whitefield's spirituality took shape in a religious society in the tradition of Spener's *collegias pietas*, the Holy Club at Oxford. He began preaching at the age of twenty-one, and his publication of sermons and journals quickly won him international fame. His experiential new-birth conversion, in which he experienced an inward change of heart, greatly influenced his theology thereafter. He promoted and practiced itinerant preaching when it was not yet accepted in many places, and partly through his influence, itinerancy became a key method of evangelical missions at home and abroad by the late eighteenth century.[98]

Whitefield's most famous sermon topic and most important theological idea for Christian cooperation was new birth as the essential marker of Christian identity, which sometimes encouraged fellowship and cooperation in missions efforts between evangelicals of different Christian denominations. His oft-printed[99] sermon, *The Nature and Necessity of Our New Birth in Christ Jesus* (1737), began with a preface exhorting fellow ministers to move their parishioners beyond the "Shell and Shadow of Religion" to an acquaintance with the "Nature and Necessity of that Inward Holiness, and

---

[96] Martin, *Evangelicals United*, chaps. 1–2; David Bebbington, "The Growth of Voluntary Religion," in *The Cambridge History of Christianity: Volume VIII, World Christianities, c.1815–c.1914*, eds. Sheridan Gilley and Brian Stanley (Cambridge: Cambridge University Press, 2006), 60; Heitzenrater, *Wesley and the People Called Methodists*, 282–98.

[97] The most recent biography of Whitefield is Thomas S. Kidd, *George Whitefield: America's Spiritual Founding Father* (New Haven: Yale University Press, 2014).

[98] Jerome Dean Mahaffey, *The Accidental Revolutionary: George Whitefield and the Creation of America* (Waco: Baylor University Press, 2011), 8.

[99] The sermon went through over twenty editions in the United States and Britain. See Jerome Dean Mahaffey, *Preaching Politics: The Religious Rhetoric of George Whitefield and the Founding of a New Nation*, Studies in Rhetoric and Religion 3 (Waco: Baylor University Press, 2007), 264 n7.

Vital Purity of Heart."[100] Taking 2 Corinthians 5:17[101] as his text, Whitefield argued that regeneration, or new birth in Christ Jesus, was the "Hinge on which the Salvation of each of us turns" and a point on which "all *sincere* Christians, of whatever Denomination, agree." Whitefield believed that justification (i.e., to have one's sins forgiven) also required sanctification (i.e., to have one's corrupt nature changed and made holy).[102] A profession of faith and a physical baptism was not enough to gain salvation. To be "born again," to "put off the old man," to be "renewed in the Spirit," and to become "new creatures" all demonstrated for Whitefield that Christianity required a "*thorough, real, inward* Change of Heart." He urged readers not to interpret these biblical phrases metaphorically, because those who did just might "interpret themselves out of their Salvation."[103] For Whitefield, as for an increasing number of evangelicals, the new birth, rather than denominational affiliation, was the quintessential marker of Christian identity.

Although Whitefield's definition of new birth as the mark of true Christians contributed to the hardening bifurcation between pro-revivalists and anti-revivalists, which caused much division in the eighteenth century, it also led to a de-emphasis on denominationalism.[104] Whitefield's nondenominationalism was manifest in a popular sermon anecdote:

> "Father Abraham, whom have you in heaven? Any Episcopalians?" "No." "Any Presbyterians?" "No." "Have you any Independents or Seceders?" "No." "Have you any Methodists there?" "No, no, no." "Whom have you there?" "We don't know those names here. All who are here are Christians—believers in Christ—men who have overcome by the blood of the Lamb and the word of his testimony." "O, is this the case?" said Whitefield; "then God help me,

---

[100] George Whitefield, *The Nature and Necessity of Our New Birth in Christ Jesus, in Order to Salvation. A Sermon Preached in the Church of St. Mary Radcliffe, in Bristol*, 2nd ed. (London: printed for C. Rivington in St. Paul's Church-yard, 1737), viii.

[101] "Therefore if any man *be* in Christ, *he is* a new creature: old things are passed away; behold, all things are become new" (KJV).

[102] Whitefield, *The Nature and Necessity of Our New Birth*, 1, 3.

[103] Ibid., 11.

[104] On the major divisions, see Noll, *The Rise of Evangelicalism*, 119–32; Martin, *Evangelicals United*, 4–9.

God help us all, to forget party names, and to become Christians in deed and in truth!"[105]

Whitefield's de-emphasis on denomination and his cooperation with Selina Hastings, countess of Huntingdon (Lady Huntingdon), contributed to a Calvinist Methodist tradition which became the most influential incubator for leaders of the interdenominational missionary society movement in the 1790s.[106] Although the divisive period of the 1770s threatened continued cooperation among evangelicals, historian Roger Martin argues that the conception of "pan-evangelicalism" survived "due to George Whitefield more than any other man." Wesley's bias toward Anglicanism and Arminianism and his prejudice against dissent made him less influential on dissenting Calvinists, Martin claims. Thus, it was Whitefield's "catholic spirit" that inspired later generations of evangelicals to cooperate.[107] Therefore, it is to Whitefield

> more than to John Wesley or regular evangelical Anglicans that we must look for the wellsprings of the late eighteenth-century pan-evangelical impulse.... The missionary-minded, undogmatic Calvinism that was the doctrinal cement of pan-evangelicalism was largely inspired by Whitefield.[108]

Indeed, it was Whitefieldian moderate Calvinists who came together to produce the great interdenominational evangelical societies of the 1790s.[109] Stephen Orchard relatedly claims that Whitefield's activity in North America is where one finds the "seminal influences which led to the flowering of Protestant missionary societies."[110]

---

[105] Cited in Mahaffey, *The Accidental Revolutionary: George Whitefield and the Creation of America*, 186; Mahaffey, *Preaching Politics*, 75–76; Joseph Beaumont Wakeley, *Anecdotes of the Rev. George Whitefield, M.A., with Biographical Sketch* (London: Hodder and Stoughton, 1872), 134–35. I have been unsuccessful in identifying the primary source.

[106] Martin, *Evangelicals United*, 12–14.

[107] Norman Sykes would agree with Martin, as he sees Wesley's contribution to ecumenism as ambiguous: "Thus the greatest religious figure of his age contributed more perhaps to the accentuating than to the healing of the divisions of the universal Church." Sykes, "Ecumenical Movements in Great Britain in the Seventeenth and Eighteenth Centuries," 165.

[108] Martin, *Evangelicals United*, 9–10.

[109] Ibid., 9–14.

[110] Orchard, "Evangelical Eschatology and the Missionary Awakening," 139.

Particularly influential in denominational mobility was Whitefield's influence on Selina Hastings, who followed Whitefield's Calvinism at the expense of her friendship with Wesley. Her college at Trevecca in South Wales trained ministers of Episcopal and non-Episcopal traditions and focused on the art of spiritual awakening, but it also came to see itself as a training ground for overseas preachers. Hastings had been interested in Whitefield's work in America, and he left her his orphanage in Bethesda, Georgia, which he had wanted to transform into an academy. Shortly after his death in the early 1770s, she made the orphanage an academy, based on the model of Trevecca College, to train evangelists to preach among the colonists, their slaves, and American Indians.[111] Hastings's Trevecca College trained many interdenominational and international missions leaders.[112]

Yet historians should not minimize the importance of the Wesleys on the ecumenical and missionary impulses upon evangelicalism. Charles Wesley (1707–1788) wrote a popular hymn in 1740 that demonstrated the ecumenical ecclesiology of the Wesleys, one which evangelicals seeking to cooperate across denominational lines for missionary purposes repeated for decades. The hymn begins by professing Christ as the perfector of the saints and the saints as Christ's "mystic body." The hymn petitions Christ to join the church in one spirit and to aid Christians in their care for one another as Christ's body. The last of ten stanzas says:

> Love, like death, hath all destroyed
> Rendered all distinctions void;
> Names, and sects, and parties fall
> Thou, O Christ, art all in all![113]

---

[111] Dorothy Eugenia Sherman Brown, "Evangelicals and Education in Eighteenth-Century Britain: A Study of Trevecca College, 1768–1792" (PhD diss., The University of Wisconsin-Madison, 1992), 227–34.

[112] At least six Trevecca students were cofounders of the London Missionary Society in 1795. Brown, "Evangelicals and Education," 211–38, 282, 303, 305, 307, 313, 318; Sykes, "Ecumenical Movements in Great Britain in the Seventeenth and Eighteenth Centuries," 165; Orchard, "Evangelical Eschatology and the Missionary Awakening," 139–44.

[113] John Wesley, *A Collection of Hymns: For the Use of the People Called Methodists* (London: Wesleyan Conference Office, 1877), Hymn 518; Bible Christian Book Committee, *A Collection of Hymns, For the Use of the People Called Bible Christians*, 2nd ed. (Plymouth: printed by S. Thorne, 1863), Hymn 495.

The last two lines of the hymn became popular in evangelical interdenominational circles, appearing in magazines and sermons in the 1790s.[114]

The same ecumenical sentiment expressed in Charles Wesley's hymn existed in other songs and sermons. For example, the name of the hymnal John Wesley published, *Hymns and Spiritual Songs, Intended for the Use of Real Christians of All Denominations* (1753), expressed tacitly what the title page and preface made unmistakable. The title page quoted Colossians 3:9–11, noting that neither ethnicity, social class, nor physical identifiers mattered after one put on the image of Christ. The preface loathed the "Spirit of Bigotry," which caused Christians to fight with one another over opinions and modes of worship, but applauded the exact opposite "Catholic Spirit." In fact, Wesley joyously observed the "Spirit of Bigotry greatly declining (at least in every Protestant Nation of *Europe*) and the Spirit of Love proportionably increasing" among people of "every Opinion and Denomination." Wesley continued, "They seem weary of tearing each other in pieces, on account of small and unessential Differences; and rather desire to build up each other, in the great Point wherein they all agree, the Faith which worketh by Love, and produces in them the Mind which was in CHRIST JESUS." Wesley hoped that his hymnal, which he said was carefully crafted along nondenominational lines, would contribute to the growing catholic spirit. "There is not an Hymn, not one Verse inserted here," Wesley assured his readers, "but what relates to the Common Salvation; and what every serious and unprejudiced Christian, of whatever Denomination, may join in."[115] This hymnal, rooted in interdenominational new birth identity, saw at least two dozen reprints in Wesley's lifetime.[116]

John Wesley also emphasized this "Catholic Spirit" in a sermon by that title, based on 2 Kings 10, which delineated the appropriate Christian disposition toward those with whom Christians disagreed. Wesley argued

---

[114] Several references are treated in later chapters. More recently, David M. Thompson borrowed the lines of verse for the title of his history of Churches of Christ in Great Britain. See David M. Thompson, *Let Sects and Parties Fall: A Short History of the Association of Churches of Christ in Great Britain and Ireland* (Birmingham: Berean Press, 1980).

[115] John Wesley, *Hymns and Spiritual Songs, Intended for the Use of Real Christians of All Denominations*, 1st ed. (London: printed by William Strahan, 1753), ii–iv.

[116] Nearly all of them are available from Eighteenth Century Collections Online. The 24th edition (London: printed by J. Paramore, 1786), retained Col 3:9–11 on the title page and the same preface as the first edition cited here.

that the limited nature of knowledge required Christians to allow liberty of opinion dictated by individual conscience. Furthermore, he encouraged Christians not to judge brothers and sisters based on types of worship or doctrinal opinions. Wesley did not swing the doors wide open, for he wanted to avoid being lumped in with the latitudinarians. Rather, a catholic-spirited person's mind should be fixed "concerning the main branches of Christian doctrine." A catholic spirit included love toward neighbor and stranger, friend and enemy, but emanated from a person who assented to right beliefs and worshiped faithfully.[117] Some editions of this sermon were included at the end of Charles Wesley's hymn, *Catholic Love*, which lamented strife created by forms and modes and names, declaring:

> Forth from the midst of Babel brought,
> Parties and sects I cast behind;
> Enlarged my heart, and free my thought,
> Where'er the latent truth I find;
> The latent truth with joy to own,
> And bow to Jesus' name alone.[118]

This ecumenism manifested itself in many ways, including John Wesley's interdenominational Society for Reformation of Manners (1757).[119]

John Wesley remained firm in this rooted-in-new-birth catholic spirit as the real key to one's Christian identity, rather than one's denominational polity, rites, and opinions. This was true even when preaching a sermon just after the death of Whitefield in 1770, though their theological differences at times caused serious discord among evangelicals. Wesley praised Whitefield's ecumenical disposition (what Wesley called "Catholic love") which Whitefield had, Wesley believed, rightly rooted in two essential doctrines of Scripture (justification by faith and new birth).[120] Wesley extolled,

---

[117] John Wesley, "Sermon XXXIX: Catholic Spirit," in *Sermons on Several Occasions by the Rev. John Wesley, M.A., Late Fellow of Lincoln College, Oxford*, New edition (Leeds: printed by Edward Baines, 1799), 515–28. Also available from the Wesley Center Online, accessed May 5, 2014, http://wesley.nnu.edu/john-wesley/the-sermons-of-john-wesley-1872-edition/sermon-39-catholic-spirit/.

[118] Charles Wesley, "Catholic Love," included with John Wesley's "Sermon XXXIX: Catholic Spirit," available at Wesley Center Online, accessed May 5, 2014, http://wesley.nnu.edu/john-wesley/the-sermons-of-john-wesley-1872-edition/sermon-39-catholic-spirit/.

[119] Martin, *Evangelicals United*, 24.

[120] John Wesley, *A Sermon on the Death of the Rev. Mr. George Whitefield. Preached at the Chapel in Tottenham-Court-Road, and at the Tabernacle near Moorfields, on Sunday, November 18, 1770* (London:

more than any other quality, Whitefield's catholic love and catholic spirit, and he exhorted the congregation to follow Whitefield's example. A person with a catholic spirit would love people as children of God and partakers in the kingdom of heaven on earth and in eternity "all of whatever opinion, mode of worship, or congregation, who believe in the LORD JESUS; who love GOD and man; [who please God, who fear God, who abstain from evil, and who are zealous to do good works]."[121] Wesley chided those who demonstrated a "party" spirit, judging others based on their choice of congregation or opinions. Catholic-spirited Christians like Whitefield loved rather than judged Christians; Wesley encouraged his hearers to do the same.

Beyond this evangelical denominational fluidity and "Catholic spirit," which admittedly did not always work out in practice as it did in theological theory, the Wesleyan tradition also supported missions, even if they were not as influential as the Whitefieldian Calvinists came to be. For example, historian Joseph Conforti noted that John Wesley was "among the first evangelicals to see the value of the *Life [of David Brainerd].*"[122] Wesley's abridged version of *Life* went through seven English editions between 1768 and 1825.[123] Although Wesley's time as a missionary for the Society for Propagation of the Gospel was brief, and even though he squelched the 1770s missions proposals of Thomas Coke (the leading architect of early Methodist missionary efforts), he was in favor of missions to all parts of the world.[124] In Coke's *An Address to the Pious and Benevolent, Proposing an Annual Subscription for the Support of Missionaries* (1786), John Wesley provided a note of approval of the project.[125] Coke even hoped to unite Calvinists and Arminians in his "Plan for the Establishment of Missions among the Heathen" (1783).[126] Coke continued a relentless effort to raise funds for foreign missions throughout his life.[127]

---

printed by J. and W. Oliver, 1770), 25.
[121] Ibid., 27.
[122] Conforti, "Jonathan Edwards's Most Popular Work," 191.
[123] Ibid.
[124] Heitzenrater, *Wesley and the People Called Methodists*, 282.
[125] Thomas Coke, *An Address to the Pious and Benevolent, Proposing an Annual Subscription for the Support of Missionaries in the Highlands and Adjacent Islands of Scotland, the Isles of Jersey, Guernsey, and Newfoundland, the West Indies, and the Provinces of Nova Scotia and Quebec* (London: n.p., 1786), 2.
[126] Martin, *Evangelicals United*, 25.
[127] John A. Vickers, "Coke, Thomas," ed. Donald M. Lewis, *Dictionary of Evangelical Biography, 1730–1860* (Peabody: Hendrickson, 2004), 1:238-39.

CONCLUSION

After three-fourths of the eighteenth century were complete, transatlantic evangelicals had constructed a missions culture that provided a compelling view of the world and the Christian's place in it. They believed that denominationalism and confessionalism often provided criteria for the essence of Christianity that focused on the intellect but neglected new-birth experience. In their advocacy of new birth as the chief criterion for Christian identity and membership in the universal church, they found fertile ground for interdenominational cooperation on a primitive gospel and ancient Christianity that preceded the denominations. They focused on Christian unity for the purpose of prayer and cooperation in missionary endeavors, hoping that Christian unity and missions to the world would usher in the latter days. Many evangelicals believed they lived in a special time when God poured out his spirit to convert people and the world, most palpably visible in the revivals throughout the eighteenth century. In this way, Puritans, Pietists, Moravians, and Methodists constructed a Christian vision of action in the world where Christian unity, prayer, missions, and eschatology were inextricably linked. As they worked to put these ideas into concrete structures and institutions, the architects of the interdenominational societies of the 1790s inherited this vision of the world and the Christian's place in it. We turn to that story in the next chapter.

Chapter Three

The Explosion of Transatlantic Evangelical Missions in the 1790s

Among those attending the exhilarating founding meetings of the London Missionary Society in September 1795 were both skeptics and supporters. One curious skeptic, who recorded his experience of the meetings under the name Iota, encountered a surprising and contagious atmosphere in the interdenominational missionary movement. After Iota experienced these solemn religious assemblies with "Christians of almost every denomination . . . together animated by *one* and the same *spirit*," he renounced his prejudices against his Christian brothers and sisters and joined the interdenominational missionary cause. Inspired by the meetings, Iota composed a poem which highlighted themes that impressed him, including pity for the "heathen," Christian unity, and the latter days.[1] If skeptics turned from caution to poetic adulation, supporters were affirmed and reported on the meetings with enthusiastic optimism. One report described the meeting like heaven after the second coming:

---

[1] Iota, "To the Editor," *The Evangelical Magazine* 3 (December 1795): 504–06; Iota, "On the Late Meeting of Ministers of Different Denominations in London, for the Establishment of a MISSIONARY SOCIETY," *The Evangelical Magazine* 3 (November 1795): 480.

Such a scene was, perhaps, never before beheld in our world, and afforded a glorious earnest of that nobler assembly, where we shall meet all the redeemed, and in the presence and before the throne of the Lamb shall sing, as in the last hymn of the service, *Crown Him, crown Him, crown Him Lord of All!*[2]

The gathering of adherents from different denominations for worship in the 1790s, during which people performed meaningful rituals together, was an extraordinary and often transformational experience for doubters and promoters alike. This chapter tells the story of the culmination and solidification of interdenominational evangelical missions in the 1790s, which found its center in the London Missionary Society and *The Evangelical Magazine*. This will provide a basis for comparison of the Campbells' experiences in Ireland, Scotland, and the United States.

The Rise of Evangelical Voluntary Societies in the 1790s

The most important transatlantic evangelical structural development in the 1780s and 1790s was the voluntary society. Although numerous societies preceded them in the eighteenth century, voluntary societies proliferated from the 1790s. The voluntary society grew out of socioeconomic, intellectual, and political contexts, and became the most important means of evangelical and social activism. Societies arose for nearly every fathomable cause, and missionary societies were among the earliest and most popular.[3] Thus it was not until the 1790s that evangelicals constructed and administered missions structures that they had been talking and praying about for over fifty years. Like a snowball rolling down a hill and continually increasing in size, the missions movement gained momentum. By the 1780s and 1790s, evangelical papers, schools, and connections had grown large enough to garner substantial support. The number of people who read and understood the words of Jonathan Edwards on prayer for missions in the last days grew. William Carey published his influential 1792 proposal of a voluntary society as a functional means for propagating the gospel to the

---

[2] "Missionary Society," *The Evangelical Magazine* 3 (October 1795): 425.

[3] By 1915, Protestants administered over 350 missionary societies, supporting about twenty-four thousand foreign missionaries. See Dana Lee Robert, *Christian Mission: How Christianity Became a World Religion* (Chichester: Wiley-Blackwell, 2009), 51.

"heathen." The General Evangelical Society (1787) organized in Dublin for Protestant evangelization of Ireland, while the Northamptonshire Baptists organized the denominational Particular Baptist Society for Propagating the Gospel Among the Heathen (Baptist Missionary Society) in 1792. In 1799, Evangelical Anglicans established what became known as the Church Missionary Society. A number of societies were explicitly interdenominational. Influential among these was the London Missionary Society, which was emulated by many smaller missionary societies in Europe and elsewhere in the transatlantic. The Religious Tract Society (1799) and the British and Foreign Bible Society (1804) were also important societies which evangelicals across denominations supported.[4]

Most individuals in 1790 still thought in terms of parish boundaries—the idea of voluntary associations of individuals joining together for a defined goal was still fairly novel. These societies were often started by unknown people, and they made space for medical and female ministries that were not possible in existing church structures. They depended on donations and regular participation of lay people just as much as they did on clergy. Therefore, the people who supported and ran them also took ownership of these societies, and sacrificed a great deal for them and their causes. Support of the voluntary societies allowed even people of modest means to perceive themselves as participants in overseas missions and other social ministries which attempted to transform culture and herald the millennium. The societies also added an "international dimension which hardly any of the churches, growing as they did within a national framework, had any means of expressing. After the age of the voluntary society, the Western church could never be the same again."[5] As Andrew Walls concludes, "By its very success, the voluntary society subverted all the classical forms of church government, while fitting comfortably into none

---

[4] R. Pierce Beaver, *Pioneers in Mission: The Early Missionary Ordination Sermons, Charges, and Instructions* (Grand Rapids: Eerdmans, 1966), 1–32; John Wolffe, *The Expansion of Evangelicalism: The Age of Wilberforce, More, Chalmers and Finney*, A History of Evangelicalism 2 (Downers Grove: InterVarsity Press, 2007), chaps. 6–7; Mark Hutchinson and John Wolffe, *A Short History of Global Evangelicalism* (Cambridge: Cambridge University Press, 2012), 70–85; Charles I. Foster, *An Errand of Mercy: The Evangelical United Front, 1790–1837* (Chapel Hill: University of North Carolina Press, 1960).

[5] Andrew F. Walls, "Missionary Societies and the Fortunate Subversion of the Church," *Evangelical Quarterly* 88, no. 2 (1988): 154.

of them."⁶ Naturally, then, voluntary societies created conflict where they took over activities that established and settled churches had previously controlled or rejected.

The social, economic, intellectual, political, and religious contexts of the late eighteenth-century transatlantic world propelled the rise of evangelical missionary societies from the 1790s onward.⁷ Maritime explorers such as James Cook "brought home to the British imagination the reality of the vastness of the world and the diversity of its peoples.... It was now more than ever apparent that the Gospel had not been preached to the ends of the earth."⁸ Imperial colonialism offered a way for Europeans to migrate and travel back and forth across the Atlantic, encounter non-Christian peoples, and establish early missions.⁹ Industrialization provided advances in communication and travel, though it also produced large-scale movements of people and urban conditions which led to increasing growth of dissenting evangelical groups such as Methodists, whose itinerants were able to serve urban and frontier areas where older parish structures were insufficient. Evangelicals from both dissenting and established groups formed voluntary religious societies which employed itinerants who could meet the needs presented by the unique societal developments in new urban areas and on the western frontier of the United States.¹⁰

The intellectual context of the Enlightenment deeply shaped both evangelicalism and the missionary enterprise throughout the eighteenth century.¹¹

---

⁶ Ibid., 147.

⁷ For in-depth analysis of the contextual factors I mention only briefly here, see David J. Bosch, *Transforming Mission: Paradigm Shifts in Theology of Mission*, American Society of Missiology Series 16 (Maryknoll: Orbis Books, 1991), 262–345; Stephen Neill, *A History of Christian Missions*, 2nd ed., The Penguin History of the Church 6 (London: Penguin Books, 1986), 208–22; Robert, *Christian Mission*, 44–48.

⁸ Stephen Orchard, "Evangelical Eschatology and the Missionary Awakening," *Journal of Religious History* 22, no. 2 (1998): 139.

⁹ "Three C's" of colonialism were often cited as Christianity, commerce, and civilization. See Bosch, *Transforming Mission*, 305.

¹⁰ Stewart J. Brown, "Movements of Christian Awakening in Revolutionary Europe, 1790–1815," in *The Cambridge History of Christianity: Volume VII, Enlightenment, Reawakening and Revolution 1660–1815*, eds. Stewart J. Brown and Timothy Tackett (Cambridge: Cambridge University Press, 2006), 577; David Bebbington, "The Growth of Voluntary Religion," in *The Cambridge History of Christianity: Volume VIII, World Christianities, c 1815–c.1914*, eds. Sheridan Gilley and Brian Stanley (Cambridge: Cambridge University Press, 2006), 60.

¹¹ On defining "Enlightenment," David Bebbington notes that the central figures and contributions to the Enlightenment included René Descartes's promotion of mathematical certainty in human knowledge; John Locke's empiricism, which argued against innate ideas and for knowledge coming from experience; and Isaac Newton's success with empirical investigation and inductive reasoning. Kerry Walters

Historians have not only debunked the idea that evangelicalism emerged as anti-intellectual and anti-rational, but recent studies by missiologist David Bosch,[12] historian Brian Stanley,[13] and historian David Bebbington[14] demonstrate that the intellectual environment of the Enlightenment directly influenced eighteenth-century evangelicalism and the missionary movement.[15]

In his seminal work on evangelicalism in Great Britain, Bebbington notes several major areas of Enlightenment influence upon evangelicalism. He argues that "Edwards derived his confidence about salvation from the atmosphere of the English Enlightenment." The Common Sense Realism philosophy of the Scottish Enlightenment animated the thought of many transatlantic evangelicals. Evangelicals adopted optimism about human progress, which translated into confidence in their ability to convert the world and the common eschatological perspective that Christ would return after the millennium (postmillennialism), since the gradual improvement of humanity would result in the millennium. Confidence in human potential, individual autonomy, and freedom of choice influenced Edwardsian moderate Calvinism, which prioritized belief in individuals, and also drove revivalism and evangelism. The flexible, tolerant, utilitarian spirit of the Enlightenment age fostered field preaching, lay preaching, and female

---

notes, "the Enlightenment worldview embraced a number of identifying beliefs. It would be a mistake to think of them as necessary and sufficient principles uniformly held by all philosophers. As historian Carl Becker noted, the ethos was more a 'climate of opinion' than an epoch of uniform agreement. But five general beliefs stand out as providing a basic orientation for most of the leading spokespersons of the Enlightenment: (1) the primacy of experience and inductive reason; (2) the importance of science, or 'natural philosophy'; (3) a deep-seated suspicion of authority; (4) an emphasis on reform; and (5) a confidence in the perfectibility of both individuals and society." Kerry Walters, "Enlightenment," in *Encyclopedia of Religion in America*, eds. Charles H. Lippy and Peter W. Williams, vol. 2 (Washington: CQ Press, 2010), 695; David Bebbington, "Enlightenment," ed. Nigel M. de S. Cameron, *Dictionary of Scottish Church History & Theology* (Downers Grove: InterVarsity Press, 1993), 294–95.

[12] Bosch devoted an eighty-two-page chapter of his magisterial missiology, *Transforming Mission*, to argue "the entire modern missionary enterprise is, to a very real extent, a child of the Enlightenment." "The entire Western missionary movement of the past three centuries," he contends, "emerged from the matrix of the Enlightenment." See Bosch, *Transforming Mission*, 274, 344.

[13] Stanley posits that "the modern Protestant missionary movement cannot be understood unless full attention is paid to the intellectual milieu within which evangelicalism was shaped. Moreover, [this book] broadly supports the now established consensus that this milieu was essentially one formed by the intellectual contours of the Enlightenment." See Brian Stanley, "Christian Missions and the Enlightenment: A Reevaluation," in *Christian Missions and the Enlightenment*, ed. Brian Stanley (Grand Rapids: Eerdmans, 2001), 4.

[14] Bebbington produced a persuasive argument that the "Evangelical version of Protestantism was created by the Enlightenment." See David W. Bebbington, *Evangelicalism in Modern Britain: A History from the 1730s to the 1980s* (London: Routledge, 1989), 42–74.

[15] For a historiographical overview on which I rely for this section, see Stanley, "Christian Missions and the Enlightenment: A Reevaluation," 1–21.

preaching, a catholic spirit, and interdenominational voluntary societies.[16] Evangelicalism was intricately related to the intellectual milieu of the Enlightenment.[17]

A number of general characteristics often identified with the Enlightenment influenced the ideas and actions of transatlantic evangelical missions proponents.[18] Reason as a central authority, combined with freedom of individual conscience, led some evangelicals, such as Philip Doddridge and some "New Lights,"[19] to oppose subscription to any creed.[20] The same tenets led to a religious toleration, which John Locke justified on grounds of Scripture, natural rights, and human psychology in his classic defense of religious toleration[21]: this caused some evangelicals to oppose the legitimacy of civil or religious authorities to compel belief.[22] Lockean and Enlightenment toleration undergirded evangelical ecumenism and the catholic spirit practiced by many early evangelicals and the 1790s missionary leaders. For many evangelicals, Enlightenment toleration reduced

---

[16] Bebbington, *Evangelicalism in Modern Britain*, 42–74.

[17] For more on the relationship of Enlightenment and evangelicalism, also see David Bebbington, "Revival and Enlightenment in Eighteenth-Century England," in *Modern Christian Revivals*, eds. Edith Waldvogel Blumhofer and Randall Herbert Balmer (Urbana: University of Illinois Press, 1993), 17–41; Mark A. Noll, *The Rise of Evangelicalism: The Age of Edwards, Whitefield, and the Wesleys*, A History of Evangelicalism 1 (Downers Grove: InterVarsity Press, 2003), 150–51; Richard T. Hughes and C. Leonard Allen, "Restoring First Times in the Anglo-American Experience," in *Illusions of Innocence: Protestant Primitivism in America, 1630–1875* (Abilene, TX: Abilene Christian University Press, 2008), chap. 1; C. Leonard Allen and Richard T. Hughes, *Discovering Our Roots: The Ancestry of Churches of Christ* (Abilene, TX: Abilene Christian University Press, 1988), chap. 7; Mark A. Noll, *A History of Christianity in the United States and Canada* (Grand Rapids: Eerdmans, 1992), 154–57; Theodore Dwight Bozeman, *Protestants in an Age of Science: The Baconian Ideal and Antebellum American Religious Thought* (Chapel Hill: University of North Carolina Press, 1977); W. Reginald Ward, "Enlightenment in Early Moravianism," in *Faith and Faction* (London: Epworth Press, 1993), 95–111.

[18] For Bosch, the contours of the Enlightenment included reason as key authority (I think therefore I am); subject-object scheme (subject [*res cogitans*] able to observe external object [*res extensa*]); the earth's ability to be occupied and subdued; the elimination of purpose and introduction of direct causality as the key to understanding reality; the belief in progress and discovery of new territories and colonialization; the ideal of modernization; the viewing of scientific knowledge as factual, value-free, and neutral; the viewing of all problems as solvable; the attitude that people are emancipated and autonomous individuals, resulting in the dominant characteristic of the modern era—radical anthropocentrism. Bosch, *Transforming Mission*, 262–67.

[19] In America, "New Lights" referred to pro-revivalists. In Ireland, "New Lights" specified those who opposed subscription to creeds. I have the latter in mind here, as discussed in I. R. McBride, "'When Ulster Joined Ireland': Anti-Popery, Presbyterian Radicalism, and Irish Republicanism in the 1790s," *Past & Present*, no. 157 (1997): 63–93.

[20] Bebbington, *Evangelicalism in Modern Britain*, 54.

[21] John Locke, *A Letter Concerning Toleration* (London: printed for Awnsham Churchill at the Black Swan at Amen-Corner, 1689).

[22] I. R. McBride, "'When Ulster Joined Ireland,'" 69–70.

or completely dissolved the cognitive dissonance that could accompany evangelical interdenominational cooperation for missions.

Numerous other Enlightenment characteristics shaped evangelical missions. Comparisons of "civilized" and "rational" Westerners with "uncivilized" and "irrational" "heathen savages" was not new to the Enlightenment era, but as Brian Stanley argues, what was "new about eighteenth-century thought was its increasing tendency to assert the *intrinsic* unity and equality of all humanity." One sees this emphasis throughout early missionary literature which attempts to provoke "pity" and "compassion" for the "heathen" destined to hell, and often rejected slavery as wrong and as an obstruction to conversion of the world. Missions advocates argued that "heathens" were not irreversibly irrational or barbarian; instead, they simply needed civilization and Christianity to manifest their God-given innate capacity to flourish. Optimism about human potential and Western progress translated into confidence in the illuminative power of education, knowledge, and rational thought, which could lead to the Christianization and salvation of the "heathen."[23] However, "civilization" versus "evangelization" was a constant conversation among missionaries and advocates; hence, the Christ- and culture-dialectic is the central theme and key problem running throughout historian William Hutchinson's *Errand to the World: American Protestant Thought and Foreign Missions*.[24] Although Enlightenment-era optimism led some ethnocentric Westerners to see "civilization" as a prerequisite to evangelization, Westerners were not monolithically ethnocentric in the missionary enterprise.

Finally, the Enlightenment ideal of toleration and individual autonomy, which led to the gradual shift of the conception of religion from the public to the private sphere, deeply shaped Western society, Christianity, and evangelical missions. Religious belief became a voluntary act of the individual rather than a public act of allegiance to the establishment, and the evangelical conversion narrative contributed to the new conception of religion. Relying on the work of Peter van der Veer, Stanley notes that the missionary movement promoted this privatization and voluntarization of

---

[23] Stanley, "Christian Missions and the Enlightenment: A Reevaluation," 10–12.
[24] William R. Hutchinson, *Errand to the World: American Protestant Thought and Foreign Missions* (Chicago: University of Chicago Press, 1987), 10–13 passim.

religion, but was also a product of it: "The locus of Christian commitment had moved from the state church to the voluntary society of 'true,' converted believers, and such societies pursued the goal of the dissemination of true Christianity both within formal Christendom and beyond it."[25] Andrew Walls argues that the evangelicalism of the 1790s calmed fears created by individualism in the modern church and society when it "reconciled the developed consciousness of individual responsibility, so characteristic of Enlightenment thought," with a close fellowship of like-minded "real" (i.e., converted rather than "nominal") Christians. Reconciling such societal and religious concerns, evangelicals added the flexible voluntary society, fueling the Protestant missionary movement and providing an outlet for evangelical activism.[26] David Bosch also points out that the voluntarism of missionary societies was driven by "social and political egalitarianism of the emerging democracies" and the "free-enterprise system."[27]

The period from the 1770s through the 1810s was a time of political upheaval in North America, Great Britain, and Europe. Enlightenment thinkers synthesized ideas that culminated in revolutions on both sides of the Atlantic and began to permeate Western political culture. The French Revolution figured prominently into eschatological speculation of evangelicals who were always looking for visible signs of the fall of Antichrist—"evangelicals all saw the sign of the latter days in the humbling of the Roman Catholic Church."[28] In this socioeconomic and political upheaval, evangelical dissent in England, Ireland, and Scotland grew at an unprecedented rate from 1790 to 1815, and these groups were important to the missionary enterprise.[29]

The religious context gave shape to and was shaped by these intellectual, political, social, and economic contexts. An important development in the religious sphere was the prior and subsequent evangelical awakenings.

---

[25] Stanley, "Christian Missions and the Enlightenment: A Reevaluation," 13; Peter van der Veer, ed., *Conversion to Modernities: The Globalization of Christianity* (New York: Routledge, 1996).

[26] Andrew F. Walls, "The Eighteenth-Century Protestant Missionary Awakening in Its European Context," in *Christian Missions and the Enlightenment*, ed. Brian Stanley (Grand Rapids: Eerdmans, 2001), 29–30.

[27] Bosch, *Transforming Mission*, 328, 334.

[28] James A. De Jong, *As the Waters Cover the Sea: Millennial Expectations in the Rise of Anglo-American Missions, 1640–1810*, 2006 reprint (Kampen: J. H. Kok, 1970), 164, 160.

[29] Brown, "Movements of Christian Awakening in Revolutionary Europe, 1790–1815," 578.

Evangelicals of the 1790s continued the conversionist revivalism of their predecessors but, painting in broad strokes, developed several key theological ideas. The Calvinism of Jonathan Edwards continued to provide what evangelicals called "moderate Calvinism," and some went further to embrace Arminianism, which was more palatable to the political and anthropological milieu of many late eighteenth-century transatlantic people.[30] John Wesley's explicit Arminianism gave credence to ideas that suited a free and confident people who were in charge of their own destinies and responsible for making their own decisions. Furthermore, postmillennialism became the most common eschatological view, and it continued its deep connection to missionary thought. According to missions scholar Charles Chaney, "Not a single sermon or missionary report can be discovered [from this era in the United States] that does not stress eschatological considerations."[31] Characteristics of evangelicals in the revolutionary 1790s included an elevated common person who was equal with all other people before God (i.e., all equally needed conversion), a lay leadership active in preaching and organizing, opposition to skepticism and materialism and some types of rationalism of the Enlightenment, and a large constituency outside the established churches.[32]

Scholars also have emphasized the inextricable connection between the evangelical awakening of the 1790s with the missionary and ecumenical movements.[33] Evangelicalism provided the international and interdenominational networks that undergirded the missionary movement. Andrew Walls notes many of these connections:

> The chain that led to William Carey's pioneering missionary initiative of 1792 was forged by a gift from a Scottish Presbyterian to an English Baptist of a book by a New England Congregationalist. Another New Englander, David Brainerd,

---

[30] On Edwardsian moderate Calvinism in the eighteenth century, see Bebbington, *Evangelicalism in Modern Britain*, 63–65.
[31] Charles L. Chaney, *The Birth of Missions in America* (Pasadena: William Carey Library, 1976), 269.
[32] Brown, "Movements of Christian Awakening in Revolutionary Europe, 1790–1815"; Noll, *The Rise of Evangelicalism*, chap. 7.
[33] Ruth Rouse, "Voluntary Movement and the Changing Ecumenical Climate," in *A History of the Ecumenical Movement, 1517–1948*, eds. Ruth Rouse and Stephen Charles Neill, 3rd ed. (Geneva: World Council of Churches, 1986), 310.

became the principal model of early British Missionary spirituality; his own work had been supported by the Society in Scotland for Promoting Christian Knowledge. An unending stream of correspondence, crisscrossing the Atlantic, reveals just how important as a missionary factor were the African-Americans and Afro-West Indians.... Magazines ... gathered and disseminated 'missionary intelligence' without regard to denomination or country of origins.... Above all, the revival supplied missionaries. There had been various earlier schemes for missions, although none went further than paper because no one was likely to undertake them. The first generation of the Protestant missionary enterprise was for practical purposes an evangelical undertaking.[34]

The contexts noted above shaped and made the missions movement possible, but the focus hereafter is to understand the evangelicals who were involved in missions on their own terms. How did they see their world? Why did missions become a central response to their perception of the world? How and why did they establish missionary societies and magazines? What were the key symbols used in missionary sermons and literature? What were the key developments in and components of transatlantic evangelical missions?

William Carey, Voluntary Missionary Societies, and Samuel Hopkins

Numerous publications during the last two decades of the eighteenth century argued for the establishment of voluntary missionary societies, sometimes organized along denominational lines and sometimes with explicit promotion of interdenominational cooperation. These appeals were typically connected to the concert of prayer for revivals and missions that began in Scotland and became widespread through the support of Jonathan Edwards and leading evangelicals in the second half of the nineteenth century. Scottish Presbyterian John Erskine (1721–1803) was key to the missionary awakening of the 1790s. He corresponded with Atlantic

---

[34] Andrew F. Walls, "The Evangelical Revival, the Missionary Movement, and Africa," in *The Missionary Movement in Christian History: Studies in the Transmission of Faith* (Maryknoll: Orbis Books, 1996), 79–80.

evangelicals throughout the eighteenth century, and promoted the 1740s revivals, the concerts for prayer, and foreign and home missions with eschatological motives. He served as a director of the Society in Scotland for Propagating Christian Knowledge, and he published and distributed the works of Jonathan Edwards. Erskine sent Edwards's *An Humble Attempt* to his English Baptist correspondents in Northamptonshire (Andrew Fuller and John Ryland, Jr.), prompting them to start concerts of prayer for revival and the spread of Christ's kingdom in 1784, from which Baptist missions developed. Erskine and the Society in Scotland for Propagating Christian Knowledge also nurtured the central leaders of the London Missionary Society.[35]

The most influential appeal for missions by way of voluntary societies came from the pen of Baptist William Carey (1761-1834), whose persuasive *Enquiry into the Obligations of Christians, to Use Means for the Conversion of the Heathens* (1792) earned widespread readership. Carey's *Enquiry* was a culmination of his experience with the Northamptonshire Baptists and his reading of Edwards's works. His effective articulation of both the "obligation" and the "means" to convert "heathens" is a chief reason for his fame as "father" of modern missions.[36]

Carey's *Enquiry* had five major sections. The first section focused on Matthew 28:19-20,[37] the so-called Great Commission, which became the chief biblical symbol for the missions movement. Carey argued that this commission of Jesus Christ to his disciples was still binding on Christians. He refuted opponents' claims that (1) "if God intends the salvation of the heathen, he will some way or other bring them to the gospel, or the gospel to them"; or (2) that the commission was only binding upon the apostles and not on Christians today; or (3) that Scriptures proved the time had not yet come for the conversion of the "heathen"; or (4) that Christians should

---

[35] De Jong, *As the Waters Cover the Sea*, 166-98; Noll, *The Rise of Evangelicalism*, 207-10; John R. McIntosh, "Erskine, John," ed. Donald M. Lewis, *Dictionary of Evangelical Biography, 1730-1860* (Peabody: Hendrickson, 2004), 1:363.

[36] Brian Stanley, *The History of the Baptist Missionary Society, 1792-1992* (Edinburgh: T&T Clark, 1992), 12.

[37] "Go ye therefore, and teach all nations, baptizing them in the name of the Father, and of the Son, and of the Holy Ghost: Teaching them to observe all things whatsoever I have commanded you: and, lo, I am with you always, even unto the end of the world. Amen" (Matt. 28:19-20 KJV).

focus on the need in their own nations.[38] In the case of number three, whose proponents also said that first "the *witnesses must be slain*, and many other prophecies fulfilled," Carey referred readers to "Edwards on Prayer," which had been recently reprinted by Sutcliffe."[39]

Carey's *Enquiry* also continued the evangelical use of eschatology as a motive for missions.[40] As James De Jong points out, basic to Carey's "theology of missions is the framework of his discussion [in *Enquiry*], namely the belief that, as promised in the prophets, history is moving toward its culmination in the kingdom of Christ."[41] Clear from the introduction, Carey encouraged Christians to pray and work for the kingdom, work which was exemplified by John Eliot, David Brainerd, and the Moravian Brethren.[42]

But Carey appealed not only to actors in history. He also found that the words of Isaiah 60 spoke definitively about his own era.[43] "In the time of the glorious increase of the church, in the latter days, (of which the whole chapter is undoubtedly a prophecy,)" Carey noted, "commerce shall subserve the spread of the gospel." Isaiah's words about navigation and trade with unknown parts of the world were being fulfilled by modern industrialism and colonialism. In the words of Isaiah 60:9, "surely the islands look to me; in the lead are the ships of Tarshish," Carey saw a fulfilled prophecy:

> The ships of Tarshish were trading vessels, which made voyages for traffic to various parts, thus much therefore must be meant by it, that *navigation*, especially that which is *commercial*, shall be one great mean [sic] of carrying on the work of God; and perhaps it may imply that there shall be a very considerable appropriation of wealth to that purpose.[44]

---

[38] William Carey, *An Enquiry into the Obligations of Christians, to Use Means for the Conversion of the Heathens* (Leicester: Printed and Sold by Ann Ireland, 1792), 7–13.

[39] Ibid., 12, n1.

[40] Stephen Neill missed this aspect of Carey's *Enquiry* when he said it was "free from eschatological speculation of the pietists." Neill, *A History of Christian Missions*, 222; De Jong, *As the Waters Cover the Sea*, 175–81.

[41] De Jong, *As the Waters Cover the Sea*, 178.

[42] Thus Carey contributed to securing their iconic status. He also mentioned John Wesley and Jonathan Edwards. See Carey, *Enquiry*, 11, 36–37, 69–71, 87.

[43] "Surely the isles shall wait for me, and the ships of Tarshish first, to bring thy [Carey has "my"] sons from far, their silver and their gold with them, unto the name of the LORD thy God . . ." (Isa. 60:9 KJV).

[44] Carey, *Enquiry*, 68.

Like Jonathan Edwards before him, Carey viewed the new navigation and commercial systems of imperial England as tools for missions, and perhaps both believed that Isaiah foresaw that there would even be a financial profit in spreading the gospel. Carey's interpretation of Isaiah 60:9 clearly demonstrates not only Carey's understanding of the nature of prophecy, but also his belief that he was living in the latter times when Isaiah's prophecies would be fulfilled.[45]

Carey provided several proposals of means for people to contribute to evangelization of the "heathen." First, the "fervent and united prayer" of all Christians would procure God's blessing. He argued that prayer could unite Christians in desiring to fulfill one of their Christian duties and perhaps secure God's blessing upon the endeavor. Indeed, Carey believed the monthly prayer meetings for the success of the gospel had been successful, and that the increase of civil and religious liberty with the decrease of "popery" would open the doors wider and wider. As evidence of success at the time of publishing, Carey cited an increase in calls to preach the gospel in places devoid of proclamation, and efforts to "abolish the inhuman Slave-Trade."[46] One year later, as discussed below, Samuel Hopkins inextricably linked missions and abolition of the slave trade.

Second, Carey proposed a voluntary missionary society, one which he likened to a trading company: "Suppose a company of serious Christians, ministers, and private persons, were to form themselves into a society, and make a number of rules respecting the regulation of the plan, and the persons who are to be employed as missionaries, the means of defraying the expence, etc." Membership to the society would be selective, only open to those who were of "serious religion," whose "hearts are in the work," and who "possess a spirit of perseverance." The society would then form a committee which would procure information on missions, receive contributions, hire missionaries, and provide for the needs of the missionaries. Carey listed several ways in which funds might be raised. The rich could give portions to the work. The common people could perhaps give one tenth of their annual income to the work, following what Carey saw as the ancient biblical and more recent Puritan practice. Congregations could open

---

[45] Ibid., 12.
[46] Ibid., 79.

subscriptions of one penny or more per week and reserve it for the propagation of the gospel. If Christians and churches used these methods, there would be enough money to support ministers at home, "*village preaching in our neighbourhods,*" and missionaries to the "heathen" world.[47] Early evangelical missionary societies used this basic method to create and run their voluntary societies like trading companies.

At the time of writing *Enquiry*, Carey did not envision an interdenominational missionary society. Instead, he proposed the society and committee be formed among his *"particular baptist denomination."* However, as Andrew Walls observes, Carey's proposal was based solely on practicality, rather than on any theological reservation about an interdenominational missionary society.[48] Carey's proposal actually had an ecumenical premise. Carey explained:

> I do not mean by this, in any way to confine it to any one denomination of Christians. I wish with all my heart, that every one who loves our Lord Jesus Christ in sincerity, would in some way or other engage in it. But in the present divided state of Christendom, it would be more likely for good to be done by each denomination engaging separately in the work, than if they were to embark in it conjointly. There is room enough for us all, without interfering with each other; and if no unfriendly interference took place, each denomination would bear good will to the other, and wish, and pray for its success, considering it as upon the whole friendly to the great cause of true religion; but if all were intermingled it is likely their private discords might throw a damp upon their spirits, and much retard their public usefulness.[49]

No doubt encouraged by correspondence with organizers of the enormous cooperative endeavors of the London Missionary Society and other societies organized along interdenominational lines for tract and Bible production and missionary endeavors, Carey's perceptions of the situation had

---

[47] Ibid., 81–87.
[48] Walls, "Missionary Societies and the Fortunate Subversion of the Church," 145–48.
[49] Carey, *Enquiry*, 84.

changed by 1806. That year, Carey proposed to Andrew Fuller, secretary of the Baptist Missionary Society, that they organize an interdenominational and international meeting in 1810 and every ten years afterward. The meetings would provide a space for missionaries and organizers to talk and understand what the others were doing—this would be a quicker method than correspondence.[50] The meeting never happened, but Carey's proposal demonstrates that he warmed to cooperation, to some degree, by 1806. Carey's evangelical Christianity was the basis of his ecumenical sentiment. He spoke of Congregational, Methodist, Moravian, and other missionaries with complete approval. They worked in the mission field for conversion of the "heathen," and in Carey's estimation, that was the central goal of Christian mission. Missions by Protestants trumped denominational affiliation, as did new birth for Whitefield and many revivalists.

For Carey, a world overrun with the chaos and darkness of paganism could be made orderly if Christians would follow Jesus's command to go and make disciples of all nations, and Carey proposed ways for Christians of all classes to participate in this great endeavor that would surely continue an outpouring of God's spirit in what seemed to be the cusp of the last days. Backed by encouragement from the Northamptonshire Baptist Association, Carey's proposal for a voluntary society prompted the formation of the Baptist Missionary Society in 1792. The Baptist Missionary Society sent him to India in 1793, and he corresponded with numerous evangelicals to continue shaping the missions environment.[51]

In the United States, Congregational minister Samuel Hopkins (1721–1803) trained at Yale College and, as a disciple of Jonathan Edwards, influenced evangelical missions with a key idea: disinterested benevolence.[52] Disinterested benevolence dated back to Edwards, though Hopkins did update the idea in *An Inquiry into the Nature of True Holiness* (1773). For Hopkins, holiness consisted of conforming to God's law, which was expressed in love. This love, or holiness, consisted of love of God and people;

---

[50] Ruth Rouse, "William Carey's Pleasing Dream," *International Review of Mission* 38, no. 2 (1949): 181–92.
[51] Stanley, *The History of the Baptist Missionary Society, 1792–1992*, chaps. 1–2; Noll, *The Rise of Evangelicalism*, 208–10.
[52] William Warren Sweet claimed Hopkins should be called the "Father of American Missions." Chaney said Sweet's assertion was an overstatement. See Chaney, *The Birth of Missions in America*, 74.

it was universal benevolence or friendly affection to all intelligent beings. Disinterested benevolence promoted selfless service for the kingdom of God, epitomized in God's giving his son to die for sinners. This selflessness for the sake of the kingdom and the glory of God was the highest good, characterizing the life of Christ and God's own holiness. The opposite of disinterested benevolence was selfishness. Missionaries like David Brainerd could be portrayed as emulating Christ in giving themselves entirely and selflessly to save others. Therefore, the missionary became a picture of disinterested benevolence. Key Calvinist motives for missions—the glory of God and the salvation of humanity—were seemingly perfectly combined in the idea of disinterested benevolence.[53]

Hopkins combined disinterested benevolence with Edwardsian post-millennial eschatology, illustrated in *A Treatise on the Millennium* (1793), to form a moderate Calvinist apology for social reform. Hopkins became one of the earliest and most vocal abolitionists and missionary advocates. Missionaries used the idea of disinterested benevolence to test the genuineness of their commitment to the gospel, and they attempted to follow Brainerd as he faced physical hardships and even death in order to spread the gospel (a chief means of loving humanity and glorifying God) to the American Indians.[54]

Hopkins's theology of missions grew out of his understanding of disinterested benevolence and abolitionism. For Hopkins, the slave trade and slavery were instruments of Satan and obstacles to Christ's command to spread the gospel; therefore, he construed justice and benevolence as key motives for both abolition and missions.[55] Christians had committed a horrendous crime by ripping people from their homelands, separating them from their families, and subjugating them to slavery. Slave traders and supporters of slavery were the "emissaries of satan," even though some

---

[53] Ibid., 82–83.

[54] Samuel Hopkins, *An Inquiry into the Nature of True Holiness* (Newport: Solomon Southwick, 1773); Samuel Hopkins, *A Treatise on the Millennium* (Boston: Isaiah Thomas and Ebenezer T. Andrews, 1793); Chaney, *The Birth of Missions in America*, 74–84; J. R. Fitzmier, "Hopkins, Samuel (1721–1803)," ed. Daniel G. Reid et al., *Dictionary of Christianity in America* (Downers Grove: InterVarsity Press, 1990), 553–54; Bosch, *Transforming Mission*, 290, 313; Joseph Conforti, "Jonathan Edwards's Most Popular Work: 'The Life of David Brainerd' and 19th-Century Evangelical Culture," *Church History* 54, no. 2 (1985): 196–97; Hutchinson, *Errand to the World*, 49–51.

[55] Samuel Hopkins, *A Discourse upon the Slave-Trade, and the Slavery of the Africans* (Providence: J. Carter, 1793), 21–22.

did not realize or believe they were servants of the evil one.⁵⁶ The slave trade was so wicked that Hopkins saw it as evidence that the sixth vial (see Rev. 16) "has been running during this time."⁵⁷ It was clear to him that the gospel was suited to root out evils such as tyranny and slavery. Hopkins believed slavery would be wholly abolished in any place where the gospel was preached, received, and obeyed. He chided the British Parliament and the United States Congress for their delay in abolishing the slave trade. He also suggested that free blacks would not be treated equally in the United States because whites had such deep-seated racism. Therefore, he proposed colonization of black people in Africa, pointing to the recent success of such endeavors in Sierra Leone. Such colonization should receive the support of the United States in reparation for its horrendous crimes against Africans. Christians should prepare black missionaries so they could spread Christianity once the freed slaves returned to Africa. In this way, Hopkins hoped that God planned to use the wickedness of slavery as a means of introducing the gospel among the nations in Africa.⁵⁸

The London Missionary Society and *The Evangelical Magazine*
Carey's and Hopkins's pleas were heard throughout the transatlantic basin, and Carey especially became a major source of inspiration for evangelical missions. The missionary movement blossomed in the wake of his *Enquiry*, with numerous magazines and societies devoted to the promotion of missions. As noted in the previous chapter, evangelical missions had always partly been a cooperative endeavor, often across denominational and national lines with an emphasis on unity based upon a simple primitive gospel. The London Missionary Society continued to infuse Christian cooperation with eschatological meaning by connecting Christian unity (unity in constitutional organizations rather than simply uniting in prayer) to previous emphases of evangelical missions. Because the London Missionary Society was so influential on evangelical missions during the period under study, and because it was the parent society of Thomas Campbell's

---

⁵⁶ Ibid., 11.
⁵⁷ Ibid., 14.
⁵⁸ Hopkins provided a six-page (unnumbered) Appendix on the proposal of colonization in Hopkins, *A Discourse upon the Slave-Trade, and the Slavery of the Africans*.

Evangelical Society of Ulster (covered in the next chapter), this section closely analyzes the formation of the London Missionary Society, its key characteristics, and its influence on transatlantic evangelicals.

Strategic use of media was crucial for the construction of evangelical missions and for promoting and funding missionary societies. Although not always entirely accurate and often run through a number of editors, the letters and other information recorded in evangelical publications became a major means of promoting the cause.[59] *The Evangelical Magazine* was instrumental in the formation of the London Missionary Society, and was a crucial conduit of international evangelical news. Founded in 1793, *The Evangelical Magazine* aimed to utilize a periodical to offer news and spread "evangelical sentiments" to thousands of people who would read magazines but had no money to buy or time to peruse large volumes. The target audience was the "more than three hundred thousand Calvinists, and many others, savingly converted to God, who trust in the merits of Christ alone for salvation." The magazine would provide a wide array of religious information—history, philosophy, poetry, prose, autobiography, obituaries, book reviews, etc. It would also relate the "Progress of the Gospel throughout the kingdom," which was a "species of information entirely new, and very important."[60]

Twenty-four evangelicals agreed to supply information to readers, and the magazine advertised these names on the front page of its volumes. These men were among the most important leaders who formed many of the evangelical societies of their day, and nearly all of them played an important role in the founding of the London Missionary Society—many were in the Whitefield Calvinist tradition.[61] Among the twenty-four were Northamptonshire Baptists John Ryland (1753–1825) and Andrew Fuller (1754–1815). English Congregationalist David Bogue (1750–1825), of Scottish birth and originally trained as a minister, also wrote for the magazine and became a key promoter of interdenominational cooperation through

---

[59] David Arnold and Robert A. Bickers, "Introduction," in *Missionary Encounters: Sources and Issues*, eds. Robert A. Bickers and Rosemary E. Seton (Richmond: Curzon Press, 1996), 4.

[60] "The Preface," *The Evangelical Magazine* 1 (1793): 1–5.

[61] For biographical information on these men, see John Morison, *The Fathers and Founders of the London Missionary Society: A Jubilee Memorial, Including a Sketch of the Origin and Progress of the Institution* (London: Fisher, Son & Co., 1844).

voluntary societies.⁶² English Congregationalist George Burder (1752–1832), who became known for his sympathies with evangelical Methodists and those in the Church of England, and whose *Village Sermons* attained widespread Atlantic readership, also contributed to the magazine as editor and author. He was one of the founders of the Warwickshire Association for the Spread of the Gospel (1793), which sought to support foreign missions and was instrumental in forming the major interdenominational missionary, Bible, and tract societies of the period.⁶³ Burder became secretary of the London Missionary Society in 1803 in succession to John Eyre (1754–1803), an Anglican clergyman who served as first editor of *The Evangelical Magazine* from 1793 to 1802. Selina Hastings sent Eyre to Trevecca College in the 1770s before he was ordained in the Church of England in 1779, and he became one of many Trevecca students who contributed to the missionary explosion in the 1790s.⁶⁴ Eyre became a founding member and secretary of the London Missionary Society.⁶⁵ Also among the twenty-four was native Welsh Independent Edward Williams (1750–1813), who, with Andrew Fuller and Samuel Hopkins, was a founder of moderate Calvinism in the tradition of Jonathan Edwards, which refuted hyper-Calvinism and provided a foundation for Calvinist missionary impetus.⁶⁶

The Evangelical Magazine took a strong interdenominational approach, both in its constituency and its message that was based on the primary Christian identity of saving faith. "Bigotry gradually diminishes," the preface of volume one declared, "and good men of all denominations, laying aside party distinctions, begin to embrace each other with fraternal affection; and we hope the present Work will accelerate the destruction of that contracted disposition, which checks the benevolent current of true godliness." The editors were "Churchmen and Dissenters of different denominations,

---

⁶² J. H. Y. Briggs, "Bogue, David," ed. Donald M. Lewis, *Dictionary of Evangelical Biography, 1730–1860* (Peabody: Hendrickson, 2004), 1:115.

⁶³ Alan Argent, "Burder, George," ed. Donald M. Lewis, *Dictionary of Evangelical Biography, 1730–1860* (Peabody: Hendrickson, 2004), 1:168–69.

⁶⁴ At least six Trevecca students were founders of the London Missionary Society. See Dorothy Eugenia Sherman Brown, "Evangelicals and Education in Eighteenth-Century Britain: A Study of Trevecca College, 1768–1792" (PhD diss., The University of Wisconsin-Madison, 1992), 211–38, 282, 303, 305, 307, 313, 318.

⁶⁵ Edwin Welch, "Eyre, John," ed. Donald M. Lewis, *Dictionary of Evangelical Biography, 1730–1860* (Peabody: Hendrickson, 2004), 1:373; Roger H. Martin, *Evangelicals United: Ecumenical Stirrings in Pre-Victorian Britain, 1795–1830* (Metuchen: Scarecrow Press, 1983), 208–09.

⁶⁶ W. T. Owen, "Williams, Edward," ed. Donald M. Lewis, *Dictionary of Evangelical Biography, 1730–1860* (Peabody: Hendrickson, 2004), 2:1194–95.

uniting their efforts in one common cause." The magazine would follow the principles of the *Gospel Magazine*, "devoid of personality and acrimonious reflections on any sect of professing Christians; as errors of mind, like diseases of the body, are rather the subjects of pity than of scorn."[67] The title page of the *Gospel Magazine* read, "The Gospel Magazine, or Treasury of Divine Knowledge, Containing Original and Select Pieces, Designed to Promote Experimental Religion, and Calculated for All Denominations."[68]

Therefore, it should be no surprise that the evangelicals who started and contributed to *The Evangelical Magazine* promoted a missionary enterprise based on motives in the evangelical tradition, with united prayer as a chief support and millennialism as a key motive. But they also magnified the ecumenical emphasis. For example, an author described only as "Horatio" utilized Edwards's *An Humble Attempt* as a guide to the signs of the times and to encourage continuation of regular prayer meetings for missions. Horatio hoped that the seventh angel would soon pour out his vial (Rev. 16:12), and he suspected the means by which the Lord would introduce that "desirable day" would be used gradually. He supposed the "*Lord will remove the* OBSTACLES *which lie in the way of the conversion of the heathen nations.*" One obstacle was the "*unhappy contentions and divisions which subsist among Christians*" because these damaged the witness of Christianity to the world. Another major obstacle Horatio named was the cruelties committed by Christians, especially the slave trade, that "infamous commerce in human blood, which has disgraced this nation for more than two hundred years." Of course, a major obstacle was pagan ignorance of Christ, which could only be remedied by sending missionaries to these nations. "For how shall they call on him in whom they have not believed? or how shall they believe in him of whom they have not heard? and how shall they hear, without a preacher? and how shall they preach, except they be sent?"[69] As historian Stephen Orchard perceptively notes, we see in the 1790s the "marching together of a millennial vision, 'The earth shall be filled with

---

[67] "The Preface," 3.

[68] This is according to the title page for volumes eight (1781) and ten (1783). I have not been able to analyze any of its other volumes.

[69] Citing Romans 10:12–15, which adorned the title page of Carey's *Enquiry*. Horatio, "Remarks on the Prophesies and Promises Relating to the Glory of the Latter Day," *The Evangelical Magazine* 1 (September 1793): 157–67; Orchard, "Evangelical Eschatology and the Missionary Awakening," 144.

the glory of the Lord,' and practical plans to bring it about."⁷⁰ Key to those plans for many evangelicals was cooperation across denominational lines.

Another key influence in the formation of the London Missionary Society was Melville Horne's (ca.1761–1841) *Letters on Missions: Addressed to the Protestant Ministers of the British Churches* (1794). Horne was an evangelical Anglican whom Wesley appointed as an itinerant preacher in 1784 and as a superintendent in 1787. He was the second chaplain in Sierra Leone in 1792, but his inability to acclimate forced his return in 1793, at which point he wrote his *Letters*—a book that influenced the formation of the London Missionary Society and Church Missionary Society.⁷¹

Beginning with commendation of Carey's *Enquiry*, *Letters* reiterated Carey's evangelical arguments for Protestant missions. He cited Carey's statistics to remind readers of the large part of the world under the darkness of paganism and Islam and to motivate disobedient Christians: "I charge you—I charge myself, with betraying the grand interests of our Maker, by refusing to propagate his gospel." He interpreted Matthew 28:19–20 as a command for all Christians, not just the apostles. Horne chided Christians for their lack of pity for the "heathen," demonstrated by their lack of support for missions even though they had the ships, money, and ministers to make missionary work a reality. Furthermore, by neglecting the command of Christ, Horne confessed, "we [Christians] are chargeable with the perdition of all the poor Heathens whom our diligence might have saved."⁷²

Horne pleaded for the establishment of missions based on the same evangelical motives covered so far, but began his letters with a persuasive exhortation to interdenominational cooperation. His first letter, for example, said that for Protestants to bicker with one another about party preferences was "to fight for Barabbas, and to crucify Jesus."⁷³ In another letter, he pleaded:

---

⁷⁰ Orchard, "Evangelical Eschatology and the Missionary Awakening," 139.
⁷¹ He describes his reasons for leaving Africa at length in the preface. See Melville Horne, *Letters on Missions: Addressed to the Protestant Ministers of the British Churches* (Bristol: printed by Bulgin and Rosser, 1794), iii–xii; W. R. Ward, "Horne, William," ed. Donald M. Lewis, *Dictionary of Evangelical Biography, 1730–1860* (Peabody: Hendrickson, 2004), 1:572–73.
⁷² Horne, *Letters on Missions*, xii, 2–5, 11–16.
⁷³ Ibid., 2.

> Let us [ministers] fly to the succor of our best mother, the
> afflicted Church of Christ. O let us no more fall out by the way.
> Let liberal Churchmen and conscientious Dissenters, pious
> Calvinists and pious Arminians, embrace with fraternal arms.
> Let the press groan no longer with our controversies; and let the
> remembrance of the petty interests we have contended for be
> buried in everlasting oblivion.[74]

Horne also advanced eschatological motives for missions: "the prophecies and promises, loudly declare the intention of God, that this last and most perfect dispensation of the everlasting gospel should be the religion of every tribe, and kindred, and tongue." Horne believed he lived in a special time that called for special measures of evangelism. "The night is far spent, and the day is at hand," he declared. "The latter ends of the world are fallen upon us, and we have many considerations to excite us, if it were possible, to more than apostolick labours." Like many evangelicals before and after him, Horne's eschatology attempted to make sense of Islamic rule over previously Christian lands, the Roman church as Antichrist, and current wars (in Horne's case, the French Revolution).[75] For Horne, the humbling of Rome during the French Revolution represented God's wrath on Antichrist and was a clear harbinger of the "latter ends of the world."[76]

Horne's *Letters* received immediate attention from *The Evangelical Magazine*, and prompted several people associated with the magazine to put forward donations for a missionary society—this culminated in the founding of the London Missionary Society. In a review of *Letters*, *The Evangelical Magazine* praised Horne's book and proposals for missions. The review crescendoed into hopeful speculation and news of an interdenominational missionary society:

> Could a new society be formed for . . . promoting the Gospel,
> and those, who now as individuals long for it, be united together,

---

[74] Ibid., 21–22.

[75] On the place of Roman Catholicism and Islam in U.S. evangelical eschatology, see Thomas S. Kidd, *American Christians and Islam: Evangelical Culture and Muslims from the Colonial Period to the Age of Terrorism* (Princeton: Princeton University Press, 2009).

[76] Horne, *Letters on Missions*, 11, 20–21; Orchard, "Evangelical Eschatology and the Missionary Awakening," 144–45.

without respect to different denominations of Christians, or repulsive distance arising from the points in dispute between Calvinists and Arminians.... Could such a society be formed upon Mr. Horne's large scale... we have pleasure to inform the Public, that one gentleman has pledged himself for an *hundred pounds*, and that we have *five hundred pounds* more engaged from another respectable minister, for the equipment of the first six persons who shall be willing to devote themselves, and be approved by such Society for a mission to the South Sea Islands.[77]

Among the twenty-four contributors to *The Evangelical Magazine* were Thomas Haweis and Samuel Greatheed.[78] Greatheed became an influential advocate of Christian unity based on the essence of the church as *one* diverse body, which should practice rituals, such as Communion, together.[79] Haweis was chaplain of Selina Hastings's chapel in Bath, and was one of the four executors of her estate upon her death in 1791.[80]

From that point on, an interdenominational missionary society became a real possibility to many evangelicals. In November 1794, leaders of *The Evangelical Magazine* began meeting with people from different denominations to consider establishing a missionary society.[81] These meetings continued in the early months of 1795, and were promoted and perceived as eschatologically significant for their missionary aim and Christian unity. "It was unanimously determined," declared a 1795 publication documenting the formation of the London Missionary Society, "that all party names and inferior distinctions should, in the prosecution of this vast design, be

---

[77] "Review of *Letters on Missions*," *The Evangelical Magazine* 2 (November 1794): 478.
[78] Stephen Orchard discovered this in Greatheed's copy of the sermons preached at the founding meeting of the London Missionary Society in 1795. Greatheed's notes in that book say that the references to contributors in the November 1794 *The Evangelical Magazine* were from Haweis (five hundred pounds) and himself (one hundred pounds), which they made after reading Horne's *Letters on Missions*. See Orchard, "Evangelical Eschatology and the Missionary Awakening," 145 n56; Richard Lovett, *The History of the London Missionary Society, 1795–1895* (London: Henry Frowde, 1899), 1:11-12.
[79] Martin, *Evangelicals United*, 30-31.
[80] Norman E. Thomas, *Missions and Unity: Lessons from History, 1792–2010*, American Society of Missiology 47 (Eugene: Cascade Books, 2010), 8.
[81] For the early history of the London Missionary Society, see Lovett, *History of the London Missionary Society*, 1:3-42; James L. Gorman, "European Roots of Thomas Campbell's *Declaration and Address*: The Evangelical Society of Ulster," *Restoration Quarterly* 51, no. 3 (2009): 131-33.

absorbed into the great Christian name and cause."[82] Finally, on February 17, 1795, thirty-three signatories agreed:

> We whose names are here subscribed, declare our earnest desire to exert ourselves for promoting the great work of introducing the Gospel and its ordinances, to Heathen and other unenlightened countries, and unite together, purposing to use our best endeavors, that we may bring forward the formation of an extensive regularly organized Society, to consist of Evangelical Ministers and Lay Brethren of all denominations, the object of which Society shall be to concert and pursue the most effectual measures for accomplishing this important and glorious design.[83]

The London Missionary Society was the culmination of evangelical missions traced to this point: it synthesized emphases of the Great Commission, interdenominational cooperation in missions based on a core or essential evangelical message, and an optimistic eschatology which considered missions to the "heathen" and conversion of the world as significant events taking place in what seemed to be—with the political revolutions, social change accompanying the Industrial Revolution and urbanization, and the establishment of united Protestant missions—the latter days. At the core of the London Missionary Society was interdenominational cooperation in missions to work toward the latter-day glory of Christ's millennial reign.[84]

Burder led efforts in 1795 to organize a constitutional meeting for the missionary society. He sent a circular letter in January of 1795, *An Address to the Serious and Zealous Professors of the Gospel, of Every Denomination, Respecting an Attempt to Evangelize the Heathen*, which challenged people to respond to the Great Commission with the "primitive zeal" of the apostles. As justification for doing something "immediately," Burder appealed to the revival of true religion over the last fifty years, Carey's *Enquiry*, Horne's *Letters*, new geographical and demographic knowledge, and a newfound desire to rectify Protestant apathy toward obeying the Great Commission.

---

[82] Thomas Haweis et al., *Sermons, Preached in London, at the Formation of the Missionary Society, September 22, 23, 24, 1795; To Which Are Prefixed, Memorials, Respecting the Establishment and First Attempts of That Society* (London: printed and sold by T. Chapman, 1795), x.

[83] Ibid., xi; Lovett, *History of the London Missionary Society*, 1:15–16.

[84] Lovett, *History of the London Missionary Society*, 1:12.

Life was short, and it was time to act. These appeals prompted meetings on September 21 to 24, 1795, when the London Missionary Society was founded, and when a number of evangelical personalities persuasively synthesized the evangelical missions culture that shaped transatlantic evangelicals over the next decades.[85]

Interdenominational cooperation for efficient missions in the last days was a key assumption that permeated the sermons and reports of the September 1795 meetings. Baptists, Independents, Congregationalists, Presbyterians, and Anglicans came together on September 21, and representatives of churches and associations read letters of support for the missionary society endeavor.[86] Over two hundred ministers congregated at Spa Fields Chapel, which belonged to Selena Hastings's connexion, on Tuesday morning, September 22, when Haweis preached on Mark 16:15–16, the first of six founding sermons.[87] Appeals to unity and interdenominational cooperation for the propagation of the gospel were ubiquitous. After an opening prayer that beseeched God to bless "all the ministers of different denominations, that they may hold the unity of the Spirit in the bond of peace, and, [be] conscious how much more important it is to spread the glorious Gospel of the ever blessed God, than to dispute about modes and forms," Haweis's sermon corroborated the ecumenical missionary message:

> The petty distinctions among us, of names, and forms; the diversities of administrations, and modes of church order, we agree, shall this day all be merged in the greater, nobler, and characteristic name of CHRISTIANS; and our one ambition be, to promote no partial interests, since Christ is not divided, but with united efforts to make known abroad, the glory of his person—the perfection of his work—the wonders of his grace—and the

---

[85] Ibid. 1:18-24.
[86] The London Missionary Society directors provided an account of the formation of the Society and its plan in Haweis et al., *Sermons, Preached in London, at the Formation of the London Missionary Society*, iii-xxxii.
[87] The other five were George Burder (on Jonah to Nineveh), Samuel Greatheed (on the Great Commission as moral law, based on Luke 10:29), John Hey (on the fullness of the times, based on Ephesians 1:10), Rowland Hill (on Matthew 24:14), and David Bogue (on objections against missions to the "heathen"). Haweis et al., *Sermons, Preached in London, at the Formation of the London Missionary Society*.

transcendent blessings of his redemption—where his adorable name hath never yet been heard.[88]

Rowland Hill proclaimed the old Charles Wesley hymn to sum up his hatred of bigotry and desire to see it subsist no more: "Let names and sects and parties fall, And Jesus Christ be all in all."[89]

David Bogue's sermon on Thursday evening expressed his awareness of how unprecedented the London Missionary Society was, and proclaimed it had accomplished what Hill had only hoped for:

> We have now before us a pleasing spectacle, Christians of different denominations, although differing in points of church government, united in forming a society for propagating the Gospel among the heathen. This is a new thing in the Christian church. Some former societies have accepted donations from men of different denominations; but the government was confined to one. But here are Episcopalians, Methodists, Presbyterians, and Independents, all united in one society, all joining to form its laws, to regulate its institutions, and manage its various concerns. Behold us here assembled with one accord to attend the funeral of *bigotry*: And may she be buried so deep that not a particle of her dust may ever be thrown up on the face of the earth.[90]

The "death of bigotry" became a slogan of interdenominational missions.

Christian unity had been a theme in evangelical missions from its inception, but the gathering of adherents from different denominations for worship, during which people performed meaningful rituals together, was an extraordinary experience for many. One such person was Iota, who appeared in the introduction of this chapter.[91] Another person recollected that epic week in September 1795, and described the response at the gathering to Bogue's proclamation of the death of bigotry:

---

[88] Ibid., 3–6.
[89] Ibid., 114–15.
[90] Ibid., 130.
[91] IOTA, "To the Editor," 504–6; IOTA, "On the Late Meeting of Ministers of Different Denominations in London, for the Establishment of a MISSIONARY SOCIETY," 480.

Another consideration that rendered these seasons unspeakably delightful, was the visible union of ministers and Christians of all denominations; who, for the first time, forgetting their party prejudices and partialities, assembled in the same place, sang the same hymns, united in the same prayers, and felt themselves one in Christ. This sentiment was so universal, that when Mr. Bogue, in the course of his sermon said, 'we are called together this evening to *the funeral of bigotry*, and he hoped it would be buried so deep, as never to rise again,' the whole vast body of people manifested their concurrence, and could scarcely refrain from one general shout of joy. Such a scene was, perhaps, never before beheld in our world, and afforded a glorious earnest of that nobler assembly, where we shall meet all the redeemed, and in the presence and before the throne of the Lamb shall sing, as in the last hymn of the service, *Crown Him, crown Him, crown Him Lord of All!*[92]

The details of the organization of the London Missionary Society, which were included not only in its publication of sermons almost immediately after its formation, but also in *The Evangelical Magazine* and other magazines, provided a guide for the formation and promotion of similar societies for years thereafter.[93] After Haweis's sermon, a portion of those gathered constituted the Society and agreed upon a plan which had been previously constructed. The Society published that plan with a story of its formation, and included the sermons preached at its founding meetings. Publication of the plan (i.e., constitution), address, and/or sermon at the founding meetings became a common feature of missionary society organization and promotion. In October 1795, Baptist John Rippon's *Baptist Annual Register* reported the news of the founding of the Society, and Philadelphia printers reproduced the account in a pamphlet with a short preface for U.S. readers in February 1796. The account praised *The Evangelical Magazine*, the September gathering for the founding of the London Missionary Society,

---

[92] "Missionary Society," October 1795, 425.
[93] Haweis et al., *Sermons, Preached in London, at the Formation of the London Missionary Society*, iii–xxxii; "Missionary Society," October 1795, 421–26; "Missionary Society," *The Evangelical Magazine* 3 (November 1795): 468–70.

and all the simultaneous concerts of prayer in the United States, Scotland, and England, which were purportedly behind the success of the Society. It included the report of the gathering and the London Missionary Society plan, as well as a number of missionary letters and a hymn.[94]

Publication of the London Missionary Society documents provided transatlantic evangelicals with a clear ideology and structure that they could emulate to create their own interdenominational evangelical and missionary societies. The plan was the basis on which people could agree to support the work, and it briefly outlined the essentials. Individuals supported the work by putting their name on the subscription list, agreeing to pay a certain amount of money per year. Article I constituted the name of the Society as "The Missionary Society." Article II stated the object: "The sole object is to spread the knowledge of Christ among heathen and other enlightened nations." Article III specified the various types of members and how much money they needed for annual subscription (e.g., individuals pay one guinea or more annually, benefactors pay ten pounds or more, executors pay fifty pounds or more, ministers or congregational representatives pay five pounds or more). Article IV delineated the general meeting schedule, which included at least an annual meeting in London in May at which at least one sermon would be preached and the various officers (directors, treasurer, secretary, and collectors) would be selected. News and matters discussed would be recorded in minutes.[95] Article V described rules concerning the directors, who were to be chosen every year. The report from the first year and Article V documented that twenty-five directors were chosen by a committee of attendees in the first year. Many of these directors were associated with *The Evangelical Magazine*.[96] No more than three-fifths could live in or near London, where monthly directors meetings took place. At least seven directors were needed to constitute a board. They were to create committees that ran basic operations, such as "managing the funds, conducting the correspondence, making reports, examining missionaries, directing the missions, etc." but the decisions of the committee were not

---

[94] *An Account of the London Missionary Society, Extracted from Dr. Rippon's* Baptist Annual Register (Philadelphia: printed by Lang & Ustick, 1796).
[95] Haweis et al., *Sermons, Preached in London, at the Formation of the London Missionary Society*, xxxi.
[96] They are listed in Ibid., xxvi.

final until ratified at a monthly meeting. Article VI described the submission of funds to the treasurer and Article VII explained salaries—the directors could give the treasurer a salary, but the directors "shall transact the business of the society without any emolument."[97]

That first week also saw a determined and successful effort on the part of Thomas Haweis to persuade the London Missionary Society meeting to set its first sights on the islands in the "South Sea" (i.e., South Pacific Ocean). Haweis prefaced his recommendations, which he gave in Surrey Chapel on September 24, 1795, with a quick postmillennial message, proposing that the London Missionary Society had assured him that the latter days were at hand. "Methinks I see the great Angel of the covenant in the midst of us, pluming his wings, and ready to fly through the midst of Heaven, with his own everlasting Gospel, to every nation, and tribe, and tongue, and people. Rev. xiv. 6." The number of people crying out like the Macedonian, "Come over into Macedonia, and help us [Acts 16:9 KJV]," had increased enormously, but "Of all the regions of the earth which are yet in heathen darkness, the South Sea Islands appear to combine the greatest prospect of success with the least difficulties to be necessarily surmounted." He laid out the necessities for the mission (e.g., ships) and the basic plan of working with the islanders to find a place to set up their mission. Haweis's talk reveals an ethnocentrism common in his day, and he was sure the islanders would be very happy to "find a body of men come to settle among them from England, purely to be a blessing to their country." Captain James Wilson offered his services due to providential leading, which Haweis recounted at length.[98] Haweis was persuasive; all agreed that the first efforts of the London Missionary Society would be to the South Pacific and approved of captain Wilson's offer to take the missionaries.[99]

---

[97] Ibid., xxxi.

[98] Thomas Haweis, "A Memoir of the Most Eligible Part to Begin a Mission, And the Most Probable Means of Accomplishing It," in *Sermons, Preached in London, at the Formation of the Missionary Society, September 22, 23, 24, 1795; To Which Are Prefixed, Memorials, Respecting the Establishment and First Attempts of That Society* (London: printed and sold by T. Chapman, 1795), 160–84, quoted from 161, 163, 168, and 175.

[99] "The Proceedings of the Second General Meeting," in *Four Sermons, Preached in London at the Second General Meeting of the Missionary Society, May 11, 12, 13, 1796 . . . To Which Are Prefixed, The Proceedings of the Meeting* (London: sold by T. Chapman, 1796), viii–x.

Haweis persuaded the attendees to commit to the islands of the South Pacific as the first target of London Missionary Society missionaries, for which they set sail in July 1796. After much deliberation of committees, the directors decided the best option for transport was to purchase a ship, which would allow them to send thirty missionaries and their wives. They purchased a vessel called the *Duff* for five thousand pounds.[100] London Missionary Society directors carefully examined candidates before choosing their missionaries, and they stated their intended plan for avoiding sending denominations or polities to the "heathen." They would leave it to the converts to "search the scriptures for themselves, and to adopt such church order and discipline as shall appear most conformable to the Apostolic model, and most conducive to their own peace and edification."[101] They also noted in their proceedings of the second, third, and fourth meetings (1796–1798) that similar societies in correspondence with the London Missionary Society had formed in Edinburgh, Paisley, Kelso, and Aberdeen, Scotland; Saxony; Holland; Switzerland; Ireland; and New York and Connecticut in the United States. On July 29, 1796, thousands attended a service to commission the twenty-nine approved missionaries, who set out with a convoy of ships headed to the East Indies. The service was a spectacle of unity: "an Episcopalian, a Presbyterian, a Seceder, an Independent, and a Methodist, united in the solemn designation of the Missionaries to their work."[102] The evening before the missionaries left, they all participated in the Lord's Supper. They managed this by predetermining that the oldest minister in attendance would lead the service. Participating in such rituals, with people of various denominations, impacted participants. The directors recalled of the interdenominational Communion: "It was surely a little specimen of what the church, in the latter days, will be, when love, like death, will level all distinctions. It was even a foretaste of heaven."[103]

---

[100] "The Report of the Directors, To the Members of the Missionary Society, Convened at the Third General Meeting," in *Four Sermons, Preached in London at the Third General Meeting of the Missionary Society, May 10, 11, 12, 1797 . . . To Which Are Prefixed, The Proceedings of the Meeting, and the Report of the Directors* (London: sold by T. Chapman, 1797), xix.

[101] "The Proceedings of the Second General Meeting," xviii.

[102] "The Report of the Directors at the Third General Meeting," xviii.

[103] Ibid., xv–xxix; quoted from xxii; "The Proceedings of the Second General Meeting," iii–xxiv; "Missionary Society," *The Evangelical Magazine* 4 (1796): 342; "The Report of the Directors to the Members of the Missionary Society, at the Fourth General Meeting, Held the Ninth Day of May, 1798," in *Four Sermons, Preached in London at the Fourth General Meeting of the Missionary Society, May 9, 10, 11, 1798*

Transatlantic Influence of the London Missionary Society

The London Missionary Society became an inspiration and a model to numerous societies in Europe and the transatlantic basin.[104] As news spread through evangelical magazines, church pulpits, and word of mouth, the ideas of William Carey, Melville Horne, and the London Missionary Society captivated the evangelical imagination and caused what Charles Chaney calls "The Missionary Explosion" in the 1790s.[105] The revolutions and awakenings in the 1790s only added more eschatological significance to the period.[106] As word about the interdenominational success of the London Missionary Society spread, missionary advocates moved to emulate its pattern of organization and action, which included relaxed strictures on membership (compared to the Society for Propagation of the Gospel in New England, the Society in Scotland for Propagating Christian Knowledge, etc.) and a focus on unity. Scholars often highlight the fact that the interdenominational aspect of these societies was short-lived, as denominations slowly took control of the societies in the 1820s and 1830s. But it is a mistake to read the 1790s documents as if the later denominational model for missions was inevitable. For the London Missionary Society and many who emulated it in the next decades, interdenominational missions were not only sustainable, but they also carried eschatological significance of a united church in a new missionary era, perhaps signaling the beginning of the latter days.

The New York Missionary Society was the first society in the United States to form based on the interdenominational pattern of the London Missionary Society.[107] Clergy and laity of the Presbyterian, Dutch Reformed, Associate Reformed, and Baptist churches met and constituted the New York Missionary Society in November 1796.[108] This Society took its theological,

---

... *To Which Are Prefixed, The Proceedings of the Meeting, and the Report of the Directors; Also Are Added, A List of Subscribers* (London: printed for T. Chapman, 1798), 9–36.

[104] Charles Maxfield, "The 'Reflex Influence' of Missions: The Domestic Operations of the American Board of Commissioners for Foreign Missions, 1810–1850" (PhD diss., Union Theological Seminary, 1995), 58–62; Brown, "Movements of Christian Awakening in Revolutionary Europe, 1790–1815," 579–80; Chaney, *The Birth of Missions in America*, 156–57; Thomas, *Missions and Unity*, 14–15.

[105] Chaney, *The Birth of Missions in America*, chap. 5.

[106] For basics on the most influential aspects and areas of these revivals, see Bret E. Carroll, *The Routledge Historical Atlas of Religion in America* (New York: Routledge, 2000), 62–63.

[107] Chaney, *The Birth of Missions in America*, 158–59.

[108] Several newspapers in New York and Massachusetts reported the event. See Centinel of Freedom, "[Last Tuesday]," *Centinel of Freedom*, November 9, 1796, News/Opinion, 2. Other papers that printed a shorter

practical, and publishing cues from the London Missionary Society, as it immediately published and advertised its founding sermon and *The Address and Constitution*.[109] Members were in awe of the design and success of the London Missionary Society. They told readers, "With a magnanimity worthy of Christians they have sacrificed the bigotries of party on the altar of Apostolic zeal." In the estimation of the New York Missionary Society, "An harmony, unparalleled, perhaps, in the modern history of the church, reigns among those who, in every denomination, love the unadulterated gospel." The success of the London Missionary Society (unity among denominations to collect a substantial amount of money, and its success in sending twenty-nine missionaries to the South Pacific on a ship that it owned) prompted the birth of the New York Missionary Society. After all, they wrote, "we are in the *habit* of praying that the kingdom of the Lord Jesus may come. But what *means* have we used for attaining the blessing?" They believed the "hearty concurrence of Christians of different denominations ... will be a token for good, that the LORD is about to build up Zion, and to appear in his glory." They mentioned the evangelical missionary heroes (Cotton Mather, John Eliot, David Brainerd, and the Moravians), appealed to compassion and pity for the "heathen" American Indians and frontier people without the gospel, and encouraged readers to form similar societies. Although it is clear that the New York Missionary Society was more concerned to safeguard certain doctrines than the London Missionary Society, members still added in their constitution that "Persons may be admitted from all religious denominations indiscriminately," and they saw interdenominational cooperation as key to the importance of the missionary enterprise of the time. Ultimately, the success of the London Missionary Society was the major motivator behind the New York Missionary Society. The London Missionary Society immediately acknowledged the New York Missionary Society, reading its address at its 1797 general meeting and, in 1798, praising the new Society, which was one of many transnational missionary societies

---

version of the announcement included *Salem Gazette* in Salem, MA and *Medley* in New Bedford, MA.

[109] New-York Missionary Society, *The Address and Constitution of the New-York Missionary Society* (New York: printed by T. and J. Swords, 1796); Alexander MacWhorter, *The Blessedness of the Liberal: A Sermon, Preached in the Middle Dutch Church, before the New-York Missionary Society, at Their First Institution, November 1, 1796* (New York: printed by T. and J. Swords, 1796). Advertisements appeared in (at least) January and February 1797 in *The Herald* (New York), *Greenleaf's New York Journal and Patriotic Register* (New York), and *The Minerva* (New York).

listed among the foreign directors who helped conduct the business of the London Missionary Society.[110]

Just as the press issued the New York Missionary Society *Address and Constitution* and founding sermon to the general public, the Northern Missionary Society announced its formation at a meeting in Lansingburgh, New York, on January 11, 1797. The Northern Missionary Society mentioned the interdenominational societies in Great Britain and the missionary heroes as inspiration, but it followed the New York Missionary Society (its "sister-society") plan and emphases. Although "Clergy and Laity, belonging to different denominations of Christians" constituted the Society, it emphasized correct "religious principles," outlined in the longest section of its constitution.[111] Early meetings occasioned sermons on Matthew 28:20 and Mark 6:10, the latter preached by Union College president John Blair Smith.[112] Numerous advertisements and announcements about the exciting meeting of clergy and laity from the northern and western parts of New York filled the papers. One anonymous reporter engaged in typical hyperbole, which reveals the degree of excitement with which many Christians met the interdenominational missions movement. The design of the institution was the "propagation of the glorious gospel of Christ" in frontier settlements and American Indian tribes. "Perhaps on no occasion," the report estimated, "did the spirit of love, zeal, and unanimity so evidently appear, as among different denominations who were convened for the promotion and advancement of this pious and benevolent object."[113] Failed attempts to unite the New York Missionary Society and the Northern Missionary

---

[110] New-York Missionary Society, *The Address and Constitution of the New-York Missionary Society*, 3, 5, 10, 16; MacWhorter, *The Blessedness of the Liberal*, 26–28; "The Report of the Directors to the Members of the Missionary Society, at the Fourth General Meeting, Held the Ninth Day of May, 1798," 18, 36.

[111] Northern Missionary Society, *The Constitution of the Northern Missionary Society in the State of New-York: To Which Is Annexed the Address of the Society to the Public* (Schenectady: printed by C. P. Wyckoff, 1797), see chap. 1, Article 3, on 3–5; Alexander Miller, *The Missionary's Short Catechism, for Children* (Albany: printed by C.R. & G. Webster, n.d.), 16. Miller's catechism, whose title page said it was "Published by Order of the Board of Directors of the Northern Missionary Society," taught infant baptism. By the time this catechism was published, therefore, the term "interdenominational" was restricted for the Northern Missionary Society.

[112] David Bassett, "Notification," *The Albany Chronicle*, January 30, 1797; The New-Jersey Journal, "[Agreeably to a general notification . . .]," *The New-Jersey Journal*, February 1, 1797.

[113] *The Weekly Museum*, February 25, 1797.

Society did not hamper their eventual merger, with other missionary societies, into the United Foreign Missionary Society in 1817.[114]

Evangelical communities continued to form denominational and interdenominational missionary societies from the 1790s forward. Although this chapter has focused on England and the United States, missions endeavors also exploded in Scotland and Ireland (this is analyzed in following chapters), including creation of the General Evangelical Society in Dublin, Edinburgh Missionary Society (1796), Glasgow Missionary Society (1796), Society for Propagating the Gospel at Home (1798), and the Evangelical Society of Ulster (1798). All of these societies and their leaders were closely connected to the London Missionary Society. The missionary voluntary society was the new means by which evangelicals would take the gospel to the world. The London Missionary Society proved to evangelicals across the globe that it was possible to bring individuals of different denominations together to fund a worldwide mission. But other types of societies also followed the interdenominational organization of the London Missionary Society, the most influential of which were the Religious Tract Society, British and Foreign Bible Society, and Society for Promoting Christianity Amongst the Jews (1809).[115]

Evangelicals in the following decades looked to society formation in the 1790s as eschatologically and organizationally significant. Although ecclesiastical bodies progressively incorporated missionary societies and their work in the nineteenth century, the interdenominational cooperation for missionary purposes in the 1790s made long-lasting impressions.[116] For example, Edward Dorr Griffin, in his 1805 missionary sermon, "The Kingdom of Christ," said that some believed they already saw the "light purpling the east" as the "dawn of a better day" approached in the wake of the founding of "numerous missionary societies . . . on both sides of the

---

[114] Chaney, *The Birth of Missions in America*, chap. 5.

[115] For these and the societies of the next two decades, see Wilbert R. Shenk, "Introduction," in *North American Foreign Missions, 1810-1914: Theology, Theory, and Policy*, ed. Wilbert R. Shenk, Studies in the History of Christian Missions (Grand Rapids: Eerdmans, 2004), 4; Brown, "Movements of Christian Awakening in Revolutionary Europe, 1790-1815," 579-80; Foster, *An Errand of Mercy*, 275-80; Martin, *Evangelicals United*; Wolffe, *The Expansion of Evangelicalism*, 155-82.

[116] Chaney, *The Birth of Missions in America*, 166-74.

Atlantic."[117] Four years later, Samuel Worcester proclaimed to a meeting of the Massachusetts Missionary Society that September 21, 1795 "will long be held in grateful remembrance, as a distinguished epoch in the annals of Christendom." Worcester believed the institution of the London Missionary Society produced "an influence more grateful than the dew of Hermon, than the dew that descended on the mountains of Zion. The holy flame there lighted from the altar of heaven, spread with rapidity in all directions." He noted that numerous societies followed the path of the London Missionary Society, and encouraged Massachusetts Missionary Society members to continue the important missions work of the Lord.[118]

CONCLUSION

Transatlantic Evangelical Missions Culture in the 1790s

The evangelical missionary movement of the late eighteenth century, although varied from one group to the next and from one decade to another, constructed a unique and identifiable religious culture by the 1790s. Its system of symbols that established powerful moods and motivations in participants, some of which have endured into the twenty-first century, did not craft an entirely new conception of the order of existence, as it retained the basic Protestant view of the world. However, the major advocates of the culture did elaborate a number of interrelated ideas that were extremely influential for the success of the missionary movement, and which became foundational to the Campbell tradition. Certainly, not all evangelicals in the 1790s agreed with all aspects of interdenominational missions summarized below, but it captivated many leaders and impacted the Campbells. Therefore, this section concludes the chapter with a summary of that culture.

Ideas foundational to interdenominational missions included (1) Christian cooperation in prayer and organization for missions fueled by evangelical new birth identity and Enlightenment toleration, (2) a simple primitive gospel—which preceded confessions and denominations—upon

---

[117] Edward Dorr Griffin, *The Kingdom of Christ: A Missionary Sermon Preached before the General Assembly of the Presbyterian Church in Philadelphia, May 23, 1805* (Philadelphia: printed by Jane Aitken, 1805), 25; Hutchinson, *Errand to the World*, 55.

[118] Samuel Worcester, "Sermon to the Massachusetts Missionary Society, May 1809," in *The Life and Labors of Rev. Samuel Worcester, D.D.*, ed. Samuel Melancthon Worcester (Boston: Crocker and Brewster, 1852), 2:72–73; Maxfield, "The 'Reflex Influence' of Missions," 58–59.

which all Christians could unite for missions, (3) pity for the "heathen," and (4) millennialism as motive for missions.

From the inception of Protestant missions, cooperation and Christian unity were central themes of missions advocates. New birth identity was key in early and mid-eighteenth-century justifications for cooperation with "real" Christians. This basic criterion of the "real" Christian was for the most part simply assumed, rather than articulated in the later nineteenth century, when toleration based on the primitive gospel became the central glue holding interdenominational missions together. Evangelical cooperation, influenced by Enlightenment religious and political toleration, was based on a simple evangelical gospel on which all agreed. Although evangelicals of the 1790s did not always agree on what this primitive core was (foundational "maxims" of Scripture; new birth conversion; a primitive, simple, or apostolic gospel; or some combination), most missions advocates agreed there was a simple evangelical gospel that transcended or preceded church polities and theological systems. An analogy would be the primitive gospel as a tree trunk from which sprouted many branches (denominations or "parties"). Denominational polities were historical additions, but they all depended and elaborated on a basic evangelical gospel trunk upon which they all ostensibly agreed, though its definition was amorphous in most writings.[119] This led missions advocates to develop types of primitivism and unity that set very different trajectories in the 1790s and afterward. This will become clear in following chapters.

From the 1740s onward, unity and cooperation had early rhetorical and visible manifestations in the concert of prayer for revivals and missions in anticipation of the last days.[120] Eighteenth-century evangelicals believed that a Christian community united in prayer and action for missions to damned "heathens" around the world really could "silence the clamour of parties

---

[119] Mather perhaps came the closest to identifying specific maxims of the primitive gospel upon which Christians could unite for missions, but even these were fairly broad in their condensed version. Some societies revealed their uneasiness about the unclear definition of an evangelical gospel by identifying "principles" members needed to believe. The more explicit these "principles" of the bottom-line gospel got, the more they took on the shape of new formularies and moved toward denominational societies.

[120] On the theme of unity and missions, see Thomas, *Missions and Unity*; Henry P. van Dusen, *One Great Ground of Hope: Christian Missions and Christian Unity* (Philadelphia: Westminster Press, 1961).

[and] confirm the truth of our holy Religion."[121] Pity for lost souls that could be saved with the simple gospel of Christ (as opposed to partyism) became a basic justification for interdenominational cooperation and motivation for missions. From Robert Millar to William Carey, evangelicals constructed a view of the world that saw "heathens" and "pagans" as people under the influence of Satan and headed to hell for eternal torment. The common view of indigenous and other world religions as evil provided powerful motivation for the missionary movement and, therefore, showed up in nearly every proposal for missionary action in the eighteenth century. For Carey, a disordered world overrun with the chaos and darkness of paganism could be made orderly if Christians would follow Jesus's command to go and make disciples of all nations. A pattern of persuasion, which moved from pity for the doomed "heathen" to motivation for mission, became a standard rhetorical device in the evangelical construction of religious meaning and duty. Converting "heathens" was such an important task that Christians not only could, but should, unite to accomplish this objective.

Unity was also linked to the millennialism of missions. Armed with an interpretation of Revelation 20 as a literal thousand-year reign of Christ, Protestant missions drew significant motivation from millennialism. The correlation of missions and millennialism was tied to interpretations of the Bible, including the assumption that all Gentiles would be brought into the church and Jews would be converted just before the millennium. Therefore, missions and millennium were intimately linked. Prayers for revival and cooperation naturally transitioned to prayers for conversion of "heathens" and for the millennial reign of Christ. Millennialism not only worked as a motive for missions, but the establishment of missionary work served as a sure sign that the last days were not far off. Christian cooperation in prayer and missions harbingered worldwide missions, conversion of the world, the millennium, and the death of bigotry. The revolutionary period and Napoleonic wars only heightened the sense of eschatological significance in this period. Industrialism, colonialism, and the voluntary society were timely developments that seemed to answer prophetic utterances about means of converting the "heathen" and the last days.

---

[121] Robert Millar, *The History of the Propagation of Christianity and Overthrow of Paganism*, 3rd ed. (London: printed for A. Miller, 1731), 2:371, 380, 394.

Evangelical missions created and solidified webs of meaning through a number of organizational structures, most potently in the voluntary interdenominational societies and magazines that represented and advertised evangelical activism and the cooperative impulse. Founded upon emerging democratic and free-market ideals, voluntary societies provided a structure which allowed individuals to organize in order to accomplish a goal without the strictures of state or denominational obstacles. This allowed creation of interdenominational membership and government, making the voluntary society a central vehicle of interdenominational cooperation. The societies utilized a number of methods for missions, especially itinerancy. Borrowing from the Methodists, evangelical missionary societies utilized itinerant ministers to reach areas lacking preachers and places of worship. These itinerants functioned as missionaries at home and abroad.

Interdenominational and transnational communication through publishing and correspondence, which provided networking channels and a sense of unity, also shaped evangelical identity and action in the world. Periodicals such as *The Evangelical Magazine* solidified interdenominational cooperation in its constituency and its news sources. The magazine also became a hub of a moderate evangelicalism that promoted the central ideas of missions, and it was the chief organ of London Missionary Society news. Publications such as William Carey's *Enquiry* and Melville Horne's *Letters* were widely disseminated and promoted in magazines. John Eliot, Cotton Mather, Jonathan Edwards, David Brainerd, Ludwig Zinzendorf, and the Moravians took on legendary status, and were frequently cited as the epitome of missionary action and disinterested benevolence. Publication of constitutions, addresses, and sermons by new societies became legitimizing symbols and a promotional technique. Voluntary societies and evangelical periodicals created a new reading public which leaders could steer toward various campaigns, such as those for morals and Sunday schools and against the slave trade, etc. The use of media to rally evangelical support for the missionary cause was crucial to missions.

A number of key rituals marked transatlantic evangelical missions. The height of ritual was worship gatherings at missionary society founding and annual meetings, where ecumenical rhetoric, Great Commission exposition, and postmillennial theology came together in founding sermons, prayers, and speeches. It was one thing to say or read that Christians should unite for action, but it was a surreal experience for Christians from different denominations to gather and perform together rituals of prayer, preaching, society creation, missionary sending, etc. It was in these rituals that the motifs and motives of evangelical missions took on a more intense and transformational character, as embodied experiences formed the outlook of participants on the world and the understanding of Christian duty and action in it. Soaring reports of London Missionary Society and Northern Missionary Society founding meetings demonstrated how ritual action affected people such as Iota. For many, experiencing these rituals with people of other denominations solidified the veracity of missions and its worldwide errand.

Interdenominational evangelical missions spread across the transatlantic and constituted a formative religious experience for many. As demonstrated in the following chapters, Thomas and Alexander Campbell were among those deeply impacted by the theology and practice of this religious culture.

Chapter Four

THOMAS CAMPBELL'S FORMATIVE BACKGROUND IN IRISH EVANGELICAL MISSIONS

AT THIRTY-FIVE YEARS OF AGE AND IN THE FIRST YEAR OF HIS ministry, Thomas Campbell's voice rang out in prayer to open the first interdenominational gathering of the Evangelical Society of Ulster on a rainy October night in 1798. He was among a dozen ministers and numerous laypeople that had gathered in an attempt to replicate the London Missionary Society in Ireland. Although small in number, these Irish ministers and laypeople created an electric atmosphere of anticipation in their little gathering, with singing, prayer, and preaching that mimicked what at least one of them—the leader, George Hamilton—experienced at London Missionary Society meetings. This sister society of the London Missionary Society, the Evangelical Society of Ulster, proved successful for the next seven years, though it also created great controversy in the various streams of the Presbyterian church in Ireland. That rainy night became perhaps the most fateful in the life of Thomas Campbell, as his leadership in the Evangelical Society of Ulster provided the inspiration and tools he eventually used to launch a similar society in the United States (i.e., the Christian Association of Washington) that eventually morphed into a reform movement. This chapter tells the story of evangelical missions in Ireland, focusing on the societies, individuals, and ideals that shaped the theology and practices of Thomas and Alexander Campbell.

Early Evangelical Missions in Ireland: The General Evangelical Society

The political and religious situation in Ireland, as in all of Western Europe, underwent massive changes from 1790 to 1840, a period in which evangelicalism experienced much growth. The Anglican Church of Ireland may have been the established church in the eighteenth century, but Catholics remained the majority, even as dissenting groups grew during the seventeenth and eighteenth centuries. England enacted laws throughout the eighteenth century that attempted to confine political rights, public office, and ownership of land to members of the established church, but the laws were only intermittently enforced. Nonetheless, these laws made Roman Catholics and dissenters into second-class citizens in many areas. Political revolutions, the intellectual milieu of the Enlightenment, and socioeconomic changes associated with the Industrial Revolution worked together to shake the foundations of state-established churches across Europe and the Americas. As Hugh McLeod puts it, it was a period of transition between the old "officially enforced religious unity of the *ancien regime* and the pluralism of the present era."[1] Two of the patterns of change that McLeod highlights were important in Ireland and Scotland: (1) a conservative established church was pitted against a variety of dissenting forces, and (2) religion provided the basis for the identity of a nation.[2] John Locke's defense of religious toleration permeated discussions about the relationship of church and state and the propriety of either church or state to compel religious belief.[3] The social, economic, political, and religious context in Northern Ireland in the late eighteenth century produced a turbulent time of challenge to traditional authorities. This context influenced the rise and reception of evangelical societies.

---

[1] Hugh McLeod, *Religion and the People of Western Europe 1789–1989*, 2nd ed. (Oxford: Oxford University Press, 1997), 15.
[2] Ibid., 15–21.
[3] I. R. McBride, "'When Ulster Joined Ireland': Anti-Popery, Presbyterian Radicalism and Irish Republicanism in the 1790s," *Past & Present*, no. 157 (1997): 69–70.

Evangelicalism found a comfortable home in this complex social arrangement, which provided a dramatic backdrop of uncertainty in which new religious ideas found room to flourish. Religious toleration of the Enlightenment saturated evangelical missions, fostering cooperation across denominational lines. Even in this complicated political arrangement, dissenting and establishment evangelicals in Ulster worked together for propagation of the gospel. The primitivism of the missionary movement sought Christian unity upon a simple apostolic gospel, and encouraged tolerance and forbearance on matters of opinion, such as polity, where rights of individual conscience, rather than civil or religious authorities, governed. Evangelicalism appealed to many people in these anxious times, evinced by an increase of evangelical activity in the late eighteenth and early nineteenth centuries.[4]

Ireland experienced some revivalist piety among Scotch-Irish settlers of the seventeenth century, but the first major proponents of evangelicalism did not arrive until the late 1740s.[5] Coming to Ireland in 1746, John Cennick had a Calvinist Methodist background in the Whitefield tradition, but he joined the Moravians in 1745. The first Secession Presbyterian minister to make his home in Ireland arrived in 1746, the same year as Cennick. Both John Wesley and George Whitefield made trips within the next five years. By the late eighteenth century, Ulster had a significant evangelical community.[6] From the late 1740s onward, prominent evangelicals committed themselves to spreading "vital religion" to Ireland. Wesley's first visit to Ireland in 1747 launched a long commitment to the country, during which he visited twenty more times. Wesleyan Methodism grew rapidly in Ireland, with fourteen thousand members by 1790.[7] The focus of Methodism on itinerancy, outdoor

---

[4] David Hempton and Myrtle Hill, *Evangelical Protestantism in Ulster Society, 1740-1890* (London: Routledge, 1992), 3-44, quoted from 23; J. C. D. Clark, "Great Britain and Ireland," in *The Cambridge History of Christianity: Volume VII, Enlightenment, Reawakening and Revolution 1660-1815*, eds. Stewart J. Brown and Timothy Tackett (Cambridge: Cambridge University Press, 2006), 54-71.

[5] For this section, I rely on Hempton and Hill, *Evangelical Protestantism in Ulster Society, 1740-1890*; David Hempton, "Evangelicalism in English and Irish Society, 1780-1840," in *Evangelicalism: Comparative Studies of Popular Protestantism in North America, the British Isles, and Beyond 1700-1900*, eds. Mark A. Noll, D. W. Bebbington, and George A. Rawlyk (New York: Oxford University Press, 1994), 156-76; Andrew R. Holmes, *The Shaping of Ulster Presbyterian Belief and Practice, 1770-1840* (Oxford: Oxford University Press, 2006); Andrew Holmes, "The Shaping of Irish Presbyterian Attitudes to Mission, 1790-1840," *Journal of Ecclesiastical History* 57, no. 4 (2006): 711-37.

[6] Hempton and Hill, *Evangelical Protestantism in Ulster Society, 1740-1890*, chaps. 1-2.

[7] Ibid., 11.

preaching, and voluntary societies became key means of evangelizing at home and abroad.[8] Calvinist Methodists also reached Ireland at this time, and they found more in common with Calvinist Presbyterians, who made up large parts of Ulster society.[9] Selina Hastings committed her resources to Ireland, based on a common perception of it lacking spirituality. In a 1773 letter, she wrote, "Poor wicked Ireland, I trust, shall yet have a Gospel day. I can't yet see how or when—but it must be; and till I find that opportunity, my eye is only waiting darkly for its accomplishment."[10]

Hastings sent popular evangelical preachers to Ireland in the 1770s and 1780s, and her preachers were influential in the creation of the General Evangelical Society, an interdenominational society founded in Dublin in 1787 to raise recruits and funds to evangelize Ireland. An early promoter of interdenominational evangelical missions in Ireland, the General Evangelical Society raised money in order to supply, in the words of G. K. Foster, a "succession of zealous and popular ministers of every denomination, who should be employed to preach occasionally wherever an opportunity should offer."[11] Anglican evangelicals Rev. John Walker and Rev. Dr. Benjamin McDowell (M'Dowall) took a leading role in the Dublin General Evangelical Society. In August 1797, Walker requested the services of an itinerant preacher in Ireland on behalf of the General Evangelical Society, which was "unconnected with any particular religious denomination."[12] During a meeting in June 1799, the General Evangelical Society made several resolutions that constituted its plan. Its goal was to send "Evangelical Preachers" with the "pure Gospel" to parts of Ireland that did not hear the gospel. Their preachers were not to spend more than one Sabbath in

---

[8] Ibid., 31, 37.

[9] On Scottish immigrants, see Steve Murdoch and Esther Mijers, "Migrant Destinations, 1500–1750," in *The Oxford Handbook of Modern Scottish History*, eds. T. M. Devine and Jenny Wormald, Oxford Handbooks (Oxford: Oxford University Press, 2012), www.oxfordhandbooks.com; Patrick Fitzgerald, "The Seventeenth-Century Irish Connection," in *The Oxford Handbook of Modern Scottish History*, eds. T. M. Devine and Jenny Wormald, Oxford Handbooks (Oxford: Oxford University Press, 2012), www.oxfordhandbooks.com.

[10] Letter from S. Huntingdon to Mr. Hawkesworth, October 13, 1773, in Jacob Kirkman Foster, *The Life and Times of Selina, Countess of Huntingdon* (London: W. E. Painter, 1839), 169.

[11] Foster, *The Life and Times of Selina*, 2:207; Hempton and Hill, *Evangelical Protestantism in Ulster Society, 1740–1890*, 15–16.

[12] J. Walker to William Cooper, August 12, 1797, in William Cooper, "Documentary Notices of the Dublin and Ulster Evangelical Societies," in *The Irish Congregational Record*, vol. 1 (Dublin: John Robertson and Company, 1834), 225.

Dublin, because they should be travelling and preaching in areas without ministers. The fifth resolution read:

> That as it is earnestly desired that no party distinctions among real Christians should prevent their cooperation in the great work of advancing the kingdom of our common Lord, the annual meeting of the Society shall be held, and the sermon preached, in different places of Evangelical worship.[13]

Walker and McDowell were assigned to "write to the Missionary Society in England for ministerial supply."[14] Clearly, the General Evangelical Society embraced evangelical missions and utilized the transatlantic networks perpetuating missions culture.

One of the first preachers that the General Evangelical Society solicited was Rowland Hill (1744–1833).[15] Influenced by the Whitefield tradition, Hill began visiting prisoners and itinerant preaching in and around Cambridge, and became a prominent evangelical Anglican promoter of interdenominational cooperation for missions. Despite his pamphlet war with Wesley and falling out with Hastings, Hill's advocacy of Christian unity on the basis of a simple gospel was key to his message, as shown by his work with the London Missionary Society and Surrey Chapel in England, the General Evangelical Society in Ireland, and the Haldane brothers in Scotland. Hill allowed evangelicals of all types to preach at his chapels. In comments about his intention for St. George's Fields chapel, he said, "Let none imagine that I mean to set up this Chapel to draw aside one individual from any other church. No, God forbid! My desire is to see all churches united in the Lord."[16] Hill's Surrey Chapel in London was perhaps the most famous interdenominational chapel in the 1780s, as he had sermons delivered there from Baptists, Anglicans, and Independents.[17] Hill was one of the thirteen committee members chosen to construct the plan for

---

[13] Ibid., 227–28.
[14] Ibid.
[15] Alan Frederick Munden, "Hill, Rowland ('Roly')," ed. Donald M. Lewis, *Dictionary of Evangelical Biography, 1730–1860* (Peabody: Hendrickson, 2004), 1:553–54.
[16] Rowland Hill, *A Sermon, Preached by the Rev. Mr. Rowland Hill, on His Laying the First Stone of His Chapel, in St. George's Fields, June 24, 1782* (London: printed for M. Folingsby, 1782), 8–9.
[17] Roger H. Martin, *Evangelicals United: Ecumenical Stirrings in Pre-Victorian Britain, 1795–1830* (Metuchen: Scarecrow Press, 1983), 13.

the London Missionary Society, and was one of the six preachers during the founding meetings of the London Missionary Society in 1795—in that sermon he proclaimed the Wesleyan verse, "Let names and sects and parties fall, And Jesus Christ be all in all."[18] Hill met the Scottish evangelical Haldane brothers in 1796, and worked closely with them thereafter.[19] In his work with the General Evangelical Society, Hill visited Ireland in 1793, 1796, 1802, and 1808.[20] Thomas Campbell heard Hill on one of those trips.[21]

The General Evangelical Society supported ministers of many denominations and worked with other evangelical societies.[22] Baptists, Anglicans, Presbyterians, and Methodists were among those associated with the General Evangelical Society. Samuel Pearce provided an account of his itinerancy in Ireland for the General Evangelical Society to John Rippon, editor of the *Baptist Register*. Rippon printed it in the *Baptist Register*, and *The Missionary Magazine* in Scotland quickly reprinted the piece, illustrating the speed and efficiency of the transatlantic evangelical networks in the 1790s. Pearce lauded a 1793 statement about the interdenominational principles of the General Evangelical Society. According to a 1795 letter announcing an upcoming meeting that Pearce received, the General Evangelical Society believed the best way to evangelize Ireland was a union of "preachers of the Gospel" in various denominations. They excluded "all distinctions of names and parties" at the meeting, exhibiting a remarkable level of tolerance.[23] Pearce expressed heartfelt approval of this meeting and wrote, "the good effects of such union are already visible. O! that in England we could rejoice in similar associations." The Baptist rejoiced that McDowell (Presbyterian) and Hill (Anglican) were both employed by

---

[18] Thomas Haweis et al., *Sermons, Preached in London, at the Formation of the Missionary Society, September 22, 23, 24, 1795; To Which Are Prefixed, Memorials, Respecting the Establishment and First Attempts of That Society* (London: printed and sold by T. Chapman, 1795), 114–15.

[19] Alexander Haldane, *Memoirs of the Lives of Robert Haldane of Airthrey, and of His Brother, James Alexander Haldane* (London: Hamilton, Adams, and Co., 1852), chaps. 8–9.

[20] Foster, *The Life and Times of Selina*, 2:207–8, 225, 229.

[21] Lester G. McAllister, *Thomas Campbell: Man of the Book* (St. Louis: Bethany Press, 1954), 47–48; Martin, *Evangelicals United*, 13; Richard Lovett, *The History of the London Missionary Society, 1795–1895* (London: Henry Frowde, 1899), 1:25, 30, 33; Lynn A. McMillon, *Restoration Roots* (Dallas: Gospel Teachers Publications, 1983), 81.

[22] Foster, *The Life and Times of Selina*, 2:208.

[23] S[amuel] Pearce, "A Short Account of THE GENERAL EVANGELICAL SOCIETY in Dublin, and of the State of Religion in That Vicinity, in a Letter from Mr Pearce of Brimingham, to Dr Rippon [Extracted from the BAPTIST REGISTER]," *The Missionary Magazine* 1, no. 4 (October 1796): 166–70.

the General Evangelical Society and winning souls. The voluntary society provided a useful means of interdenominational cooperation for preaching an evangelical gospel in Ireland by the 1790s.[24]

Ecumenical Missions: The Evangelical Society of Ulster and Thomas Campbell

The Evangelical Society of Ulster, an Irish version of the London Missionary Society, and the General Evangelical Society were at the heart of Irish evangelical missions in the 1790s. Furthermore, its structure and principles exerted tremendous influence not only on Irish Christianity, but also on U.S. Christianity when one of the founding members, Thomas Campbell, laid the foundations for a new religious movement in the United States that was indebted to the Evangelical Society of Ulster's constitutional forms, principles, and view of a united Christian mission.[25]

The ecclesiastical context in Ulster shaped and was shaped by the political and social world of the 1790s. In County Armagh in southern Ulster, the population was divided almost equally between Catholics and Protestants, and both groups had become economically empowered through the growing linen industry until population growth, land enclosure, and increasing rent payments led to the formation of secret societies that engaged in

---

[24] Pearce, "A Short Account of THE GENERAL EVANGELICAL SOCIETY in Dublin, and of the State of Religion in That Vicinity, in a Letter from Mr Pearce of Brimingham, to Dr Rippon [Extracted from the BAPTIST REGISTER]," 166–70.

[25] The connection of the Evangelical Society of Ulster to Campbell prompted several scholarly studies of the Evangelical Society of Ulster in the 1980s from David Thompson, Joseph Thompson, and Hiram Lester. These scholarly contributions enhance historical understanding of the Evangelical Society of Ulster, but much of the story of the Evangelical Society of Ulster remains untold. I am especially indebted to the discoveries of Hiram Lester and his careful collection of those materials in the T. W. Phillips Memorial Library, Bethany College, Bethany, WV, Archives and Special Collections, Hiram Lester Papers. See David M. Thompson, "The Irish Background to Thomas Campbell's *Declaration and Address*," *Journal of the United Reformed Church History Society* 3, no. 6 (1985): 215–25; David M. Thompson, "The Irish Background to Thomas Campbell's *Declaration and Address*," *Discipliana* 46 (1986): 23–27; Joseph Thompson, "The Evangelical Society of Ulster," *The Bulletin of the Presbyterian Historical Society of Ireland*, no. 17 (March 1988): 1–29; Hiram J. Lester, "Alexander Campbell's Early Baptism in Ecumenicity and Sectarianism," *Restoration Quarterly* 30 (1988): 85–101; Hiram J. Lester, "An Irish Precursor for Thomas Campbell's Declaration and Address," *Encounter* 50, no. 3 (1989): 247–67; Hiram J. Lester, "The Case Against Sectarianism," *The Disciple* 17, no. 3 (1990): 10–12; Hiram J. Lester, "The Form and Function of the *Declaration and Address*," in *The Quest for Christian Unity, Peace, and Purity in Thomas Campbell's Declaration and Address: Text and Studies*, eds. Thomas H. Olbricht and Hans Rollmann, ATLA Monograph Series 46 (Lanham: Scarecrow Press, 2000), 173–92; Hempton and Hill, *Evangelical Protestantism in Ulster Society, 1740–1890*, 37–40, 70; Holmes, "The Shaping of Irish Presbyterian Attitudes to Mission, 1790–1840" passim; Holmes, *The Shaping of Ulster Presbyterian Belief and Practice, 1770–1840*, 41, 117, 133, 153, 195–96.

acts of intimidation and destruction in the 1780s and 1790s.[26] In Ulster, Presbyterians were the dominant dissenting group. The General Synod of Ulster had 180 congregations, the largest number in Ulster. Influenced by religious toleration as articulated by John Locke, some General Synod ministers opposed requiring subscription to the *Westminster Confession of Faith* on grounds of the rights of individual conscience, liberty of mind, and the nature of church authority. These "New Lights" had control of two-thirds of the presbyteries (i.e., they did not require subscription) by the 1770s, and some used the same grounds of individual rights of conscience to refute the union of church and state in Ireland. At the other end of the spectrum, the two conservative Secession synods (Burgher and Antiburgher[27]) and the tiny Reformed presbytery (Covenanters) held rigidly to the formularies, and typically opposed episcopacy and Erastianism.[28]

The 1790s in Ulster saw heightened social conflict as anti-Catholic sentiment grew among Protestants and as the Catholic Defenders organized and demanded rights for the Catholic community under the Anglican establishment. Many Protestants perceived Irish Catholicism as a serious threat, and all the more so when rumors circulated that the revolutionary French supported the Irish Catholics. On the other hand, even prejudiced Protestant reformers articulated a growing conviction of the injustice of

---

[26] Michael Staunton, *The Voice of the Irish: The Story of Christian Ireland* (Mahwah: HiddenSpring, 2003), chap. 6; Joseph Coohill, *Ireland: A Short History*, 4th ed. (London: Oneworld, 2014), chap. 2; John O'Beirne Ranelagh, *A Short History of Ireland*, 3rd ed. (Cambridge: Cambridge University Press, 2012), chap. 2.

[27] The General Assembly in the National Church of Scotland passed an act in 1730 which deprived members of congregations of choosing their ministers and gave that authority to people who were often Episcopalians. Four men were discontent with this act and subsequently established the Associate Presbytery (the Seceders). The Seceders further divided into Burgher and Antiburgher factions in 1747 because they disagreed about whether oaths required of burgesses in some Scottish cities, which bound them to support "the religion presently professed within the realm," were wrong. In April of 1747, the two groups separated and met in different places, each calling themselves the true "Associate Synod" and each perceiving the other as the divisive group. To the Antiburghers, the oath resembled the very thing the Seceders had fought against. This division among the Seceders was transported to Ireland even though the Burgher oath was not required there. On the Secession divisions, see David Stewart, *The Seceders in Ireland: With Annals of Their Congregations* (Belfast: Presbyterian Historical Society, 1950), 42–53, 107–09, 193, 199–203; John M. Barkley, *A Short History of the Presbyterian Church in Ireland* (Belfast: Publications Board, Presbyterian Church in Ireland, 1959), 31–32; Robert Richardson, *Memoirs of Alexander Campbell: Embracing A View of the Origin, Progress and Principles of the Religious Reformation Which He Advocated*, vol. 1 (Cincinnati: Standard Publishing Company, 1890), 51–58; Thompson, "The Irish Background to Thomas Campbell's *Declaration and Address*," 1986, 25; Stewart J. Brown, "Religion and Society to c.1900," in *The Oxford Handbook of Modern Scottish History*, eds. T. M. Devine and Jenny Wormald, Oxford Handbooks (Oxford: Oxford University Press, 2012), oxfordhandbooks.com.

[28] McBride, "'When Ulster Joined Ireland,'" 63–93. Erastianism is the belief that the state should have supremacy in ecclesiastical matters.

excluding Irish Catholics from political life.[29] Despite the Catholic Relief Acts, social unrest in the 1790s led to the Irish Rebellion of 1798, which represented a revolution against British rule and perceived oppression. "Of the minority of Presbyterian clergymen who made the transition from constitutional agitation to armed rebellion," historian Ian McBride notes, "the orthodox and latitudinarian ["New Light"] parties were present in roughly even numbers, with the Seceders once more isolated in their vocal loyalism."[30] Perhaps newly motivated by the 1780 repeal of the sacramental test for dissenters and the 1784 attainment of a share of the *regium donum* (a regular payment from the state to ministers), Seceder conservatism of the period led most ministers into political quietism that was more focused on inward evangelical religion than on outward transformation of the state.[31] Great Britain crushed the rebellion, and the Acts of Union in 1800 created the United Kingdom of Great Britain and Ireland.[32]

The chief instigator behind the establishment of the Evangelical Society of Ulster was a Burgher Presbyterian minister named George Hamilton. Hamilton received "the truth as it is in Jesus" when he heard Rowland Hill preach in 1793 during Hill's first itinerancy in Ireland for the General Evangelical Society. At that time, Hamilton was a probationer with the Burghers.[33] The fourth annual meeting proceedings of the London Missionary Society in May 1798 mentioned the spark of missionary fervor in Ireland, which the directors learned about from a letter Hamilton had written. His congregation in Armagh sent the London Missionary Society over twenty-one pounds that year, and Hamilton was listed as one of four

---

[29] For example, the United Irishmen emerged in the wake of the French Revolution as a radical political coalition in which Catholics and Protestants cooperated for rights.

[30] McBride, "'When Ulster Joined Ireland,'" 74.

[31] McBride argues, "although the overwhelming majority of Presbyterians were in favour of parliamentary reform, there were profound disagreements over the question of Catholic enfranchisement, and some Seceding ministers had even identified themselves publicly with the government" (Ibid., 73). Only two Seceders joined the conflict. Bebbington argues that evangelicalism during this period typically—with exceptions for their common liberal stances on antislavery and support of the American Revolution and religious liberty—blended political quietism and loyalism. Ibid., 73–85; David W. Bebbington, *Evangelicalism in Modern Britain: A History from the 1730s to the 1980s* (London: Routledge, 1989), 72–74; Ian McBride, *Scripture Politics: Ulster Presbyterians and Irish Radicalism in the Late Eighteenth Century* (Oxford: Clarendon Press, 1998), 108.

[32] McBride, "'When Ulster Joined Ireland,'" 63–93; James Kelly, "Inter-Denominational Relations and Religious Toleration in Late Eighteenth-Century Ireland: The 'Paper War' of 1786-88," *Eighteenth-Century Ireland / Iris an Dá Chultúr* 3 (January 1, 1988): 39–67; McBride, *Scripture Politics*; Staunton, *The Voice of the Irish*, chap. 6; Coohill, *Ireland*, chap. 2.

[33] Cooper, "Documentary Notices of the Dublin and Ulster Evangelical Societies," 226.

directors of the London Missionary Society in Ireland. Other Ireland directors included John Walker (Anglican at the time) and Benjamin McDowell (Presbyterian), two of the architects of the late-eighteenth-century evangelical revival in Dublin.[34]

The meeting to establish the Evangelical Society of Ulster took place on October 10, 1798, and it was no doubt an impressionable experience for those who worshipped with people from several denominations.[35] A number of laypeople, as well as thirteen ministers from four denominations (Burgher, Antiburgher, Church of Ireland, and Synod of Ulster), attended the meeting after worshiping together. Notable ministers who participated in the meeting included George Maunsell, Rector of Drumcree in the diocese of Armagh, who chaired.[36] Maunsell was an influential figure in Ireland who could garner prestige for the burgeoning Evangelical Society of Ulster. Thomas Campbell, Antiburgher minister at Ahorey, and Maunsel accounted for two of the four ministers who, with seven laypeople, were chosen as "members of Committee."

At the founding meeting, Hamilton preached a soaring sermon, *The Great Necessity of Itinerant Preaching*, which epitomized evangelical interdenominational missions and provoked backlash from Presbyterian Synods. Hamilton argued for the necessity of an interdenominational approach to evangelizing Ireland and the world. For Hamilton, faithful ministers of

---

[34] Besides serving as directors in Ireland for the London Missionary Society, McDowell and Walker supported the General Evangelical Society and Walker the Evangelical Society of Ulster. See "The Proceedings of the Second General Meeting," in *Four Sermons, Preached in London at the Second General Meeting of the Missionary Society, May 11, 12, 13, 1796 . . . To Which Are Prefixed, The Proceedings of the Meeting* (London: sold by T. Chapman, 1796), xxiii–xxiv; Missionary Society, *Four Sermons, Preached in London at the Fourth General Meeting of the Missionary Society, May 9, 10, 11, 1798 . . . To Which Are Prefixed, The Proceedings of the Meeting, and the Report of the Directors; Also Are Added, A List of Subscribers* (London: printed for T. Chapman, 1798), 35, 169; Myrtle Hill, "McDowell, Benjamin," ed. Donald M. Lewis, *Dictionary of Evangelical Biography, 1730–1860* (Peabody: Hendrickson, 2004), 2:716–17; Timothy C. F. Stunt, "Walker, John," ed. Donald M. Lewis, *Dictionary of Evangelical Biography: 1730–1860* (Peabody: Hendrickson, 2004), 2:1151.

[35] Following the pattern of the London Missionary Society, Hamilton published the narrative of the creation of the Society and its foundational sermon in George Hamilton, *The Great Necessity of Itinerant Preaching: A Sermon Delivered in Armagh at the Formation of the Evangelical Society of Ulster, on Wednesday, 10th of Oct. 1798. With a Short Introductory Memorial, Respecting the Establishment and First Attempt of the Society* (Armagh: Printed and Sold by T. Stevenson, and by each Member of the Committee, 1799). I quote a copy available at Archives and Special Collections, T. W. Phillips Memorial Library, Bethany College, Bethany, WV, Hiram Lester Papers, Folder 0304. My thanks also to Jean Cobb and, more recently, Sharon Monigold, for assistance with this and other documents in the Archives and Special Collections at Bethany.

[36] Alan R. Acheson, "Maunsel, George," ed. Donald M. Lewis, *Dictionary of Evangelical Biography: 1730–1860* (Peabody: Hendrickson, 2004), 2:755.

Christ "never preach for a party, or to promote the interest of any particular sect.... Their language is, Let names, and sects, and parties fall, And Jesus Christ be all in all." Hamilton thought denominational proselytizing actually hindered the spread of the gospel because it advanced parties instead of conversion to Christ and hindered a united effort for missions: "Let now the fire of brotherly love, and of pure christian [sic] zeal, consume the hay and stubble of party distinctions."[37]

Hamilton's sermon advanced other themes of evangelical missions. Although he admitted that itinerant preaching could be disorderly, he found his commission in the Bible, which "we hold to be alone the rule of ministerial usefulness and exertion." Hamilton trumped denominational rule with the primary "rule." He also pointed to signs of the times (political revolutions and evangelical missions) to invoke millennialism as a motive for missions (he cited Rev. 14:6, 8): "Behold, my brethren, the peculiar aspect of the present times! Does not the shaking of the nations indicate, that he is on his way to receive the heathen for his inheritance? ... Are we not told, that in troubleous times, Zion shall be built up? And are not the present times of this very description?" He quoted Cotton Mather to persuade his readers to see with eschatological eyes: "I am well satisfied that if men had the wisdom to discern the signs of the times, every hand would be at work to spread the name of our adorable Jesus into all the corners of the earth." Hamilton's interpretation of prophecies in Scripture led him to see political events, missionary endeavors, interdenominational cooperation, and effective itinerancy as signs of the last days, and it seems Thomas Campbell believed him.[38] After worship, the group approved the plan for the Evangelical Society of Ulster, which became the blueprint for the plan of Campbell's Christian Association of Washington in 1809. The Society's goal and methods to achieve it were to "make the Gospel known in those Towns and other places where it may be judged necessary; by introducing the Preaching of the Word, setting up Prayer meetings, distributing Bibles and Evangelical tracts among the poor." Membership dues would fund itinerant preachers. The Society would cooperate with the other missionary societies in Great Britain and elsewhere and "Unite with approved

---

[37] Hamilton, The Great Necessity, 14–16.
[38] Ibid., 27, 34–35.

Evangelical Ministers, and private Christians, respectable in their moral conduct, and of every Denomination." The Evangelical Society of Ulster's plan and mission were similar to the London Missionary Society's—they were staunchly interdenominational efforts to convert sinners to a nondenominational, primitive, evangelical gospel.[39]

The Evangelical Society of Ulster quickly built a base of evangelical support and made plans to fund itinerant preachers. Hamilton wrote to the London Missionary Society in January 1799, and requested that the London Missionary Society send two of its itinerant preachers to Ireland that spring. Hamilton's letter, reprinted in *The Evangelical Magazine* to garner more support, said that about twenty evangelical ministers were Evangelical Society of Ulster members, and he was hopeful that annual subscriptions would soon total around one hundred pounds. He assured the directors of the London Missionary Society that fields in Ireland were "white unto harvest," but that the Irish church needed laborers.[40]

Though it had experienced quick success, the Evangelical Society of Ulster soon faced early opposition. Some feared the Society was "inimical to the outward distinctions which prevail amongst us." Hamilton explained that those with such fears did not understand the purpose of the Society carefully, because its members had "solemnly disclaimed all intention of interfering directly, or indirectly, with the internal arrangements, or distinguishing peculiarities of any Christian denomination." Yet he continued with words which no doubt prompted more of the same charges:

> But be it so, that our association should set the wood, the hay, and the stubble [i.e., denominational peculiarities] in a blaze; what we would ask, are the sibboleths and shibboleths of sects and parties, compared with the extensive spread of the Gospel, and gathering of precious souls to the Lord Jesus. 'We seek not our own but the things of Christ; and if he be exalted, (says a

---

[39] The plan of the London Missionary Society's plan is provided in Ibid., xv–xvii; Lovett, *History of the LMS*, 1:30-32; Lester, "The Form and Function of the *Declaration and Address*," 173–92.

[40] George Hamilton, "Letter from Mr. Hamilton to the Secretary of the Missionary Society: Armagh, January 2, 1799," *The Evangelical Magazine* 7 (March 1799): 126–27. This letter is housed at the Archives of the London Missionary Society, School of Oriental and African Studies, University of London. A copy of the letter is in Archives and Special Collections, T. W. Phillips Memorial Library, Bethany College, Bethany, WV, Hiram Lester Papers, Folder 0304.

pious Dissenter),[41] let forms crumble back into their original chaos, and distinctions among Christians be obliterated and forgotten.'[42]

To those who asked how it was possible to associate with people of other denominations, Hamilton argued that Presbyterian vows did not and should not preclude them from working with the faithful in other denominations. Furthermore, if there were any such "anti-scriptural vows" among the Presbyterians, then "we refuse to recognize their obligation."[43]

In March 1799, William Cooper received a letter from Hamilton on behalf of the Evangelical Society of Ulster, inviting him to spend four months that summer itinerating in Ireland. Cooper decided to go to Ireland in 1799, after much deliberation led him to believe God willed it.[44] The quest was considered dangerous, because smoke from the 1798 rebellion was still clearing and dissenter animosity was running high. Cooper's friends and family tried to persuade him not to go, but after serious reflection, Cooper came to believe that the preaching tour was providential. Cooper left London with Hamilton and J. J. Richards in May 1799 after the London Missionary Society annual meeting.[45]

Cooper preached a sermon based on Revelation 14:6 entitled *The Flying Angel* on May 27 at Hamilton's Armagh church before the committee of the Evangelical Society of Ulster, and publication of the sermon in Ireland and England received attention.[46] Cooper utilized allegorical interpretation to

---

[41] Demonstrating the connections facilitated by publishing, this quote comes from Rev. George Lambert's sermon at the second London Missionary Society annual meeting in 1796. See Missionary Society, *Four Sermons, Preached in London at the Second General Meeting of the Missionary Society, May 11, 12, 13, 1796 . . . To Which Are Prefixed, The Proceedings of the Meeting* (London: sold by t. Chapman, 1796), 40–41.

[42] Hamilton, *The Great Necessity*, xii–xiii.

[43] Ibid., iii–xvii.

[44] For an overview of this type of providence, see Holmes, *The Shaping of Ulster Presbyterian Belief and Practice, 1770–1840*, 85–88.

[45] "Memoir of William Cooper," 3–4.

[46] For correspondence of the London Missionary Society missionaries in Ireland, see the letters available in the Archives of London Missionary Society, School of Oriental and African Studies, University of London. I am working from copies of these letters which are available at Archives and Special Collections, T. W. Phillips Memorial Library, Bethany College, Bethany, WV, Hiram Lester Papers, Folder 0304. The letters include: William Cooper to John Eyre on June 20, 1799; George Hamilton to John Eyre on June 20, 1799; William Cooper to John Eyre on July 18, 1799; George Hamilton to John Eyre on October 9, 1799; John Lowry to John Eyre on October 10, 1799; and John Eyre to William Cooper, October 19, 1799. For context, also see William Cooper, *The Flying Angel: A Sermon, Delivered in the New Meeting House*

suggest that the angels flying represented the itinerant missionaries of the London Missionary Society and similar societies. He believed he preached in the last days, and postmillennialism provided a major motivation for his missionary fervor. For Ireland, he prophesied, "I do think the set time is come for God in Mercy to Visit this Land."[47]

But his evangelical message was caustic at points. He aggressively pitted the experientially converted against the unconverted, he ridiculed those who read sermons to audiences, he downplayed ecclesiastical ordination, and he derided opponents of itinerant preaching.[48] His opposition to party zeal in favor of Christian union to spread an evangelical gospel was a prevalent theme also in his letters that summer. This missionary of the London Missionary Society and Evangelical Society of Ulster embodied an abrasive version of evangelical missions in the 1790s.

Cooper's rhetoric was well-remembered. Alexander Campbell, for example, remarked over thirty years later that he had listened to Cooper's preaching as a lad with pleasure.[49] However, "THE EVANGELIST OF IRELAND," to use the epithet that Cooper had earned for his oratory, was challenged by the leadership of both the Antiburgher and Burgher synods.[50] They raised concerns about his methods of spreading the gospel since he was acting in a "manner not consonant to Presbyterian Principles & Obligations." After investigating the matter fully through committees, and when they had spoken with the Evangelical Society of Ulster participants, the Burgher committee members were persuaded of their sincerity and of the "Purity of their Intercourse with Ministers and People of different Denominations, & of Evangelical Principles in private Ordinances such as Prayer Praise christian Conference & the like." The synod then stated that although interdenominational cooperation for missions may be expedient in certain circumstances, when the itinerants were "duly qualified,"

Armagh, Ireland, before the Committee of the Evangelical Society of Ulster, on Monday, the 27th of May, 1799 (London: Printed by S. Rousseau; for T. Chapman, 1799), 3; "Memoir of William Cooper," 1–7.

[47] William Cooper to John Eyre on July 18, 1799, 2.

[48] It is not difficult to understand why Cooper turned down episcopal ordination in July 1801, even though Haweis and Dublin evangelicals encouraged him to accept a bishopric—the ordination he received from Haweis was scriptural and he needed no other ordination besides. "Memoir of William Cooper," 5–6.

[49] Alexander Campbell, "Letter to William Jones, No. V.," *Millennial Harbinger* 6 (July 1835): 306.

[50] "Memoir of William Cooper," 4–7.

Yet in Faithfulness to our Trust who are to confirm the Churches over which the Holy Ghost hath made us Overseers, we recommend it to the different Pbys under our Inspection to be cautious against Allowing any Infraction or Delirection [i.e., dereliction] of any Part of that scriptural Reformation to which thro' the Blessing of Christ our Head on us & our Forefathers, we have attained in on Form of Gospel Doctrine, Discipline & Worship, that we may mind the same Things & walk by the same Rule as being of one Mind & one Judgment.[51]

Their comments revealed the tension between the unique denominational formularies of the synod that separated it from other denominations and the ideals of evangelical missions, which pushed for interdenominational cooperation. Cooperation among denominations was expedient, but the presbyteries should be cautious of ministers neglecting the formularies of the Burgher fellowship.

The 1799 Antiburgher Synod rejected the Evangelical Society of Ulster more decisively than the 1799 Burgher Synod, though only one Antiburgher minister was involved—Thomas Campbell. Rejecting what he perceived as the cold formality of the Anglicanism of his father, Campbell was drawn to the Presbyterian church. In his youth, he experienced evangelical conversion, and eventually sought ordination with the Seceders.[52] In 1787, he married Jane Corneigle, with whom he had seven children. Campbell completed the courses required for divinity from the University of Glasgow in 1792, where he imbibed the intellectual influences of the Scottish Enlightenment, and entered Divinity Hall in Whitburn, Scotland, an Antiburgher Presbyterian school run by Archibald Bruce. Campbell travelled there for an eight-week

---

[51] *Minutes of the Associate (Burgher) Synod of Ireland* (1799), (unnumbered) pages 6–7. For both the Burgher and Antiburgher *Minutes*, I quote from copies of the originals available at Archives and Special Collections, T. W. Phillips Memorial Library, Bethany College, Bethany, WV, Hiram Lester Papers, Folder 0106. According to Hiram Lester's research, the Burgher and Antiburgher minute books are located in the library of Union Theological College in Belfast, Northern Ireland. Microfilms of the original manuscripts are available from the Public Record Office of Northern Ireland in Belfast. For some of the relevant Presbyterian minutes and further discussion on them, see Thompson, "The Evangelical Society of Ulster," 15–16, 24–29; Stewart, *The Seceders in Ireland*, 104–07.

[52] Thomas Campbell experienced "effectual calling," as described in the *Westminster Confession of Faith* (chapter 10). For a description of his experience, see Richardson, *Memoirs of Alexander Campbell*, 1890, 1:23.

summer session each year for five consecutive years.[53] After successfully passing all the required exams, he became a probationer until he received a position at the Ahorey congregation in 1798, a town near two major centers of Evangelical Society of Ulster activity—three miles from Rich Hill and eight miles from Armagh.[54] Campbell embraced evangelical missions by becoming a leader of the Evangelical Society of Ulster from its beginning.[55]

At the end of the second day of the Antiburgher Synod, which took place from July 30 to August 1, 1799, the synod turned to two questions. First, "Is the Evangelical Society of Ulster constituted on Principles consistent with the Secession Testimony?" Second, "What shall be done with respect unto a Member of this court who took an Active part in forming that society & promoting its Interests?" The "Member" referred to in the second question was Thomas Campbell. In order to make well-founded judgments, the synod read the printed Evangelical Society of Ulster papers, including the August 1798 circular letter, Hamilton's *Great Necessity of Itinerant Preaching*, and a few other documents. Campbell "illustrated at length" the contents of the Evangelical Society of Ulster papers, after which members of the synod discussed their opinions as to the consistency of the Society's principles with the Secession *Testimony*. The minutes state, "A charitable opinion of the Piety & Zeal of their Society was entertained," but the

> principles of their Constitution were completely Latitudinarian whereby the truth of the Gospel is in Danger of Being Destroyed & the practice of Godliness overthrown where they have been established in the providence of God so that while the zeal of this Society would carry them out to the Enlargement of the

---

[53] Dates for Thomas Campbell's education are debated. Lester McAllister and Robert Richardson assume his education at the University of Glasgow was completed around 1786, and that he entered Divinity Hall in 1787. Eva Jean Wrather argues for a later date, assuming Campbell completed courses at the University of Glasgow in 1792 just before he entered Divinity Hall in 1792. David Stewart has records that Thomas Campbell entered Divinity Hall in 1792 and that he was not ordained until 1798, making Wrather's argument more probable. See Ibid., 1:25–27; Stewart, *The Seceders in Ireland*, 437.

[54] Measurements according to Google Maps (maps.google.com). One can find more information and pictures at http://www.therestorationmovement.com/_international/ireland/ahorey.htm.

[55] For bibliography of Thomas Campbell, see Lester G. McAllister, "Campbell, Thomas (1763–1854)," ed. Douglas A. Foster et al., *The Encyclopedia of the Stone-Campbell Movement* (Grand Rapids: Eerdmans, 2004), 138–42; McAllister, *Thomas Campbell*; Richardson, *Memoirs of Alexander Campbell*, 1890, 1 passim; Eva Jean Wrather, *Alexander Campbell: Adventurer In Freedom—A Literary Biography*, ed. D. Duane Cummins, vol. 1, 3 vols. (Fort Worth: Texas Christian University Press and the Disciples of Christ Historical Society, 2005).

Kingdom of our Lord Jesus Christ on one side it eventually Destroyed & undermined it on Another.[56]

Like the Burghers, the Antiburghers disliked the aggressive anti-party spirit of the Evangelical Society of Ulster. This "latitudinarianism" undermined the Antiburgher understanding of the gospel.

It was late by the time they arrived at this decision, so the synod established a committee to "converse with Rev Thos. Campble on the subject of his connexion with the Evangelical Society of Ulster." The synod reconvened the next morning, and got the report from the committee concerning the second question. The minutes contained the following responsive statement from Thomas Campbell:

> I am willing to receive the advice of the Synod respecting my connexion with the Evangelical Society of Ulster to take it under my most serious consideration & to endeavor in all things to see eye to eye with the Revd. Synod—& in the meantime to desist from any official intercourse with the Society only remaining a simple subscriber.[57]

It was a carefully worded statement that conceded very little to the synod. Although Campbell agreed to seriously consider advice of the synod and endeavor to agree with its ruling, he clearly did not agree. Ironically, although he gave up his role as a member of the Evangelical Society of Ulster committee, he remained a subscriber—subscribers were the life source of the Society, as without them it had no money to hire itinerants. So Campbell committed to funding operations of the Society when the synod had just ruled that its principles were completely latitudinarian. Nonetheless, "after some conversation the foregoing Declaration was accepted as satisfactory."[58]

The Antiburgher Synod meeting the next year in July of 1800 expressed alarm at the progress of itinerant preaching and their members hearing preaching from non-Antiburgher ministers.[59] The Synod did question

---

[56] *Minutes of the Associate (Antiburgher) Synod of Ireland* (1799), 117–18.
[57] Ibid., 119.
[58] Ibid., 120.
[59] William Gregory, *Visible Display of Divine Providence, or, The Journal of a Captured Missionary Designated to the Southern Pacific Ocean, in the Second Voyage of the Ship Duff*, 2nd ed. (London: Printed by J. Skirven, 1801), 163–66.

"whether or not persons of our communion are unwarily engaged in a course of separation from their brethren, while they continue as members of praying societies under the inspection of said Evangelical Society of Ulster, and not under the pastors to whom they profess to adhere?" The Synod decided "without a dissenting voice" (i.e., Campbell did not oppose) that Antiburgher members involved in Evangelical Society of Ulster praying societies were in fact engaged in an act of separation. Therefore, those engaged in praying societies not under the inspection of Antiburgher pastors should be admonished to withdraw from those societies, and undergo censure if they refused.[60]

Several factors probably influenced Campbell to refrain from another plea on behalf of the legitimacy of the Evangelical Society of Ulster. Campbell's thorough defense of the Evangelical Society of Ulster the previous year was his first Synod meeting as an ordained pastor, and the 1800 Synod was his second. Although he was thirty-seven years old, he was new to the ministry. Furthermore, a concern not to jeopardize his long road to ordained ministry, combined with the unanimous Synod opinion against the Evangelical Society of Ulster, no doubt influenced his lack of opposition to the charges against a society he cofounded and against evangelical missions principles he still valued. In addition, one can assume that, given Campbell's later leadership in the union efforts among the Irish Seceders, the possibilities of uniting with the Burghers provided hope and balanced his disappointment concerning the Evangelical Society of Ulster. Whatever the case, after a member of the synod motioned for the reading of the 1799 minutes concerning Campbell's connection with the Evangelical Society of Ulster, Campbell "gave full satisfaction as to his seeing eye to eye with the synod in this matter, having even declared that he had not paid the last year's subscriptions to that society."[61] Although Campbell would continue fraternizing with Evangelical Society of Ulster leaders and traveling itinerants from various denominations, he was willing in 1800 to refrain from membership and official association with the Society in order to retain his Antiburgher identity and pastorate at Ahorey.

---

[60] *Minutes of the Associate (Antiburgher) Synod of Ireland* (1800), 131–33.
[61] Ibid., 134.

The success of Evangelical Society of Ulster itinerants and opposition to the Society continued through the first half of the first decade of the nineteenth century. The Evangelical Society of Ulster received itinerants not only from the London Missionary Society, but from the Society for Propagating the Gospel at Home, an interdenominational missions organization in Scotland that is discussed in the next chapter. This Society was run by James and Robert Haldane, Scottish Presbyterians who were Independents by 1801. In two 1801 letters, a Society for Propagating the Gospel at Home itinerant to Ireland praised the Evangelical Society of Ulster for its denominational diversity and Ireland for its attentive audiences. The letter carried news of a meetinghouse in Moy for the "reception of evangelical preachers, which is expected to be finished in the course of the summer."[62] James Haldane eventually toured Ireland in September 1801 with Hamilton. The Haldanes must have held Hamilton and the Evangelical Society of Ulster in high regard, as they had him teach at their Irish seminary which trained itinerant missionaries.[63] Hamilton reported in 1801 that the Evangelical Society of Ulster had twenty-one itinerants holding Sabbath services that were well attended.[64]

As the Evangelical Society of Ulster enjoyed famous itinerants and support from England and Scotland, the Burgher Synod continued questioning methods of the Society in 1801 and 1802, leading Evangelical Society of Ulster leaders to leave the Burgher Synod and become Independents or Congregationalists. In 1801, the synod constructed a committee for a "friendly conference" with members of the Evangelical Society of Ulster (including George Hamilton, John Lowry, and John Gibson). The committee and Evangelical Society of Ulster members constructed three declarations to limit the actions of Burgher ministers in the Evangelical Society of Ulster. First, the synod would not give encouragement to lay preaching. James Haldane was a lay preacher, and the Society for Propagating the Gospel at Home, with leading evangelicals in Scotland, had argued for its legitimacy.

---

[62] "Extracts of Letters from One of the Preachers Sent (by Request from the Evangelical Society) to Ireland, by the Society for Propagating the Gospel at Home.—Feb. 5, 1801," *The Missionary Magazine* 6 (June 15, 1801): 260–61.

[63] Haldane, *Memoirs of the Lives of Robert and James Alexander Haldane*, 329–32.

[64] George Hamilton, "Plan of a Proposed Itinerancy from Mr. H----'s Church at Armagh," *The Missionary Magazine* 6 (August 17, 1801): 346–47.

Second, the synod disapproved of Evangelical Society of Ulster preachers going into Burgher congregations without their consent. Third, the synod would not "Countenance promiscuous Communion, in the Ordinance of the Lord's Supper."[65]

The synod voted to adopt the declarations, but in 1801, seven ministers formally protested this adoption. The protest carried over to 1802, when protestors presented six arguments to the synod about why the declarations were too lenient in allowing ministers to fraternize with the Evangelical Society of Ulster. These arguments pointed to lack of doctrinal standards, polity, ordination, and unity, concerns similar to those of the Antiburgher opposition. The Burgher protestors conceived it

> disengenious in [Evangelical Society of Ulster members] to profess Presbyterian Principles, & at the same Time exert themselves in promoting Sectarian Measures to the Distraction of our Congregations, to the Infringement of Uniformity, & the Alienation of Christian Affection.[66]

Evangelical Society of Ulster members were supposed to respond in 1802, which was pushed back to 1803, but a response was never recorded, probably because key leaders such as George Hamilton and John Gibson left the Burghers. The Evangelical Society of Ulster argued for unity based on a primitive gospel which preceded denominational confessions and disciplines, but for many Irish Seceders, that version of unity seemed both divisive and latitudinarian.

In the face of this kind of opposition, a number of transatlantic evangelicals broke from Presbyterianism after being influenced by the interdenominational and evangelical characteristics of missions, opting for a less-restricted congregational polity. Hamilton, who found the congregational form of church government to foster interdenominational cooperation, left the Burgher Synod in 1802.[67] Gibson also exchanged

---

[65] *Minutes of the Associate (Burgher) Synod of Ireland* (1801), 6-8; Thompson, "The Evangelical Society of Ulster," 25; Holmes, *The Shaping of Ulster Presbyterian Belief and Practice, 1770–1840*, 195–96.

[66] *Minutes of the Associate (Burgher) Synod of Ireland* (1802), (unnumbered) page 5.

[67] Stewart, *The Seceders in Ireland*, 187–90; James Seaton Reid and W. D. Killen, *History of the Presbyterian Church in Ireland: Comprising the Civil History of the Province of Ulster, from the Accession of James the First*, new ed. (Belfast: William Mullan, Donegall Place, 1867), 3:416–17; Thomas Witherow,

Burgher Presbyterianism for Independent congregational polity in order to participate in interdenominational missions. In 1802, the Burgher Synod charged Gibson with "holding Communion with Persons disaffected to the Presbyterian Form of Church Government." The synod recognized this as a symptom of the deeper problem of Gibson's association with the Evangelical Society of Ulster and, therefore, gave him an ultimatum:

> That Mr Gibson be allowed untill the next Meeting of the Pby to consider the Matter of his Connection with the Evangelical Society of Ulster, that [he] be InJoined at that Meeting explicitly to renounce the Principles, and abandon the Connection of that Society, otherwise the Pby are authorized to declare him no Member of our Communion, & that at present he promise not to promote the Measures of that Society in the mean Time.[68]

The 1802 minutes give no more information, but the 1803 minutes briefly noted he was no longer a member of the Burghers.[69] Hamilton and Gibson were only two of the many evangelicals in Ireland, Scotland, England, and the United States who followed a similar path out of the Presbyterian church for freedom to work with all Christians in spreading the simple apostolic gospel.

Gibson became an Independent minister in Rich Hill and a friend of Thomas Campbell, who shared a love of interdenominational missions, even though he remained in the Presbyterian fold in the midst of the Evangelical Society of Ulster conflicts. As Campbell's early biographer noted, the Independents at Rich Hill knew Campbell well enough to give him a facetious nickname (they called him Nicodemus, "who came to Jesus by night," because he usually arrived at the Independent congregation at night after he had completed services at his own church in Ahorey). Gibson's Rich Hill Independent congregation became a standard stop for evangelical itinerants, which allowed Campbell to hear Rowland Hill, James Haldane,

---

Historical and Literary Memorials of Presbyterianism in Ireland (London: William Mullan and Son, 1880), 310–11; Thompson, "The Evangelical Society of Ulster," 18.

[68] *Minutes of the Associate (Burgher) Synod of Ireland* (1802), (unnumbered) page 13.

[69] "Received a Report from the Pby of Armagh, respecting their Proceedings concerning Mr. Gibson, whom, they according to the Overture of Synod, declared no longer a member of our Communion." Ibid., (1803), (unnumbered) page 3.

John Walker, and others involved in developing and disseminating evangelical missions. Like Gibson, Campbell eventually started an Independent congregation after ostracizing himself from a Presbyterian synod in 1809 for practicing a more open invitation to Communion, among other charges.[70]

As many Evangelical Society of Ulster members left their Presbyterian synods and became Independents, the Evangelical Society of Ulster remained an important link in the evangelical network of missionary societies through 1805. Not only did the London Missionary Society continue a strong relationship with the Evangelical Society of Ulster, the Society for Propagating the Gospel at Home also sent itinerants to work under the direction of the Evangelical Society of Ulster. According to the Society report for January of 1802 to May of 1803, the organization sent fifteen missionaries to Ireland at around the beginning of January 1802, the majority of whom were placed under the direction of the Evangelical Society of Ulster.[71] In 1803, Hamilton sent a letter to *The Missionary Magazine* in Scotland, declaring that during the last year, operations of the Evangelical Society of Ulster throughout the north had been "crowned with remarkable success," noting the work of itinerants, Sabbath schools, and prayer meetings.[72] Hamilton wrote a state-of-the-society letter in September 1803, delineating the successes of the Evangelical Society of Ulster—its ministers supplied regular preaching in eight places, they built a place of worship in one of those places and planned to build in three other places the ensuing summer, and the General Evangelical Society and Evangelical Society of Ulster had distributed Bibles in Ireland which they acquired from the Society for the Propagation of Christian Knowledge.[73] The Evangelical Society of Ulster had big plans for the following year as well—it would employ seven ministers, as it had the past two years.[74]

---

[70] Richardson, *Memoirs of Alexander Campbell*, 1890, 1:59–60.

[71] "Report by the Society for Propagating the Gospel at Home, from January 1802 to May 15, 1803," *The Missionary Magazine* 8 (July 18, 1803): 313–16.

[72] George Hamilton, "Extract of the REPORT of the EVANGELICAL SOCIETY of Ulster, North of Ireland, March 12, 1803," *The Missionary Magazine* 8 (April 18, 1803): 190–91.

[73] *The Advocate of Revealed Truth, And Inspector of the Religious World* 4, no. 1 (1804): 189–92.

[74] George Hamilton, "Some Account of the Evangelical Society of Ulster in Ireland, in a Letter from Mr. Hamilton of Armagh, Dated 5th September 1803," *The Missionary Magazine* 8 (October 17, 1803): 479; D. C., "Extract of a Letter from One of the Preachers under the Ulster Society, to a Friend in Edinburgh, Dated 15th June 1803," *The Missionary Magazine* 8 (October 17, 1803): 479–80.

The most thorough and apologetic report the Evangelical Society of Ulster published was in *The Missionary Magazine* for February 1804. The anonymous author (probably Hamilton) argued that the Evangelical Society of Ulster was completing its goals, but needed more money. Despite pledges of support from the London Missionary Society of one hundred pounds, an Edinburgh collection of one hundred pounds, and other financial and itinerant support from Scotland, the author said funds were exhausted.[75] In 1804, *The Missionary Magazine* urged readers to support efforts of the Evangelical Society of Ulster to distribute Bibles in Ireland.[76] Later, Hamilton provided a statement dated January 1, 1805, to *The Missionary Magazine*, reporting the substantial amount Scottish churches had given to the Evangelical Society of Ulster the previous year.[77] At that point, Hamilton was secretary and John Gibson was chairman.[78]

Although it appears neither the Presbyterian Synod of Ulster nor the Anglican Church of Ireland launched opposition to the Evangelical Society of Ulster that was equivalent to that of the Seceders, individuals from both denominations were involved with evangelical missions, and some split from the denominations in favor of a congregational polity that allowed for more interdenominational cooperation and "promiscuous communion."[79] In this category, two of the most influential figures on evangelicalism in general and on the Campbells in particular were Alexander Carson and John Walker. Carson received his bachelor of arts and master of arts

---

[75] The author provided a brief financial statement of the money received and expended from 1799 to 1803. The Evangelical Society of Ulster raised more than one hundred pounds annually. During its most active period (October 1801 to March 1803), the Society received 358 pounds and expended 416 pounds. In February 1804, the Society had a balance of 28 pounds. See "Report of the Evangelical Society of Ulster in Ireland," *The Missionary Magazine* 9 (February 20, 1804): 81–86.

[76] "Ulster Evangelical Society," *The Missionary Magazine* 9 (July 16, 1804): 333–35.

[77] Edinburgh Tabernacle gave over one hundred pounds, Mr. Aikman's Chapel gave 53 pounds, Glasgow Tabernacle 44 pounds, Mr. Wardlaw's Chapel 30 pounds, and tabernacles in Dundee, Perth, and Dunkel provided over 33 pounds. These churches were affiliated with the Haldanes, the Society for Propagating the Gospel at Home, and the missionary movement in Scotland. James Haldane ministered at the Edinburgh Tabernacle and Greville Ewing at the Glasgow Tabernacle, both of which Robert Haldane owned. Aikman closely associated with the Haldanes and the Society for Propagating the Gospel at Home from James Haldane's first itinerant preaching tour in 1797. See Chapter Five for more on these connections.

[78] *The Missionary Magazine* 10 (1805): 47.

[79] The Synod of Ulster did pass restrictions on itinerant preachers in 1789, and in 1804, the synod made membership a prerequisite to officiating in their congregations, though this did not necessarily preclude "occasional hearing" of ordained Protestant ministers. Thompson, "The Evangelical Society of Ulster," 16–17; *Records of the General Synod of Ulster: From 1691 to 1820* (Belfast: General Assembly of the Presbyterian Church in Ireland, 1898), 3:112, 279.

degrees from the University of Glasgow, and was ordained in the Synod of Ulster in 1798. A former schoolmate and friend of Greville Ewing, who led evangelical missions in Scotland with the Haldanes in the 1790s, Carson embraced evangelical missions in Ireland. He met James Haldane when the lay preacher itinerated in Ireland in 1801, and Carson eventually taught for a Haldane seminary in Ireland.[80] Carson followed the route of the Haldanes and Ewing from Presbyterian to Independent polity, a route influenced by the interdenominational primitivism prevalent in evangelical missions. Carson's published defense for leaving, *Reasons for Separating from the General Synod of Ulster* (1805), likely influenced Thomas Campbell.[81] Yet Carson's primitivism, like that of the Haldanes and later the Campbells, eventually led him to a belief that the New Testament supported only believer's baptism, which in turn led all of them to affiliation with Baptists for at least a period of time. Carson was a lifelong friend of the Haldane brothers and an advocate of the Baptist Missionary Society.[82] The Campbells heard Carson in Ireland and knew of his theological positions then and later, when Alexander Campbell talked of him kindly as late as the 1820s.[83]

John Walker, another central figure in Irish missions, retained his Anglican identity while leading evangelical missions in Dublin until 1804. Educated at Trinity College, Dublin, the center of early Anglican evangelicalism in Ireland, Walker was one of the most influential evangelicals during the late eighteenth and early nineteenth centuries. He served as chaplain of Bethesda Chapel in Dublin from 1793 until 1804. Walker took a leading role in the General Evangelical Society in Dublin, supported the Evangelical Society of Ulster, and served as a London Missionary Society

---

[80] Richardson, *Memoirs of Alexander Campbell*, 1890, 1:170.

[81] Thompson, "The Irish Background to Thomas Campbell's *Declaration and Address*," 1986, 27.

[82] Mark A. Noll, *The Rise of Evangelicalism: The Age of Edwards, Whitefield, and the Wesleys*, A History of Evangelicalism 1 (Downers Grove: InterVarsity Press, 2003), 205-07; Martin, *Evangelicals United*, 210; Haldane, *Memoirs of the Lives of Robert and James Alexander Haldane*, 301-04; Thompson, "The Evangelical Society of Ulster," 19; Joshua Thompson, "Carson, Alexander (1776-1844)," *The Oxford Dictionary of National Biography* (Oxford: Oxford University Press, 2004), http://www.oxforddnb.com/view/article/4775; Thompson, "The Irish Background to Thomas Campbell's *Declaration and Address*," 1986, 27; George C. Moore, *The Life of Alexander Carson* (New York: Edward H. Fletcher, 1851), 97, 110, 151; Lynn A. McMillon, "The Quest for the Apostolic Church: A Study of Scottish Origins of American Restorationism" (PhD diss., Baylor University, 1972), 155-56; Joshua Thompson, "Carson, Alexander," ed. Donald M. Lewis, *Dictionary of Evangelical Biography, 1730-1860* (Peabody: Hendrickson, 2004), 1:202-03.

[83] Richardson, *Memoirs of Alexander Campbell*, 1890, 1:60, 82, 183, 187; Robert Richardson, *Memoirs of Alexander Campbell: Embracing A View of the Origin, Progress and Principles of the Religious Reformation Which He Advocated*, vol. 2 (Cincinnati: Standard Publishing Company, 1890), 132.

director in Ireland. Like many others, the context of the 1790s and early 1800s led Walker to study the principles of Christian fellowship in the primitive church. This led him to separate from the Church of Ireland in 1804 because he concluded it was an erroneous departure from apostolic Christianity. David Hempton and Myrtle Hill note, "The tendency of 'bible' Christians to disregard the finer distinctions of their church in the wider interests of a gospel mission undermined both the hierarchical structure and the wider authority of the established church."[84] Jettisoning tradition and promoting cooperation for evangelism led some into a cooperative primitivism, but for others such as Walker, it led to a sectarian restorationism that sought a New Testament pattern for church order. When "precepts" about that pattern were viewed as positive laws from God, primitivism morphed from an ecumenical to a sectarian character.[85]

Walker wielded much influence on evangelicalism and the Campbells. Although evangelicals had remained friendly with the establishment up to that point, "Walker's secession was not only a body-blow to that tradition, but made interdenominational cooperation among evangelicals far more difficult to defend," because he used "principled or doctrinaire arguments," rather than self-restraint and pragmatism of the earlier evangelicals.[86] Walker made "quite a strong impression on the mind of young Alexander [Campbell]," according to Campbell's biographer Robert Richardson.[87] The Campbells heard Walker preach at Gibson's Independent congregation in Rich Hill, and enjoyed religious conversation with him at Gibson's house. Although evidence does not reveal why he was there, Thomas Campbell preached in Dublin in 1802 (on three different texts) and 1803, perhaps encountering Walker on those trips.[88] Alexander Campbell read three of Walker's works in 1811 and 1812, including his *Expostulatory Address to*

---

[84] Hempton and Hill, *Evangelical Protestantism in Ulster Society, 1740–1890*, 15, 65; quoted from 65.
[85] E. I. Carlyle and David Huddleston, "Walker, John (1769–1833)," *Oxford Dictionary of National Biography* (Oxford: Oxford University Press, 2004), http://www.oxforddnb.com/view/article/28502; Hempton and Hill, *Evangelical Protestantism in Ulster Society, 1740–1890*, 15, 65; John Walker and Alexander Knox, *An Expostulatory Address to the Members of the Methodist Society in Ireland: Together with a Series of Letters to Alexander Knox, Esq. M.R.I.A.*, 4th ed. (Edinburgh: J. Ritchie, 1806).
[86] Hempton and Hill, *Evangelical Protestantism in Ulster Society, 1740–1890*, 65.
[87] Richardson, *Memoirs of Alexander Campbell*, 1890, 1:60–61, 82.
[88] Campbell recorded the Scripture text of his sermons preached from 1800 to 1806, including the year and the place. Those are available at T. W. Phillips Memorial Library, Bethany College, Bethany, WV, Archives and Special Collections, Campbell Papers, Part 14—Manuscripts, *Manuscript L*, 369–74. Also see Carisse Mickey Berryhill, "A Descriptive Guide to Eight Early Alexander Campbell Manuscripts" (research

Members of the Methodist Society in Ireland.[89] In fact, Alexander Campbell recorded excerpts of this work in his 1809 journal.[90] Ironically, Walker's exclusivist restorationism got its start in the irenic primitivism of evangelical missions, which used a pragmatic primitivism for cooperation, rather than exclusion. Interestingly, Walker's transition is not entirely unlike Alexander Campbell's transition in the 1810s and 1820s, discussed in Chapters Six and Seven.

The Hibernian Society Replaces Local Evangelical Societies

Although the Evangelical Society of Ulster was clearly active through 1805, I have found no reference to the Evangelical Society of Ulster after 1805, because it seems the Hibernian Society (1806) and other Hibernian auxiliaries practically replaced it. The Evangelical Society of Ulster disappeared from *The Evangelical Magazine* and *The Missionary Magazine*, both of which had promoted it, whereas the Hibernian Society became ubiquitous in the pages of these interdenominational magazines.[91] As many of the same leading evangelicals and publications which had supported the Evangelical Society of Ulster and General Evangelical Society began supporting the larger, well-funded Hibernian Society,[92] the Hibernian Society was able to bring efforts of local and regional societies into a central hub by using the same individuals and networks in Ireland.[93] The Evangelical Society of Ulster

---

paper, Memphis, 2000), 6–7, http://web.archive.org/web/20120114232220/http://www.mun.ca/rels/restmov/texts/acampbell/acm/ACM00A.HTM.

[89] Richardson, *Memoirs of Alexander Campbell, 1890*, 1:61, 82, 172, 177, 444–47; Walker and Knox, *An Expostulatory Address*.

[90] Alexander Campbell, *Manuscript B: Juvenile Essays on Various Subjects*, 158–59. Lester McAllister transcribed and published Manuscript B as Alexander Campbell and Lester G. McAllister, *Alexander Campbell at the University of Glasgow 1808–1809* (Nashville: Disciples of Christ Historical Society, 1971), 89–92; Richardson, *Memoirs of Alexander Campbell, 1890*, 1:444–47; Walker and Knox, *An Expostulatory Address*, ix–xii and 44. McAllister, in the introduction to this journal, assumed Campbell took notes when he heard Walker address the Methodists (5), but Richardson correctly notes that Campbell was taking notes from Walker's book (1:444). The quotes in this paragraph come from Walker, ix–xii and 44.

[91] For example, see *The Evangelical Magazine* 13 (1805): 571–73; *The Evangelical Magazine* 14 (1806): 87–88, 231, 567–69, 574; *The Evangelical Magazine* 16 (1808): 93, 229–30, 269–70, 402–03, 448–49, 535–36; *The Evangelical Magazine* 17 (1809): 168, 260–62; *The Evangelical Magazine* 18 (1810): 39–40, 251–52, 254, 495; *The Missionary Magazine* 11 (1806): 514–17; *The Missionary Magazine* 12 (1807): 84, 206–09, 474; *The Missionary Magazine* 13 (1808): 81, 172, 295, 423–24, 474–75; *The Missionary Magazine* 14 (1809): 117–18; *The Missionary Magazine* 15 (1810): 233–34.

[92] Founded in 1806, the Hibernian Society sought information from knowledgeable evangelicals in Ireland, utilizing the advice of Hamilton and others. See *The Missionary Magazine* 12 (1807): 208.

[93] For an example of funding, in 1808 the Hibernian Society received funds of nearly one thousand pounds. See *The Missionary Magazine* 14 (1809): 117–18.

and General Evangelical Society had typically acted as a unified movement of people who were separated by location, but shared resources, such as London Missionary Society itinerants. The smaller societies sent funds to one another, to larger societies, and vice versa. They shared responsibility of Sunday schools, religious tract and Bible distribution, itinerancy, etc. When the interdenominational Hibernian Society emerged with powerful and wealthy donors in London and elsewhere who had the same goals and evangelical faith,[94] it was natural for the smaller societies to work closely with the Hibernian Society and share resources, as this fulfilled a cooperative goal articulated in their constitutions. As Hempton and Hill note, 1800–1850 was a period during which major evangelical societies in London established Hibernian auxiliaries, permitting the use of London assets to "convert the Irish and civilize their country."[95] The Hibernian Society in 1806 was an important beginning to that process.

The Hibernian Society perpetuated evangelical missions. Interdenominational cooperation among "true" Christians (e.g., those who had "vital religion") for spreading an evangelical gospel was the main goal of the Hibernian Society. The Society sent a deputation, which included London Missionary Society leader David Bogue, to survey the religious landscape of Ireland. The deputation pledge stated that the object of the Society was "to associate real christians of different sects, for the purpose of diffusing that vital religion, which may be traced among them all, apart from which, no sect is worth upholding."[96] The deputation encouraged the adherents of existing denominations to be tolerant of diversity and embrace the essential unity of Christians: "Why should diversity so often generate discord? At least, why should those who are essentially one, grieve each other, and gratify the common foe; by mutual surmises and provocations?"[97]

---

[94] The plan of the Hibernian Society stated its goals as the diffusion of religious knowledge in Ireland by means of the "Ministry of the Gospel, by the dispersion of the Holy Scriptures and Religious Tracts, by the formation and support of schools, and by every other lawful and prudent measure calculated to promote pure religion, morality, and loyalty." Committee members at the time of institution included some familiar names involved in the London Missionary Society, such as George Burder and Rowland Hill. Hibernian Society, *Report of a Deputation from the Hibernian Society, Respecting the Religious State of Ireland: To Which Is Annexed a Plan of the Society, Together with a List of Its Officers* (London: printed for the benefit of the Society by T. Rutt, 1807), 62, 64.

[95] Hempton and Hill, *Evangelical Protestantism in Ulster Society, 1740–1890*, 47.

[96] Hibernian Society, *Report of a Deputation from the Hibernian Society*, 17.

[97] Ibid., 35.

Thomas Campbell's Unity Efforts

As the Hibernian Society perpetuated evangelical missions in the first decade of the nineteenth century, Thomas Campbell became the leading Antiburgher advocate for unity among Irish Seceders. Seceders had split into Burgher and Antiburgher factions over the Scottish Burgher oath, which did not exist in Ireland, rendering the split superfluous there.[98] Conversations in synods from 1800 led to a movement to dissolve the Irish connection with the General Associate Synod of Scotland and unite the Irish Seceders.[99] The Burgher and Antiburgher synods each appointed three men to committees which discussed union in October 1804 and March 1805. Campbell was one of the three Antiburgher representatives, and he addressed the Antiburgher Synod with the propositions that the October 1804 committee had constructed. He described the Seceder division in Ireland as an "evil of no small magnitude" because it was "inconsistent with the genius and spirit of the Christian religion, which has union, unity, and communion in faith, hope, and love, for its grand object upon earth." The Seceder division produced a "party spirit," and was embarrassing because the "subject-matter of our difference is not to be found either in the Old or New Testament." One fourth of Campbell's address to the synod was a harangue against division, some of which he reiterated later in his *Declaration and Address*, which also included four propositions that the committee constructed for both Seceders in Ireland and the General Associate Synod of Scotland.[100]

Campbell was chosen to present the Antiburgher Seceders' case to the General Associate Synod of Scotland in Glasgow in 1806, though he was as unable to convince the Scottish Synod of the propriety of Irish union as he was to convince the Irish Antiburghers of the propriety of the "latitudinarian" principles of the Evangelical Society of Ulster. At the synod in Scotland, Campbell presented a compelling case, but was outvoted.[101]

---

[98] Stewart, *The Seceders in Ireland*, 42–53, 107–09, 193, 199–203; Barkley, *A Short History of the Presbyterian Church in Ireland*, 31–32; Richardson, *Memoirs of Alexander Campbell*, 1890, 1:51–58; Thompson, "The Irish Background to Thomas Campbell's *Declaration and Address*," 1986, 25; Brown, "Religion and Society to c.1900."

[99] *Minutes of the Associate (Antiburgher) Synod of Ireland* (1800), 129–30; Stewart, *The Seceders in Ireland*, 107, 193–94; Thompson, "The Evangelical Society of Ulster," 25.

[100] Alexander Campbell, "Address of Thomas Campbell to the Synod of Ireland, Met at Belfast, County Down, A. D. 1804," in *Memoirs of Elder Thomas Campbell, Together with A Brief Memoir of Mrs. Jane Campbell* (Cincinnati: H. S. Bosworth, 1861), 210–14.

[101] Richardson, *Memoirs of Alexander Campbell*, 1890, 1:58, see asterisk footnote.

However, in 1818, ninety-seven Burgher and Antiburgher congregations united into one Irish Seceder synod. Less than twenty years had passed since the Seceders vehemently opposed the Evangelical Society of Ulster, but the unified Secession Synod reflected its commitment to evangelical missions by supporting the London Missionary Society and the Hibernian societies that it had earlier opposed.[102] Campbell was not in Ireland to celebrate the union or Antiburgher support of evangelical missions, for, looking to improve his health and opportunity, he had joined the Scotch-Irish immigration to the United States on April 18, 1807. His experiences in Ireland deeply impacted his course of action in the United States, a story I will pick up in Chapter Six.[103]

CONCLUSION

This chapter has shown that the evangelical missions which emerged in Ireland and powerfully shaped Thomas Campbell were inextricably connected to broader transatlantic evangelical missions. Campbell's synod perceived the interdenominational missions endeavor in Ireland as latitudinarian; yet Campbell revealed his admiration for the ideals, form, and function of the Evangelical Society of Ulster not only in his defense to the Irish Synod, but also in his replication of the Society in the United States, which later chapters cover. Missions in Ireland promoted cooperation among Christians of various denominations through voluntary societies for the expansion of a simple evangelical Christianity. The basis upon which "true," "real," or converted Christians of different denominations could cooperate was a primitive or apostolic gospel, which was purer and simpler than confessional Christianity as developed in the Protestant traditions. The intellectual milieu of the Enlightenment fostered the toleration and forbearance that undergirded missions in Ireland, and it lauded attempts to jettison tradition for a pure, apostolic, primitive Christianity. Some missions advocates turned a pragmatic primitivism which began with a

---

[102] Hempton and Hill, *Evangelical Protestantism in Ulster Society, 1740-1890*, 50, 70.

[103] Stewart, *The Seceders in Ireland*, 42–53, 107–09, 193, 199–203; Barkley, *A Short History of the Presbyterian Church in Ireland*, 31–32; Richardson, *Memoirs of Alexander Campbell*, 1890, 1:51–54; Thompson, "The Irish Background to Thomas Campbell's *Declaration and Address*," 1986, 25; Brown, "Religion and Society to c.1900."

goal of ecumenical missions into a sectarian primitivism for the end of a restored New Testament church—this was partly the case with Walker and Carson, both of whom influenced the Campbells. The interdenominational missions featured a pragmatic primitivism and ecumenism that could be worked to very different ends, depending on the individual leaders and their divergent contexts. The same was true for the evangelicals in Scotland, to whose story we turn in the next chapter.

Chapter Five

THE INFLUENCE OF SCOTTISH EVANGELICAL MISSIONS ON ALEXANDER CAMPBELL

In October 1808, Alexander Campbell (1788–1866) and the rest of the Campbell family embarked on a journey to join Thomas Campbell in the United States, but they took an unexpected detour. As the family set sail on the ship *Hibernia* in 1808, their journey became nearly fatal when their boat ran upon some rocks off the coast of Scotland. Alexander wrote about that night in his diary: "The vessel was almost on her side & for a little me thought the drowning flood must be the inevitable fate of every soul on board."[1] However, everyone made it ashore, and they even managed to save some luggage. In the following weeks, the Campbell family made their way to Glasgow, where Greville Ewing, one of the most influential advocates of evangelical missions in Scotland from the 1790s to the middle of the nineteenth century, became Alexander's mentor. We know very little about the nine months the Campbells spent in Glasgow, but we know a great deal about the people who influenced Alexander and Thomas Campbell, as well as a host of transatlantic evangelicals through

---

[1] See Alexander Campbell, *Manuscript D*, 21. All the manuscripts of Alexander Campbell used in this book are available at Archives and Special Collections, T. W. Phillips Memorial Library, Bethany College, Bethany, WV, Campbell Papers, Part 14—Manuscripts.

their leadership in Scottish evangelical missions. This chapter tells the story of evangelical missions in Scotland and focuses on the societies, individuals, and ideals that influenced the Campbells.

Scottish Churches and Evangelical Missions

The moderate party[2] in the Presbyterian Church of Scotland dominated the ecclesiastical context in Scotland until the 1830s, when the evangelicalism that had been growing throughout the eighteenth century finally constituted a majority in the General Assembly. After a chaotic sixteenth and seventeenth century, the Church of Scotland became Presbyterian in 1690 and has remained so since. Evangelicalism and missions had some existence in Scotland from their inceptions, as discussed in Chapters Two and Three. George Whitefield and John Wesley had itinerated in Scotland, and the Cambuslang Revival during the Great Awakening acquired international fame. John Erskine led evangelicals and the missionary movement in Scotland during the eighteenth century. Numbers of dissenting Baptists and Congregationalists began growing in the late eighteenth century; and Presbyterian dissenting groups, who were often evangelical, also grew in the nineteenth century, making up one-third of the Christians in main cities by 1835. Numerous evangelicals in Scotland, led by Greville Ewing and the Haldane brothers, embraced missions in the 1790s and early 1800s, joining the interdenominational networks to convert the "heathen" abroad and at home. Nonetheless, the missionary movement created serious conflict in the 1790s, illustrated by the General Assembly's rejection (by a small

---

[2] The moderate party in the Church of Scotland resembled the latitudinarians in the Church of England. The moderates dominated in the General Assembly by the mid-eighteenth century. They supported political accommodation (e.g., supporting lay patronage) and intellectual respectability, yet they retained the doctrines in the *Westminster Confession*. Moderate control of education fostered the Scottish Enlightenment and a politically respectable version of Christianity, which could appeal to the new cosmopolitan upper classes emerging from economic opportunities of the Industrial Revolution. Moderates typically favored tolerance, reasonableness, and other Enlightenment ideals, though an uneasy tension existed between Enlightenment openness and Westminster orthodoxy. Moderates were suspicious of dissent and "enthusiasm," so they were often at odds with evangelicals in and out of the Church of Scotland. Evangelicals often viewed moderates as prioritizing reason over experience and piety, and dissenting evangelicals among the Seceders viewed lay patronage as abandoning the Presbyterian principle of honoring the will of local congregations. See Camille K. Dean, "Evangelicals or Restorationists? The Careers of Robert and James Haldane in Cultural and Political Context" (PhD diss., Texas Christian University, 1999), chap. 1.

majority) of missions in 1796 and the subsequent conflicts about missions within the establishment.³

The intellectual context in Scotland during the 1790s made evangelical missions both appealing and controversial. Evangelicals and moderates both embraced aspects of the Scottish Enlightenment, which influenced missions, though many moderates disliked evangelical approaches to missions, causing a decades-long debate in the General Assembly.⁴ In the broader view, historian Brian Stanley argues that "the Enlightenment that did most to mold English-speaking evangelicalism in general and the missionary movement in particular was that in Scotland."⁵ Likewise, historian Camille Dean's analysis of the Haldane brothers in Scotland emphasizes the influence of the Enlightenment, radical social change, and revolutionary political ideas on the missionary movement.⁶ Yet the Scottish Enlightenment had an ambivalent role on missions because Enlightenment ideals, like those of ecumenical primitivism, could develop in very different directions. Even so, the intellectual milieu of the Enlightenment was an important aspect of the culture of missions, and it became a dominating influence in the Campbell Movement.⁷

In the wake of the founding of the London Missionary Society in 1795, Scottish evangelicals continued the historically strong Scottish

---

³ David Bebbington, "Evangelicalism," ed. Nigel M. de S. Cameron, *Dictionary of Scottish Church History & Theology* (Downers Grove: InterVarsity Press, 1993), 306–07; John H. S. Burleigh, *A Church History of Scotland* (London: Oxford University Press, 1960), 261–333. Evangelicals did eventually come to dominate in the General Assembly in the 1830s under leadership of missionary advocates such as Thomas Chalmers. In the 1820s and 1830s throughout the transatlantic, denominations took over the missionary movement, changing its character from the interdenominational approach it had from its inception.

⁴ Ian Douglas Maxwell, "Civilization or Christianity? The Scottish Debate on Mission Methods, 1750–1835," in *Christian Missions and the Enlightenment*, ed. Brian Stanley (Grand Rapids: Eerdmans, 2001), 123–40; Hugh Miller, "The Debate on Missions," in *The Headship of Christ, and the Rights of the Christian People: A Collection of Essays, Historical and Descriptive Sketches, and Personal Portaitures* (Boston: Gould and Lincoln, 1870), 144–99.

⁵ Brian Stanley, "Christian Missions and the Enlightenment: A Reevaluation," in *Christian Missions and the Enlightenment*, ed. Brian Stanley (Grand Rapids: Eerdmans, 2001), 17.

⁶ Camille Dean explains each of these three influences. "The Enlightenment furnished evangelicals a wider worldview, a respect for other cultures and languages, and a less introspective, meliorist Calvinism that stressed gospel grace more than predestined reprobation. The widespread enunciation of political freedom and human rights translated to a conviction that all people have a right to hear the gospel." Camille Dean, "Robert and James Alexander Haldane in Scotland: Evangelicals or Restorationists?" *Restoration Quarterly* 42, no. 2 (2000): 101–02.

⁷ David Bebbington, "Enlightenment," ed. Nigel M. de S. Cameron, *Dictionary of Scottish Church History & Theology* (Downers Grove: InterVarsity Press, 1993), 294–95; Carisse Mickey Berryhill, "Common Sense Philosophy," ed. Douglas A. Foster et al., *The Encyclopedia of the Stone-Campbell Movement* (Grand Rapids: Eerdmans, 2004), 230–31.

involvement in evangelical missions—from 1795 to 1800, they produced about a dozen interdenominational voluntary missionary societies and *The Missionary Magazine* (1796). All these missionary societies worked closely with the London Missionary Society, and twenty-eight Scots were London Missionary Society directors from 1796 to 1800, representing the Church of Scotland (14), Associate (Burgher) Synod (7), General Associate (Antiburgher) Synod (1), Independents (3), and the Relief Church (1). Most Presbyterian synods and assemblies eventually frowned upon or rejected the voluntary societies. The Antiburghers in Scotland judged the constitutions of the interdenominational societies to be "latitudinarian," just as their Irish colleagues resolved.[8] Camille Dean concludes that the Seceders were "out of step with the intellectual spirit of their times," but evangelicals in the Church of Scotland gained ground for their ability to adapt to new socio-intellectual contexts and appeal to popular evangelical piety.[9] Indeed, evangelicals in the Church of Scotland led the dissemination of interdenominational missions in Scotland, though some left the establishment and became Independents in the face of opposition. In other words, missions immediately took root among many Scottish evangelicals, but some denominations or groups within denominations (e.g., the moderates in the Church of Scotland and the Scottish Antiburghers) opposed missions and/or voluntary missionary societies. In Scotland, as in other places throughout the transatlantic, interdenominational societies conducted the overwhelming amount of missionary work until the denominations took over missions in the 1820s and 1830s.[10]

---

[8] John Roxborough, *Thomas Chalmers, Enthusiast for Mission: The Christian Good of Scotland and the Rise of the Missionary Movement*, Rutherford Studies in Historical Theology (Edinburgh: published for Rutherford House by Paternoster Press, 1999), 170.

[9] Dean, "Evangelicals or Restorationists?" 56, 59. On the contexts Dean has in mind, other than the Scottish Enlightenment: "By the end of the century, the course of industrialization and the democratizing influences of the American and French revolutions reinforced a trend toward greater popular participation in both religion and politics in Scotland" (56). Dean capitalizes "Evangelical" when referring to evangelicals in the Church of Scotland.

[10] Roxborough, *Thomas Chalmers*, chap. 9 and Appendices 6–7; James A. De Jong, *As the Waters Cover the Sea: Millennial Expectations in the Rise of Anglo-American Missions, 1640–1810*, 2006 reprint (Kampen: J. H. Kok, 1970), chap. 5; William Brown, *History of the Propagation of Christianity Among the Heathen Since the Reformation*, 3rd ed. (London: T. Baker, 1854), 415–503; Esther Breitenbach, "The Impact of the Victorian Empire," in *The Oxford Handbook of Modern Scottish History*, eds. T. M. Devine and Jenny Wormald, Oxford Handbooks (Oxford: Oxford University Press, 2012), oxfordhandbooks.com.

Greville Ewing: Early Architect of Scottish Evangelical Missions

Greville Ewing was perhaps the most influential leader of interdenominational missions in Scotland in the 1790s. Ewing received a Scottish Enlightenment education at the University of Edinburgh, and then trained for ministry. He was ordained in 1793 in the Church of Scotland as associate minister of Lady Glenorchy's Chapel in Edinburgh, where his homiletical skill quickly made him a popular preacher. Ewing read *The Evangelical Magazine* and even contributed an article under the pseudonym "Onesimus," which compared Arminianism and Calvinism in 1794, arguing that the two groups could disagree on the important doctrines at stake and yet cooperate for important work.[11] The editors of *The Evangelical Magazine* requested his address, and he responded with a letter offering his services.[12] This marked the beginning of a long relationship, as Ewing became a trustee listed on *The Evangelical Magazine* title page from 1804 until 1840 (the year before his death). In Scotland, Ewing held membership in the Society in Scotland for Propagating Christian Knowledge, before which he preached a missionary sermon in 1796.[13] Also in 1796, he supported the establishment of the Edinburgh (later Scottish) Missionary Society, and became its first secretary. With a Baptist named Charles Stuart, Ewing cofounded *The Missionary Magazine* in 1796, the first interdenominational missions periodical in Scotland, and he served as editor for its first three years.[14] Ewing found his pastoral home at the center of evangelical missions.

Formed in March 1796, just six months after the London Missionary Society, the Edinburgh Missionary Society drew support from leading evangelicals in Scotland for interdenominational missions. It was fitting that seventy-five-year-old John Erskine, who had led Scottish evangelical

---

[11] Onesimus, "A Comparative View of Calvinism and Arminianism," *The Evangelical Magazine* 2 (November 1794): 453–61; J. J. Matheson, *A Memoir of Greville Ewing, Minister of the Gospel, Glasgow* (London: John Snow, Paternoster Row, 1843), 623–29.

[12] Greville Ewing to the editors of *The Evangelical Magazine*, December 8, 1794, in J. Matheson, "Memoir of the Late Rev. Greville Ewing, of Glasgow," *The Evangelical Magazine, and Missionary Chronicle* 19 (October 1841): 54–55.

[13] Ibid., 123–24.

[14] For biography, see W. G. Blaikie and David Huddleston, "Ewing, Greville (1767–1841)," *The Oxford Dictionary of National Biography* (Oxford: Oxford University Press, 2004), http://www.oxforddnb.com/view/article/9018; Matheson, "Memoir of Greville Ewing"; Kenneth J. Stewart, "Ewing, Greville," ed. Donald M. Lewis, *Dictionary of Evangelical Biography, 1730–1860* (Peabody: Hendrickson, 2004); Dean, "Evangelicals or Restorationists?" 4."

missions from the 1740s to the 1790s, presided at the first meeting.[15] Erskine presided at the first Edinburgh Missionary Society meeting, while the younger Ewing became the first secretary of the Society. The Edinburgh Missionary Society replicated the interdenominational nature and goals of the London Missionary Society, and planned to cooperate with it as well as the Society for Propagation of the Gospel, Society for the Propagation of Christian Knowledge, Society in Scotland for Propagating Christian Knowledge, and other Scottish missionary societies. By February 1797, the Edinburgh Missionary Society and London Missionary Society had joined together for a mission to West Africa, and the Edinburgh Missionary Society had given funds to the Baptist Society for its translation of the Bible into Bengali and supported the United Brethren Society in London.[16] From its start, the Edinburgh Missionary Society sought interdenominational cooperation for missionary endeavors.

Ewing led interdenominational missions not only through the missionary society in Edinburgh, but also via *The Missionary Magazine*. The content of the magazine reveals its ardent support for interdenominational cooperation for missions based upon primitive Christianity and motivated by eschatology. The common evangelical missions eschatology donned the title page: "And this Gospel of the kingdom shall be preached in all the world for a witness unto all nations, and then shall the end come. Mat. xxiv.14." The magazine further revealed its ideology in a proposal to missionary societies, which included translating the Bible, purchasing slaves (they sought to free slaves, because they thought slavery was wrong and

---

[15] While the Seceders condemned the Cambuslang Revival in the early 1740s, Erskine defended it. He served as a director of the Society in Scotland for Propagating Christian Knowledge, published and distributed the works of Jonathan Edwards, and sent Edwards's *An Humble Attempt* to his English Baptist correspondents in Northamptonshire (Andrew Fuller and John Ryland, Jr.), starting a series of events which influenced the start of Baptist missions. Erskine and the Society in Scotland for Propagating Christian Knowledge also nurtured the central leaders of the London Missionary Society. Erskine represented evangelical missions at the General Assembly of the Church of Scotland in 1796, responding to opposition from the moderate party to missions proposals. See Dean, "Evangelicals or Restorationists?" 59, 90–91; De Jong, *As the Waters Cover the Sea*, 166–98; Mark A. Noll, *The Rise of Evangelicalism: The Age of Edwards, Whitefield, and the Wesleys*, A History of Evangelicalism 1 (Downers Grove: InterVarsity Press, 2003), 207–10; John R. McIntosh, "Erskine, John," ed. Donald M. Lewis, *Dictionary of Evangelical Biography, 1730–1860* (Peabody: Hendrickson, 2004), 1:363; Roxborough, *Thomas Chalmers*, 169; Miller, "The Debate on Missions," 168.

[16] Greville Ewing, *A Defence of Missions from Christian Societies to the Heathen World: A Sermon, Preached before the Edinburgh Missionary Society, on Thursday, Feb. 2, 1797* (Edinburgh: printed by J. Ritchie, 1797), 81–84.

an obstruction to the expansion of Christianity in Africa), converting the Jews ("Their conversion will perhaps precede the *fullness of the Gentiles*"), and collecting "A fund for *premiums* to excite the discussion of Missionary subjects—the meaning of prophecies which relate to the progress of the Gospel—the signs of the times—obstructions to Christianity, &c. how to remove them, &c."[17] Like evangelicals throughout the transatlantic, eschatology motivated missions in Scotland, and leaders sought to remove obstacles to "heathen" reception of the gospel.

Eschatology certainly motivated Scottish missions, but interdenominational cooperation, primitivism, and networking with transatlantic missions culture were even more ubiquitous in *The Missionary Magazine*. The preface of the first volume announced that the magazine belonged to private individuals who fiercely opposed the "industrious spirit of party" while hoping to procure "favour from the Friends of SIMPLE REVEALED TRUTH."[18] This cooperation among denominations for missions filled the pages of the periodical, which reported on Baptist, Methodist, Moravian, Congregational, and Presbyterian missions efforts with impartiality, and printed letters and reports from missions leaders in many of these groups. The first issue in July 1796 reported, with adulation, the proceedings of the London Missionary Society annual meeting, noting the numerous societies in the transatlantic which were joining the London Missionary Society or working for the same goals independently. The London Missionary Society and the Edinburgh and Glasgow missionary societies created a "spiritual union" more "perfect" than the political union, as the London Missionary Society allowed the Scottish societies to use its ship to take missionaries anywhere in the world. London Missionary Society news got as much space as anything in *The Missionary Magazine*, though news of the Edinburgh and Glasgow missionary societies and the Society in Scotland for Propagating Christian Knowledge was commonplace. The magazine experienced quick success, selling five thousand to six thousand copies of each month's issue in the first year.[19]

---

[17] "Proposals to Missionary Societies," *The Missionary Magazine* 1 (September 1796): 141.

[18] "Preface," *The Missionary Magazine* 1 (July 1796): i–ii.

[19] "Proceedings of Missionary Societies," *The Missionary Magazine* 1 (July 1796): 45–47; Matheson, "Memoir of Greville Ewing," footnote on 126.

Sermons preached at missionary society gatherings were among the most important rituals for bringing Christians of different denominations together to construct an interdenominational evangelical identity with the key motive of missions, and Ewing contributed his homiletical skills to these meaning-making events.[20] Ewing's *Defence of Missions from Christian Societies to the Heathen World*, preached before the Edinburgh Missionary Society in 1797, provided a clear statement of how he shaped and was shaped by missions. Taking Romans 10:11ff as his text, Ewing found similarities between the new interdenominational missions and Paul's audacious message that "there is no difference between the Jew and the Greek." Just as Paul's Jewish contemporaries saw it as "presumptuous in a young man ... to depart from the beaten track of his brethren and fathers," so did Christians entrenched in partyism view the interdenominational efforts for missions. However, both Paul and the new missionary advocates discerned God's will correctly. Ewing's sermon argued that the best missions method was voluntary societies sending translators and itinerant preachers of the primitive gospel alone (i.e., not denominational Christianity, which would only confuse the hearers) to "heathen" lands.[21]

Ewing's involvement in the interdenominational missionary movement and his public advocacy of itinerant and field preaching even by lay people led to conflict and, ultimately, to his resignation from the Church of Scotland in 1798. In the midst of his advocacy for missions and itinerancy, the Church of Scotland opposed these means of spreading the gospel. Despite John Erskine's best efforts at the 1796 General Assembly, the moderate majority rejected, by a vote of 58 to 44, the evangelical proposals to start missions in the Church of Scotland and to authorize a general collection to support interdenominational missionary societies. Traditional moderates in the Church of Scotland typically rejected the burgeoning missionary movement, and they nixed the two proposals in 1796 on one or more of the following grounds: (1) "heathens" must be civilized before assenting to truth, (2) interdenominational cooperation and itinerancy were beyond the control

---

[20] Some of these sermons were printed and sold in order to disseminate the culture to Christians and to raise funds for missions. See "Proceedings of Missionary Societies," *The Missionary Magazine* 1 (August 1796): 94.

[21] Ewing, *A Defence of Missions from Christian Societies*.

of the church courts, and (3) some linked missionary enthusiasts with radical politics. Ewing said these events and future opposition to itinerancy in Scotland weakened his attachment to the established church because they used their authority over ministers and congregations to stop people from preaching the gospel. In ways similar to those of evangelical Presbyterians in Ireland who committed themselves to the ideas and practices of missions, Ewing and others traded their Presbyterian polity for a more flexible independent congregational polity.[22]

Robert and James Haldanes' Society for Propagating the Gospel at Home

Ewing's move to a congregational polity created space for him to develop his relationship with the Haldane brothers, whom he had known since the late 1770s when they attended the same high school in Edinburgh.[23] Robert Haldane and James Haldane were among the most committed supporters of evangelical missions in the 1790s and early 1800s. The Haldanes were aristocrats who received education at the University of Edinburgh, where Scottish Enlightenment thinkers left an indelible mark. Robert served in the Royal Navy from 1780 to 1783, and James worked for the East India Company from 1785 to 1794. Around the mid-1790s, both brothers committed to an evangelical faith. This happened under the influence of future London Missionary Society leader and Congregational minister David Bogue in Gosport, England. During stays in London, the Haldanes encountered Bogue, a family friend and expatriate Scot who, from the early 1780s, produced in them empathy for dissenters.[24] In Scotland, Bogue's missions influence on the Haldanes was redoubled by Ewing, William Innes (Ewing's brother-in-law), John Erskine, John Campbell, and others. James Haldane met William Carey in India, and Carey's work inspired both brothers to join the missionary movement. Shortly after Bogue declared the funeral of bigotry at the initial meeting of the London Missionary Society in 1795,

---

[22] Roxborough, *Thomas Chalmers*, 171; Maxwell, "Civilization or Christianity? The Scottish Debate on Mission Methods, 1750–1835," 123–40; Miller, "The Debate on Missions," 144–99; Dean, "Evangelicals or Restorationists?" 90–91; Matheson, "Memoir of Greville Ewing," 159.

[23] Alexander Haldane, *Memoirs of the Lives of Robert Haldane of Airthrey, and of His Brother, James Alexander Haldane* (London: Hamilton, Adams, and Co., 1852), 20.

[24] Ibid., 23.

the Haldanes began to devote their lives and fortune to the interdenominational missionary endeavor.[25] Robert Haldane served as a Scottish director of the London Missionary Society by 1796, and filled that role for the next nine years.[26] The first decade of the Haldanes' evangelicalism centered in interdenominational missions, though, as historians have demonstrated, the Haldanes moved from interdenominational primitivism to a more exclusionary primitivism that resembled Glasite restorationism, and ultimately created to a "restorationist evangelical synthesis."[27]

The Haldanes worked with the most influential evangelicals in missions from the very start of their commitment to the effort. In 1796, Robert conceived of a plan to sell his estate of Airthrey to defray the expenses of a mission to India. He invited Innes, Bogue, and Ewing, all of whom agreed, but the directors of the East India Company repeatedly refused Haldane's proposal for permission to travel because of the Company's economic interests. The directors also suspected Haldane's and other dissenting evangelicals' political leanings.[28] Instead of India, the Haldanes turned their attention to home missions in Scotland through the Society for Propagating the Gospel at Home, educating itinerant preachers and missionaries, and building the Congregational movement in Scotland. James accompanied visiting Cambridge scholar Charles Simeon (1759–1836) on a three-week itinerant preaching tour in the Highlands in 1796.[29] He also cooperated

---

[25] For a biography of the Haldanes, see Deryck Lovegrove, "Haldane, Robert (1764–1842)," *The Oxford Dictionary of National Biography* (Oxford: Oxford University Press, 2004), http://www.oxforddnb.com/view/article/11896; Deryck Lovegrove, "Haldane, James Alexander (1768–1851)," *The Oxford Dictionary of National Biography* (Oxford: Oxford University Press, 2004), http://www.oxforddnb.com/view/article/11895; Dean, "Evangelicals or Restorationists?"; Haldane, *Memoirs of the Lives of Robert and James Alexander Haldane*.

[26] "The Proceedings of the Second General Meeting," in *Four Sermons, Preached in London at the Second General Meeting of the Missionary Society, May 11, 12, 13, 1796 . . . To Which Are Prefixed, The Proceedings of the Meeting* (London: sold by T. Chapman, 1796), xxiv; Roxborough, *Thomas Chalmers*, 264.

[27] Dean, "Evangelicals or Restorationists?" 2–3, 8; Dean, "Robert and James Alexander Haldane in Scotland," 100; Deryck W. Lovegrove, "Unity and Separation: Contrasting Elements in the Thought and Practice of Robert and James Alexander Haldane," in *The Stone-Campbell Movement: An International Religious Tradition*, eds. Michael W. Casey and Douglas A. Foster (Knoxville: University of Tennessee Press, 2002), 520–43; Dyron Daughrity, "Glasite Versus Haldanite: Scottish Divergence on the Question of Missions," *Restoration Quarterly* 53, no. 2 (2011): 65–79.

[28] The Edinburgh Missionary Society focused on its Africa mission in which the Glasgow and London missionary societies partnered, so it could not support the Haldane-Innes-Ewing-Bogue mission. The East India Company did not support missions until forced by Parliament in 1811. Matheson, "Memoir of Greville Ewing," chapter 2; Dean, "Evangelicals or Restorationists?" 89.

[29] Dean, "Evangelicals or Restorationists?" 92–93; Haldane, *Memoirs of the Lives of Robert and James Alexander Haldane*, 132–40.

with Church of Scotland evangelical leader John Campbell (1766–1840) to establish dozens of Sabbath schools for religious instruction to young and working-class people.[30] Campbell worked to form the Religious Tract Society in Edinburgh (1793), associated closely with the Haldanes, and served as London Missionary Society director for eight years and as its inspector to South Africa on two occasions.[31]

James Haldane became president of the Edinburgh Missionary Society by 1797, the same year he preached his first sermon, and he and two other laymen (John Aikman, a divinity student, and Joseph Rate, a student from Bogue's Gosport Academy) undertook an itinerant trip into the Highlands from July to November of that year.[32] Although they encountered much opposition to their itinerancy and lay preaching, they experienced great success, preaching to as many as six thousand on one occasion and distributing more than twenty thousand religious tracts.[33]

Due to opposition, the three itinerants used the introduction of the published journal of the trip to defend lay and itinerant preaching and to answer objections.[34] They argued

> that it is not only lawful, but the bounden duty of every Christian to preach the gospel. . . . Whether a man declare those important truths to two or two hundred, he is in our opinion a preacher of the gospel, or one who declares the glad tidings of salvation, which is the precise meaning of the term *preach*.[35]

---

[30] At these Sabbath schools, people learned the catechism and Scripture, sung songs, heard exhortations, and prayed. Dean, "Evangelicals or Restorationists?" 94–95; James Ross, *A History of Congregational Independency in Scotland* (Glasgow: James MacLehose & Sons, 1900), 48.

[31] Andrew C. Ross, "Campbell, John," ed. Donald M. Lewis, *Dictionary of Evangelical Biography, 1730–1860* (Peabody: Hendrickson, 2004), 1:189–90; Roxborough, *Thomas Chalmers*, 262; Robert Philip, *The Life, Times, and Missionary Enterprises of the Rev. John Campbell* (London: John Snow, 1841), 119–21.

[32] Dean, "Evangelicals or Restorationists?" 96–102; Lynn A. McMillon, "The Quest for the Apostolic Church: A Study of Scottish Origins of American Restorationism" (PhD diss., Baylor University, 1972), 147–48; Haldane, *Memoirs of the Lives of Robert and James Alexander Haldane*, chap. 7; James Alexander Haldane, *Journal of a Tour through the Northern Counties of Scotland and the Orkney Isles, in Autumn 1797: Undertaken with a View to Promote the Knowledge of the Gospel of Jesus Christ* (Edinburgh: printed by J. Ritchie, 1798).

[33] For the names of tracts and numbers distributed, see Haldane, *Journal of a Tour through the Northern Counties of Scotland*, 35.

[34] John Ritchie, early secretary of the Society for Propagating the Gospel at Home, printed the journal for the benefit of the Society for Propagating the Gospel at Home, as noted on the title page. Haldane, *Journal of a Tour through the Northern Counties of Scotland*.

[35] Ibid., 5–6.

They took issue with opponents who argued that Scripture stipulated that one needs a license or ordination to preach. Although they supported ordination, they also supported the "duty of Christians to exhort one another" as following "apostolic practice."[36] This included women, though propriety required they preach only to their own sex in private.[37] The great reformers, they argued, had no license; just as necessity justified the reformers' unlicensed preaching, so it justified "lay-preaching at present, when thousands are perishing for lack of knowledge."[38] Furthermore, they supported lay administration of baptism and the Lord's Supper, appealing to positive law hermeneutics and pointing to Acts 10:47–48 to argue that the apostles preached and commanded others (e.g, lay people) to baptize.[39] It is worth mentioning that Alexander Campbell recorded reading James Haldane's *Journal of a Tour* in 1811 or 1812.[40]

Although their defense of itinerant lay preaching had a more acerbic tone, the three authors clearly embraced interdenominational evangelical missions. They believed "the true church is not found in one sect or denomination, but scattered among all who have heard the gospel."[41] Christian charity and cooperation suggested the last days were upon them. The lack of bigotry and surplus of liberality and affection the itinerants encountered led them to "contemplate that glorious day of gospel-light, which we trust has begun to dawn, when Christians shall agree to differ in lesser matters, and shall cordially embrace in the arms of Christian affection all

---

[36] They cited Ephesians 4:15; Hebrews 3:13, 10:24–25; 1 Peter 4:10; Acts 18:25; and more throughout the introduction.

[37] Haldane, *Journal of a Tour through the Northern Counties of Scotland*, 12.

[38] Ibid., 14.

[39] One gets an idea of James Haldane's restorationism at this time from his argument that Scripture teaches "the Lord will have mercy and not sacrifice; that he prefers the benefit of his creatures to positive or ceremonial commands" (Ibid., 10). However, he does use positive law to justify lay preaching. He also employed the Reformed regulative principle for publicly reproving open sinners or offences: "We have both apostolic precept and example in Scripture for publicly reproving open offenders" (24). On Reformed and restorationist positive law as well as the regulative principle, see *Westminster Confession of Faith*, 1.6 and 21.1; John Mark Hicks, "The Gracious Separatist: Moral and Positive Law in the Theology of James A. Harding," *Restoration Quarterly* 42, no. 3 (2000): 129–47; Michael W. Casey, "The Origins of the Hermeneutics of the Churches of Christ Part One: The Reformed Tradition," *Restoration Quarterly* 31, no. 2 (January 1, 1989): 75–91; Michael W. Casey, "The Origins of the Hermeneutics of the Churches of Christ Part Two: The Philosophical Background," *Restoration Quarterly* 31, no. 4 (January 1, 1989): 193–206.

[40] Robert Richardson, *Memoirs of Alexander Campbell: Embracing A View of the Origin, Progress and Principles of the Religious Reformation Which He Advocated*, vol. 1 (Cincinnati: Standard Publishing Company, 1890), 443.

[41] Haldane, *Journal of a Tour through the Northern Counties of Scotland*, 25.

who hold the head [i.e., Christ]."⁴² The authors twice appealed to Luke 14:23—the passage George Hamilton took for his sermon on the necessity of itinerancy at the founding of the Evanglical Society of Ulster in Ireland the same year—to justify missions by itinerancy, arguing that preachers could no longer simply expect people to come into the church; rather, they had to proclaim the gospel in the fields and streets.⁴³ The Scots ought to replicate the English dissenters, whose zeal drove them out of the churches and into the neighborhoods preaching the gospel. The authors hoped the journal would provoke others to join the work in Scotland, so pity for the wretched state of religion and perishing Scots permeated the pages. "The people, almost in every place, seem willing to receive, and thankful for instruction," so more itinerants were needed to warn Scots to "flee from the wrath to come." The authors hoped readers would hear "Come over and help us" crying from these pages.⁴⁴

Encouraged at the successes of their itinerant trip and the increasing number of Sabbath schools, the Haldanes, John Campbell, and twelve others met on December 20, 1797, to establish the Society for Propagating the Gospel at Home, which added to the more than thirty voluntary societies established in Great Britain in the 1790s.⁴⁵ *The Missionary Magazine* of 1797 had substantial articles on propagation of the gospel at home and use of the "Sunday School" or "Sabbath School." Similar to the persuasions used by Christians throughout the transatlantic, some in Scotland argued that Scots "ought first to use means for the conversion of the Heathen at home" before focusing on the "heathen" abroad.⁴⁶ Sabbath schools were a key means of spreading the gospel at home, especially among the new industrial poor working class. Therefore, "many of the praying societies in various denominations in Edinburgh, and its neighbourhood, established a monthly meeting for prayer, for the revival of religion at home, and for the

---

⁴² Ibid., 30–31.

⁴³ They gained larger crowds by using drums and bells to announce they were preaching. Responding to charges that they disturbed the peace, they argued that more people came from curiosity than were offended by the disturbingly loud drums. Ibid., 28–29.

⁴⁴ Ibid., 94–95.

⁴⁵ Society for Propagating the Gospel at Home, *An Account of the Proceedings of the Society for Propagating the Gospel at Home, From Their Commencement, December 28, 1798, to May 16, 1799* (Edinburgh: J. Ritchie, 1799), 6; Dean, "Evangelicals or Restorationists?" 104.

⁴⁶ "To the Editor of the *Missionary Magazine*: [ON SUNDAY SCHOOLS]," *The Missionary Magazine* 2 (1797): 242–44, quoted from 242.

success of the Gospel abroad." They created societies to collect funds and garner financial support so children could attend for free. These enlightened evangelicals were convinced that "Vice is the unavoidable consequence of ignorance," so education was a means of civilizing, moralizing, and evangelizing Scotland. By May 1797, *The Missionary Magazine* reported schools in half a dozen towns, and listed regulations people could use to start more of these schools. The first rule was that they "consist of serious people of every denomination."[47] The Society for Propagating the Gospel at Home tapped into interdenominational missions to reach uneducated "heathens" through Sunday schools.

Like other voluntary societies, the Society for Propagating the Gospel at Home published a pamphlet with an account of the origin of the Society, an address to readers and potential supporters, and the plan and rules of the Society.[48] The Society "had no plan of forming a new sect, but wished that Christians of all denominations should join, in seeking to promote pure and undefiled religion."[49] The Society preached the "pure unadulterated doctrines of the gospel." Christians found common ground not because of denominational affiliation, but because of true evangelical beliefs. Following the foundational pattern and organizational content of other evangelical missions societies, the group appointed a committee to work out the documents, including an "Address from the Society," which explained the Society's design and introduced the four-page "Plan and Rules of the Society."[50]

Several high-profile itinerants, such as Greville Ewing and Rowland Hill, contributed to the growing success of the Society. On December 24, 1797, Ewing preached *A Defence of Itinerancies and Field Preaching* before the Society for Gratis Sabbath Schools at Lady Glenorchy's Chapel. The sermon

---

[47] "SOCIETIES FOR SABBATH-EVENING SCHOOLS," *The Missionary Magazine* 2 (May 1797): 186-87.

[48] Society for Propagating the Gospel at Home, *An Account of the Proceedings of the Society for Propagating the Gospel at Home*. This account also includes narratives of numerous itinerants of the organization (including Ewing's itinerancy from December 14 to 25, 1798, on pp. 71–76), catechists, letters of instruction to itinerant preachers and catechists, lists of SPGH tracts distributed, and financial reports.

[49] Ibid., 2.

[50] Society for Propagating the Gospel at Home, *An Account of the Proceedings of the Society for Propagating the Gospel at Home*, 7–15; Society for Propagating the Gospel at Home, "Plan of the Society for Propagating the Gospel at Home," *The Missionary Magazine*, no. 3 (February 19, 1798): 57–63; "Society for Propagating the Gospel in Scotland," *The Evangelical Magazine*, no. 6 (February 1798): 73–74.

prompted opposition and made him a "marked man" in the establishment, because Ewing supported lay itinerant preaching with numerous biblical justifications. Ewing printed the sermon with a preface written in February 1799, intimating his surprise that the leading objection against his sermon came not from Scripture, but from the notion that "it was imprudent for any man in his situation, to preach such a sermon at all." Ewing disagreed with this reasoning, stating his primitivist position: "In all questions of Christianity, he [Ewing] deems it the first object to ascertain the doctrine of scripture, and the second, to declare that doctrine."[51] His support of the evangelical missions and lay preaching led to trouble. After the establishment censured him, he resigned from the Presbytery of Edinburgh and the Church of Scotland in December 1798.[52]

Similarly, Rowland Hill made two preaching tours in Scotland for the Society for Propagating the Gospel at Home, which provoked sharp responses from Presbyterians and exacerbated the issue of itinerancy in Scotland. In August 1798, Hill conducted his first preaching tour of Scotland, and published the travel log of his journey in early 1799.[53] Ironically, the comments Hill made in his journal that most incensed his opponents emerged from his hostility to sectarian zeal and promotion of the "grace of love among serious Christians of every denomination." Hill told readers:

> no ill design could have influenced my mind on the free remarks made on different parties; my only aim being to unite those who are separated.... I love all of my Master's family wherever I find them, and however unhappily disjointed and divided among themselves, ... I ardently long for that day when the uniting spirit of the Gospel may constrain us to be all as one in him our 'living Head.'[54]

---

[51] Greville Ewing, *A Defence of Itinerant and Field Preaching: A Sermon, Preached before the Society for Gratis Sabbath Schools, on the 24th of December 1797, in Lady Glenorchy's Chapel, Edinburgh* (Edinburgh: printed by J. Ritchie, 1799), vii–viii.

[52] Resignation letter and germane correspondence provided in Matheson, *A Memoir of Greville Ewing, Minister of the Gospel, Glasgow*, 177–80.

[53] Rowland Hill, *Journal of a Tour through the North of England and Parts of Scotland: With Remarks on the Present State of the Established Church of Scotland and the Different Secessions Therefrom. Together with Reflections on Some Party Distinctions in England; Shewing the Origin of These Disputes, and the Causes of Their Separation. Designed to Promote Brotherly Love and Forbearance among Christians of All Denominations* (London: printed by T. Gillet, 1799).

[54] Ibid., x–xii.

Nonetheless, Hill's rhetorical invective against churches which refused Communion with Christians of other denominations provoked outrage. For example, in a letter to James Haldane, prefaced to the "Observations and Remarks" section of his *Journal*, Hill combined primitivism, ecumenism, and missions to rebuke opposition to the missions culture:

> In preaching through England, Scotland, Ireland, and Wales, I always conceived *I stuck close to my parish*. We are to 'preach the Gospel to every creature, even to the end of the world.' Go on, my Sir, be the maul of bigotry, and of every sectarian spirit among all denominations; declare vengeance against the unscriptural innovations of narrow-minded bigots, who, finding the Word of God uncompliant to designs like theirs, have combined together to support their dogmas, according to certain rules of their own creating: and all these, as contrary to the sacred designs of God, that all Christians should be brethren, and love as such; as the designs of Christianity can be to those of Mahomet, the Pope, or the Devil.[55]

Obviously, Hill's comparison of opponents to Muslims, Catholics, and Satan provoked severe responses.[56]

Opposition, Independence, and Internal Division

Although interdenominational missions garnered support from Christians across the denominational spectrum, itinerant preaching at home differed in category and repercussion from itinerant preaching in foreign places. Dissenting and some establishment evangelicals could agree on missions to the "heathen" abroad, but itinerant preaching at home created problems for the establishment and other denominations such as the Seceding Presbyterians, who regarded ordination and parish boundaries as important

---

[55] Ibid., 67–68; Haldane, *Memoirs of the Lives of Robert and James Alexander Haldane*, 225–26.
[56] One published response to Hill's journal came from leading Edinburgh Antiburgher John Jamieson in 1799, to which Hill responded the following year with *A Plea for Union and for a Free Propagation of the Gospel* (1800) addressed to the Society for Propagating the Gospel at Home. See John Jamieson, *Remarks on the Rev. Rowland Hill's Journal, In a Letter to the Author, Including Reflections on Itinerant and Lay Preaching* (Edinburgh: printed for J. Ogle, 1799); Rowland Hill, *A Plea for Union and for a Free Propagation of the Gospel: Being an Answer to Dr. Jamieson's Remarks on the Late Tour of the Rev. R. Hill, Addressed to the Scots' Society for Propagating the Gospel at Home* (London, 1800).

and sometimes even sacrosanct structures. But many of these lay itinerants not only preached the gospel; they also publicly rebuked moderate ministers who did not preach up to the pure primitive gospel standards of the evangelicals.

Furthermore, the moderate majority in the Church of Scotland perceived lay itinerancy as a political threat. Rules of the Society for Propagating the Gospel at Home clearly prohibited public and even private conversations about politics, but in the perception of moderates who sought to preserve conservative establishments and hierarchies, lay itinerancy and a disregard for conservative establishments smacked of political liberalism. These itinerants often drew converts from the poor and working class, whom the itinerants and catechists encouraged to read and think independently—all of this lent credence to conservative suspicions of the political subversiveness of the Society. In politically conservative eyes, the transatlantic revolutions, with their liberal ideology of the equality of all individuals and disregard for traditional authority, were manifesting themselves in lay itinerancy, lay catechists, and lay performance of the sacraments.[57] Thanks to evangelical publications such as *The Missionary Magazine* and frequent publication of itinerants' journals, the opposition could easily follow every move of the evangelicals.

By May 1799, the moderate majority in the Church of Scotland officially responded to perceived political and ecclesiastical threats from the Society for Propagating the Gospel at Home. The General Assembly required Act XI, "Pastoral Admonition," to be read in every pulpit in the Church of Scotland.[58] The General Assembly argued that the activity of the itinerants fulfilled the prophecy "that in the last days perilous times were to come, when many false teachers should arise, scoffers walking after their own lusts, and when men should turn away their ears from the truth."[59]

---

[57] Both Ewing and Robert Haldane published pamphlets on the Christian's duties to civil government, revealing their subservience to government. Matheson, *A Memoir of Greville Ewing, Minister of the Gospel, Glasgow*, 175.

[58] They also published an act attacking the Sunday schools of the Society of Propagating the Gospel at Home. General Assembly of the Church of Scotland, "XII. Report Concerning Vagrant Teachers and Sunday Schools," in *The Principal Acts of the General Assembly of the Church of Scotland, Convened at Edinburgh, the 23d Day of May 1799: Collected and Extracted from the Records by the Clerk Thereof* (Edinburgh: printed by James Dickson, 1799), 42–45.

[59] Apparently combining 1 Timothy 3:1, 4:4; and 2 Peter 3:3.

The Pastoral Admonition pointed to the anti-Christian end of the French Revolution, and equated the "empty sound of Liberty" with tyranny in both civil and ecclesiastical governments. In doing so, the Pastoral Admonition connected Society itinerants (who, according to the Pastoral Admonition, egregiously presumed to be universal "missionaries") with innovation, disorder, tyranny, intrusion, and even sedition (noting that the Sunday schools had "secret meetings" and corresponded with other societies in the neighborhood). The act combined ad hominem attacks, along with appeals to the tradition and formularies of the Church of Scotland and its careful rules for ordination, to convey to parishioners that it hoped to protect them from false teachers "in these giddy times," when too many were deceived by the "spirit of innovation" to break away from established forms in civil and ecclesiastical matters.[60]

After the May 1799 acts of the General Assembly against itinerancy and Sunday schools, many evangelicals, embracing missions as manifested in the Society for Propagating the Gospel at Home, broke away from the established church and adopted independent or congregational polity, though Ewing had left the church six months earlier. Concerning the establishment, Camille Dean notes, "The Evangelical party in the Established Church of Scotland, and even the Relief Church, joined the dominant Moderate party in opposing lay preaching and condemning its practice by the Haldanes."[61] Dissenters largely took over field and street preaching in Scotland. Ewing, William Innes, the Haldanes, and many others left the established church for new horizons in independent congregational churches.[62]

Independent and inspired, Ewing, the Haldanes, and others who embraced evangelical missions in Scotland produced new networks and structures to disseminate and propagate the gospel at home. The Haldanes built large venues called "tabernacles" or "missionary" churches in Edinburgh, Glasgow, and Dundee, where James Haldane, Ewing, and Innes became ministers. Haldane adopted the "tabernacle" scheme from George

---

[60] General Assembly of the Church of Scotland, "XI. Pastoral Admonition, Addressed by the GENERAL ASSEMBLY OF THE CHURCH OF SCOTLAND, Met at Edinburgh, May 23, 1799, to All the People under Their Charge," in *The Principal Acts of the General Assembly of the Church of Scotland, Convened at Edinburgh, the 23d Day of May 1799: Collected and Extracted from the Records by the Clerk Thereof* (Edinburgh: printed by James Dickson, 1799), 38–42; Dean, "Evangelicals or Restorationists?" 113.

[61] Dean, "Evangelicals or Restorationists?" 108.

[62] Ross, *A History of Congregational Independency in Scotland*, 57–58.

Whitefield's plan, having "large places of worship, where as great variety as possible is kept up in the preaching, by employing different ministers, in order to excite and maintain attention to the gospel, especially in such as are living in open neglect of religion."[63] The Haldanes saw the tabernacles more as missionary centers for gospel preaching in the Whitefieldian tradition than as churches of either a new sect or indigenous Scottish Independents (e.g., Glasites or Old Scots Independents). For example, James Haldane said of the Edinburgh Tabernacle that it:

> in fact, was no separation from the Establishment. It was merely opening another place of worship for preaching the Gospel without regard to *forms* of external arrangement of Church order, and where the pastor and many of the members showed their catholic spirit by going to the Sacrament in the Established Church.[64]

The Haldanes had preachers from Congregational (David Bogue), Baptist (Andrew Fuller), and Anglican (Rowland Hill) fellowships at the interdenominational tabernacles. Yet, the tabernacles naturally seemed congregationalist in as much as they held to local congregational autonomy and the gathered church of disciplined believers (rather than of all citizens). Ewing drew up a statement of principles for the tabernacles, which outlined an attempt to do everything according to the Scriptures.[65]

The Haldanes also utilized seminaries to provide well-trained itinerant preachers for Scotland and abroad. Ewing taught the first class of thirty students, which began in Edinburgh in January 1799. In May 1799, Ewing

---

[63] Robert Haldane, *Address to the Public, Concerning Political Opinions, and Plans Lately Adopted to Promote Religion in Scotland* (Edinburgh: J. Ritchie, 1800), 69–70; Ross, *A History of Congregational Independency in Scotland*, 56–57, 64–65; McMillon, "The Quest for the Apostolic Church," 151.

[64] Quoted in Haldane, *Memoirs of the Lives of Robert and James Alexander Haldane*, 352.

[65] These principles eventually included New Testament authority, plurality of elders, deacons to administer a weekly collection to the poor, and weekly Lord's Supper. Dean, "Evangelicals or Restorationists?" 129–33; Haldane, *Memoirs of the Lives of Robert and James Alexander Haldane*, 214–17; McMillon, "The Quest for the Apostolic Church," 150–51; Matheson, *A Memoir of Greville Ewing, Minister of the Gospel, Glasgow*, 171, 194–220; Greville Ewing and Robert Haldane, *Facts and Documents Respecting the Connections Which Have Subsisted between Robert Haldane, Esq. and Greville Ewing, Laid before the Public, in Consequence of Letters Which the Former Has Addressed to the Latter, Respecting the Tabernacle at Glasgow* (Glasgow: printed by James Hedderwick, 1809), 15, 64; Ross, *A History of Congregational Independency in Scotland*, chap. 6; Lynn A. McMillon, "Ewing, Greville (1767–1841)," ed. Douglas A. Foster et al., *The Encyclopedia of the Stone-Campbell Movement* (Grand Rapids: Eerdmans, 2004), 324.

moved to Glasgow, where he ministered at the Glasgow Tabernacle. Innes also taught students, along with meeting his responsibilities as minister at the Dundee Tabernacle. Numerous others in Scotland were involved, and George Hamilton also taught a cohort in Armagh, Ireland. The last of more than ten cohorts in the Haldane seminaries completed their studies in 1808, together totaling more than three hundred students trained for evangelical missons at home and abroad.[66]

Despite their comradery in the interdenominational missionary movement in Scotland during the late 1790s and early 1800s, Ewing and the Haldanes grew apart, and due to numerous disagreements and conflicts rooted in the Haldanes' shifting theology and practice, eventually parted ways. The Haldanes changed course from a unitive evangelism in the 1790s to a strict restorationism and embrace of separation of church and state by 1808, a transformation which explains the diverse historiography—one end of the spectrum paints the Haldanes as advocates of ecumenical Christianity, and the other end as innovators whose critical spirit led to division, disappointment, and failure.[67] The Haldanes' 1790s characteristics of unity for evangelism were indebted to evangelical missions, as was the seed of primitivism that morphed into an exclusive restorationism. Historian Camille Dean recounts the Haldanes' "transformation from Enlightenment-era aristocrats, to lay evangelists, to leaders of a new Scottish Independency, to implementers of restorationist church order and advocates of believer's baptism."[68] This seemingly drastic shift was common among evangelical missions advocates. Historian Lynn McMillon points to the explanation Ewing provided for the Haldanes' shift: inspired by the works of John Glas and Robert Sandeman, they moved toward a more exclusivist restorationism.[69] McMillon demonstrates that James Haldane's reliance on Glas

---

[66] Haldane, *Address to the Public, Concerning Political Opinions, and Plans Lately Adopted to Promote Religion in Scotland*, 82–85; McMillon, "The Quest for the Apostolic Church," 151–53; Haldane, *Memoirs of the Lives of Robert and James Alexander Haldane*, 329–32.

[67] Lovegrove, "Unity and Separation," 2002, 520–43; Deryck W. Lovegrove, "Unity and Separation: Contrasting Elements in the Thought and Practice of Robert and James Alexander Haldane," in *Protestant Evangelicalism: Britain, Ireland, Germany and America c 1750–c1950: Essays in Honour of W. R. Ward* (Oxford: Basil Blackwell, 1990), 153–77.

[68] Dean, "Evangelicals or Restorationists?" 1–2.

[69] On Glas and Sandeman, see McMillon, "The Quest for the Apostolic Church," chaps. 3–4; Lynn A. McMillon, *Restoration Roots* (Dallas: Gospel Teachers Publications, 1983), chaps. 3–5; Dean, "Evangelicals or Restorationists?" chap. 5.

emerges clearly in *A View of Social Worship and Ordinance Observed by the First Christians* (1805).[70]

The Haldanes' restorationism that sought to create a facsimile of the New Testament church, combined with practical and personal disagreements, exacerbated differences between the Haldanes and Ewing, which led to an official break in 1808 among the eighty-five churches in the Scottish Congregationalist network. Although Ewing had advocated for lay itinerancy, he disagreed with the Haldanes' growing disregard for distinctions between laity and a trained clergy. Furthermore, problems arose regarding Robert Haldane's ability to relinquish control of his investments in the Congregational churches. By 1809, this led Ewing to rebuke Robert Haldane as the "POPE of independents."[71] Finally, when the Haldanes accepted believer's baptism in 1808, James Haldane produced a thorough defense of his change in position.[72] Although he apparently intended to continue ministering at the Edinburgh Tabernacle after this decision, viewing the change as secondary in importance and assuming those who adhered to believer's and infant baptism could worship together in forbearance, the majority of the congregation left, and longtime supporters such as John Aikman started new congregations. Rejection from the Congregational movement that the Haldanes co-built and had largely funded, whether by paying itinerants or owning church buildings, led to bitter financial disputes. After the division, the Haldanes formed a new body of Baptists in Scotland and Ewing led the Congregational churches. Numerous publications from both sides attempted to explain their positions.[73]

---

[70] James Alexander Haldane, *A View of the Social Worship and Ordinances Observed by the First Christians: Drawn from the Sacred Scriptures Alone, Being an Attempt to Enforce Their Divine Obligation and to Represent the Guilt and Evil Consequences of Neglecting Them* (Edinburgh: printed by J. Ritchie, 1805); McMillon, "The Quest for the Apostolic Church," 152–55; Daughrity, "Glasite Versus Haldanite," 65–79; Dean, "Evangelicals or Restorationists?" 159–76. McMillon notes the similarities between Haldane and Glas—absolute authority of Scripture, restoration of New Testament model or pattern for Christian worship, local congregational autonomy, plurality of elders with no distinction between teaching and ruling elders, deacons and lay ministers in each local congregation, civil authority with no authority over God's church, and weekly Lord's Supper. Differences included Haldane's more charitable dealing with those of other theological persuasions and more evangelistic zeal.

[71] Ewing and Haldane, *Facts and Documents*, 249.

[72] James Alexander Haldane, *Reasons of a Change of Sentiment and Practice on the Subject of Baptism: Containing A Plain View of the Signification of the Word, and of the Persons for Whom the Ordinance Is Appointed; Together with a Full Consideration of the Covenant Made with Abraham, and Its Supposed Connexion with Baptism* (Edinburgh: printed by J. Ritchie, 1809).

[73] Dean, "Robert and James Alexander Haldane in Scotland," chap. 6.

Although Ewing and the Haldanes vehemently debated about church polity and baptism, both remained committed to the evangelistic endeavor for the rest of their lives. In the case of Ewing, for example, the same year he published *Facts and Documents* (1809), representing his and the Haldanes' history and split, he also wrote a book at the request of the directors of the London Missionary Society.[74] Furthermore, from 1804 until 1840 (the year before he died), *The Evangelical Magazine* listed Ewing on the title page among the "Trustees and Stated Contributors," a veritable all-star list in interdenominational missions, which included David Bogue, George Burder, William Cooper, Andrew Fuller, Thomas Haweis, Rowland Hill, Alexander Waugh, and two dozen more. His portrait appeared at the beginning of the February 1806 issue of *The Evangelical Magazine*, and upon his death in 1841, the publication venerated him in a biography that constituted the first seven pages of the October issue. Ewing served as a director of the London Missionary Society for twenty-four years, more than any of the other 155 Scottish directors of the Society from 1796 to 1842.[75] After the breakup of the Haldanes' seminaries, Ewing founded Glasgow Theological Academy in 1811, "perhaps the most influential of the seminaries that trained missionaries for the LMS" after Bogue's Gosport Academy (Gosport Academy trained 40 percent of the London Missionary Society missionaries sent out in the first thirty years).[76] Despite their new advocacy of separation and focus on restoring primitive church order, which created tension with their earlier emphasis on unity, the Haldanes remained committed to evangelism and the missionary movement.[77]

Alexander Campbell's Brief but Influential Encounter with Scottish Evangelicals

As noted previously, the Campbell family experienced a near-fatal boat accident in October 1808 when they attempted to travel to the United

---

[74] *The Evangelical Magazine* 17 (1809): 124. The work was on the Jews and the law, which was reviewed in *The Evangelical Magazine* 17 (1809): 339.

[75] Roxborough, *Thomas Chalmers*, 261–67.

[76] Stanley, "Christian Missions and the Enlightenment: A Reevaluation," 18–19. Bogue and Ewing were conduits of the influence of the Scottish Enlightenment on missions.

[77] Blaikie and Huddleston, "Ewing, Greville (1767–1841)"; Stewart, "Ewing, Greville"; Dean, "Evangelicals or Restorationists?" chaps. 1, 7–8; Daughrity, "Glasite Versus Haldanite," 76–77; Matheson, "Memoir of Greville Ewing," 477–83; Dean, "Robert and James Alexander Haldane in Scotland," 106–08; Lovegrove, "Unity and Separation," 2002, 520–43."

States to join Thomas. Although Alexander was only twenty at this time, he had gained an excellent reputation as a teacher at the school his father started in Rich Hill in 1804. Alexander assisted from the age of seventeen, and controlled the school after his father's departure to the United States in 1807. He received most of his education at the feet of his father and from his own rigorous study of Scripture, languages, moral philosophy, and poetry. Like his father, Alexander experienced evangelical Reformed conversion—at that time a central characteristic in evangelical culture—in his late teens during his teaching years.[78] He then became a member of the Ahorey Presbyterian Church, started studying for the ministry, and kept teaching at Rich Hill until the family migrated to the United States. After the Campbells' U.S.-bound ship wrecked off the coast of Scotland,[79] they made their way from the coast to Glasgow, where they spent the winter.

In Glasgow, Campbell immediately sought out Greville Ewing, who became his mentor during the family's ten-month stay in the city and helped him attend the University of Glasgow. He went to Ewing first because one of his hosts during the journey from the shipwreck to Glasgow gave him a letter of introduction to Ewing.[80] Ewing introduced Campbell to some of the professors at the University of Glasgow, where Campbell gained entrance to classes that were beginning in November, and Ewing helped the Campbell family acquire lodging.[81] Campbell took courses in Greek, literature, French, and philosophy.[82] George Jardine, a disciple of Thomas Reid, taught both Alexander and Thomas Campbell the Common Sense

---

[78] Alexander recalled that this involved a period of struggle and distress "under the awakenings of a guilty conscience.... I was enabled to put my trust in the Saviour of sinners, and to *feel* my reliance on him as the only Saviour of Sinners. From the moment I was able to feel this reliance on the Lord Jesus Christ, I obtained and enjoyed peace of mind." Richardson, *Memoirs of Alexander Campbell*, 1:1:49; Leroy Garrett, "Campbell, Alexander (1788-1866)," ed. Douglas A. Foster et al., *The Encyclopedia of the Stone-Campbell Movement* (Grand Rapids: Eerdmans, 2004), 116-18.

[79] Alexander Campbell, *Manuscript D*, 21. All the manuscripts of Alexander Campbell used in this book are available at Archives and Special Collections, T. W. Phillips Memorial Library, Bethany College, Bethany, WV, Campbell Papers, Part 14—Manuscripts.

[80] Campbell recorded getting letters of introduction from Mr. George Fulton to Rev. Greville Ewing in Glasgow, from Mr. Hector Simson to William Harley, a manufacturer in Glasgow, and from Rev. Mr. McKintosh to Rev. Mackinzie in Glasgow. See Alexander Campbell, *Manuscript D*, 29.

[81] Alexander Campbell, *Manuscript D*, 36.

[82] Campbell attended the University of Glasgow from November 1808 to May 1809. Alexander Campbell, *Manuscript B*, includes Campbell's notes and journal from his study at Glasgow. See Alexander Campbell and Lester G. McAllister, *Alexander Campbell at the University of Glasgow 1808-1809* (Nashville: Disciples of Christ Historical Society, 1971).

Philosophy that made the Scottish Enlightenment so popular among transatlantic evangelicals.[83]

Campbell encountered leaders of evangelical missions not only in Ewing's company, but also in area pulpits. He said the family did not attend the same place of worship regularly, but visited numerous places: "We heard Mr. Mittes for the most part, Mr. Ewing frequently, Mr. Mitchel sometimes, Mr. Balfore, and Dr. Hat once, with a number of probationers in all the churches."[84] "Mr. Balfore" in Campbell's journal is probably Robert Balfour, a leader in the evangelical missions scene in Glasgow. Balfour delivered missionary sermons before the Society in Scotland for Propagating Christian Knowledge and the London Missionary Society. When opponents of the missionary endeavor launched their common charge that the "time for the conversion of the heathen is not yet come, because the Millennium" is still at a distance, Balfour pointed them to David Bogue's 1795 London Missionary Society sermon, which provided a postmillennial answer motivated by the Great Commission and pity for the "heathen."[85] These experiences proved influential in Campbell's early formation.

Campbell's biographer, Robert Richardson, claimed that his stay in Glasgow worked an "entire revolution in his views and feelings in respect to the existing denominations," and that this revolution "seems to have been occasioned chiefly through his intimacy with Greville Ewing." Campbell "frequently" had dinner or tea at Ewing's house, and "formed many agreeable intimacies with the guests . . . , and acquired . . . an intimate knowledge of Mr. Ewing's previous religious history, and that of his coadjutors, the Haldanes and others." All of this produced a "lasting effect upon his mind." Richardson ascribed extraordinary influence on Ewing as a "cause" of Campbell's nondenominationalism. Richardson said the movement in Scotland "may be justly regarded, indeed, as the *first phase* of that religious reformation which he subsequently carried out."[86] Campbell resolved that

---

[83] Berryhill, "Common Sense Philosophy," 231.

[84] Alexander Campbell, *Manuscript D*, 38.

[85] De Jong, *As the Waters Cover the Sea*, 173–74, 187; David Bogue, "Objections Against A Mission to the Heathen, Stated and Considered," in *Sermons, Preached in London, at the Formation of the Missionary Society, September 22, 23, 24, 1795; To Which Are Prefixed, Memorials, Respecting the Establishment and First Attempts of That Society* (London: printed and sold by T. Chapman, 1795), 126–27.

[86] Richardson, *Memoirs of Alexander Campbell*, 1:147–49; McMillon, "The Quest for the Apostolic Church," 155–60.

Ewing's Congregationalism was better than Presbyterianism. According to Richardson, Campbell could not even partake in the semiannual Communion with the Seceders in Scotland due to this conviction.[87]

The studious Campbell probably knew many of the names he encountered at Ewing's congregation and in the area churches from his experiences in Ireland, though even if he did not, he became acquainted with their beliefs and practices during conversations at Ewing's house and elsewhere. In Ireland, the Campbells heard a number of people affiliated with the London Missionary Society, the Scottish evangelical magazines, and the Scottish missionary societies, as itinerants working for or with the Evangelical Society of Ulster often stopped at the Rich Hill congregation, where Thomas frequently attended the evening meetings and special events. In this sense, it must have been an exhilarating experience for the young Campbell to be mentored by Ewing, who utilized his missionary paper, missionary societies, congregations, and various networks to promote and support the Evangelical Society of Ulster that his father cofounded. The Haldanes and Ewing had invested in seminary education, and George Hamilton even taught for one of their seminaries in Ulster. Ewing's magazine and the Haldane-Ewing congregations regularly sent money and missionaries to help the Evangelical Society of Ulster. One assumes these connections had to come up around the table during Campbell's time with Ewing.

Campbell's stay in Glasgow exposed him to evangelical missions, which shaped his actions in the United States. In Glasgow, he lived in an urban and unfamiliar context in which he was able to visit many churches and have conversations with leading evangelicals and academics in Ewing's house and at the University of Glasgow. Furthermore, his close association with Ewing, a leader of new missions not just in Scotland but in the entire United Kingdom, must have been exhilarating for a twenty-year-old person living in the midst of these monumental shifts in the Christian understanding of voluntary missions that did not rely on denominational structures. Ewing had become something of an international celebrity for his role in the evangelical missionary movement and as a leader of Congregationalism in Scotland. Although historians have largely focused on the restorationism of

---

[87] Richardson, *Memoirs of Alexander Campbell*, 1:186–90.

the Haldanes and Ewing, which was obviously influential to the Campbells, it is clear that the larger missions culture that produced both Ewing and the Haldanes provides a more holistic context that explains not just the Campbells' restorationism, but also their interdenominational promotion of simple evangelical Christianity for the propagation of the gospel.

Alexander's lessons at the University of Glasgow finished in May, and the Campbell family made preparations to complete their voyage to the United States, finally arriving to their father's embrace on the other side of the Atlantic in autumn of 1809.

CONCLUSION

This chapter advances the argument I have been making: the evangelical missions culture that arose throughout the eighteenth century and solidified from the 1790s is the religious and historical context most helpful for understanding the origins of the Campbell Movement. As demonstrated in the previous pages, the Campbells, along with thousands of evangelicals, were riding a wave of missionary enthusiasm that led them to attempt to minimize differences so they could cooperate with others in spreading a primitive and simple evangelical gospel at home and abroad. They formed voluntary societies that were typically outside the reach of established churches, which allowed diverse individuals to work together in communicating the gospel through itinerant preaching, Bible and tract distribution, Christian education through Sabbath schools, and prayer meetings and society meetings, where excitement soared with impassioned preaching about unity, the Great Commission, converting the "heathen," and the last days. The basis upon which "true," "real," or converted Christians of different denominations could cooperate was a primitive or apostolic gospel, which was purer and simpler than confessional Christianity as developed in the Protestant traditions. Numerous contextual factors made this cooperation easier, such as toleration influenced by the Enlightenment era, which also lauded attempts to jettison tradition for a primitive Christianity, to view evangelical identity as "converted," united in that conversion rather than being divided by denomination, and to use voluntary societies as a means for diverse individuals to organize and accomplish goals.

Pragmatic cooperation for missions could, in theory, congeal around agreement on a pure and primitive apostolic gospel that was stripped of the historical additions of Christian tradition, but this pragmatic primitivism and ecumenism could be worked to aim at very different ends, depending on the individual leaders and their divergent contexts. The pure and primitive gospel could become divisive when proponents moved in a restorationist direction, shifting from an ecumenical to a patternist impetus for primitivism. In Ireland, Scotland, and elsewhere, some advocates of interdenominational missions transformed pragmatic primitivism for the end of ecumenical cooperation into sectarian primitivism for the end of a restored New Testament church—this was partly the case with John Walker, Alexander Carson, the Haldane brothers, and eventually the Campbells in the United States.

Historians have noted the influence of both Ewing and the Haldanes on the Campbells' primitivism, but viewing these connections within broader evangelical missions, which defined the worldview of Ewing and the Haldanes, provides fresh insight into the Campbells' early encounters of broader missions which brought unity, millennialism, and primitivism into a coherent view of the world and Christian activism in it. Ideas about missions, itinerancy, interdenominational cooperation, the church's essential unity in diversity, pity for the "heathen," and millennialism amalgamated in these Scottish evangelical missions advocates just as it did throughout the transatlantic. The Scottish evangelicals who influenced the Campbells were involved in all the central evangelical networks and provided important missions impressions, especially on Alexander's young mind when he lived in Glasgow under the mentorship of Ewing.

Tensions emerged as those swept up in evangelical missions dealt with unity, tolerance, politics, the establishment, separatism, primitivism, restoration, itinerancy, and millennialism. The tensions were as significant on the U.S. frontier as they were in Ireland and Scotland, though the unique democratic context in the United States provided a different type of fertile soil in which evangelical missions could grow.

Chapter Six

FROM THE BRITISH ISLES TO THE UNITED STATES:
The Christian Association of Washington, 1809–1812

WHEN THOMAS CAMPBELL ARRIVED IN THE UNITED STATES in 1807, transatlantic evangelical missions still captivated the minds of many in the new nation. In 1805, Edward Dorr Griffin said in a sermon that some already saw the "light purpling the east" as the "dawn of a better day" approached in the wake of the founding of "numerous missionary societies . . . on both sides of the Atlantic."[1] Likewise, in 1809, the same year that Thomas Campbell wrote the *Declaration and Address*, Samuel Worcester proclaimed to a meeting of the Massachusetts Missionary Society that the day the London Missionary Society was founded (September 21, 1795) "will long be held in grateful remembrance, as a distinguished epoch in the annals of Christendom."[2] Worcester and Griffin were just two of the

---

[1] Edward Dorr Griffin, *The Kingdom of Christ: A Missionary Sermon Preached before the General Assembly of the Presbyterian Church in Philadelphia, May 23, 1805* (Philadelphia: printed by Jane Aitken, 1805), 25; William R. Hutchinson, *Errand to the World: American Protestant Thought and Foreign Missions* (Chicago: University of Chicago Press, 1987), 55.

[2] Samuel Worcester, "Sermon to the Massachusetts Missionary Society, May 1809," in *The Life and Labors of Rev. Samuel Worcester, D.D.*, ed. Samuel Melancthon Worcester (Boston: Crocker and Brewster, 1852), 2:72–73; Charles Maxfield, "The 'Reflex Influence' of Missions: The Domestic Operations of the American Board of Commissioners for Foreign Missions, 1810–1850" (PhD diss., Union Theological Seminary, 1995), 58–59.

many missions advocates who continued to look back at the creation of the interdenominational missionary societies in the 1790s to persuade their listeners in the early nineteenth century to continue the important work of interdenominational missions in an eschatologically significant time.[3]

Like Griffin and Worcester, Campbell believed the progress of evangelical missions in interdenominational unity for the evangelization of the world was eschatologically significant, and he continued to shape that culture by institutionalizing it in 1809. The ideas, practices, and forms of evangelical missions were at the center of the earliest organization, documents, principles, and actions in the Campbell Movement.

Evangelical Missions in the United States

As discussed in Chapter Two, the excitement of the interdenominational London Missionary Society captivated the evangelical imagination and caused what Charles Chaney calls "The Missionary Explosion" in the 1790s in the United States. From the founding of the London Missionary Society in 1795 to the establishment of the American Board of Commissioners for Foreign Missions in 1810, U.S. church leaders spread missions awareness through sermons, periodicals, concert for prayer, interdenominational voluntary societies, and biographies that portrayed missionaries as symbols of disinterested benevolence. Inspired by the London Missionary Society, new missionary societies such as the New York Missionary Society (1796) and the Northern Missionary Society (1797) praised the interdenominational efforts as eschatologically significant, remembered the missionary heroes (Cotton Mather, John Eliot, David Brainerd, and the Moravians), appealed to compassion and pity for "heathen" American Indians and frontier people without the gospel, and encouraged readers to form similar societies. Societies for missions, Bibles, tracts, and education developed into what historian Charles Foster calls a "united front" which generated a benevolent empire in the United States that was still largely interdenominational in the late 1820s, though denominations took over many of the missionary societies in the 1820s and 1830s.[4]

---

[3] Charles L. Chaney, *The Birth of Missions in America* (Pasadena: William Carey Library, 1976), 166–74.

[4] Maxfield, "The 'Reflex Influence' of Missions," 58–62; Stewart J. Brown, "Movements of Christian Awakening in Revolutionary Europe, 1790–1815," in *The Cambridge History of Christianity: Volume*

Although transatlantic connections remained influential, the U.S. context created some unique characteristics for Christianity and missions. The United States had just gained its independence, and it had created a democracy that also relinquished an established national church. A wave of revivals known as the Second Great Awakening created religious excitement that led to new worship experiences and religious movements. Furthermore, movement of people in the 1790s and 1800s created an ever-expanding western frontier. These contexts fostered revivalism and democratization of Christianity in an expansive and religiously unregulated nation, and encouraged missions at home more than abroad. In fact, the numerous missionary societies created in the United States before 1810 were devoted to home missions; the American Board of Commissioners for Foreign Missions was the first U.S. society devoted to foreign missions. Some of the societies were interdenominational and others denominational, but they typically focused on evangelizing frontier populations, American Indians, and blacks. The Edwardsean New Divinity, whose leaders such as Samuel Hopkins championed a moderate Calvinism in the tradition of Jonathan Edwards, led the missions efforts in many areas around the turn of the century. Although many people practiced interdenominational cooperation in regional missionary societies and in the Plan of Union (1801), which encouraged forbearance on polity (e.g., Congregational and Presbyterian) for the sake of cooperation among Reformed Christians to evangelize the frontier, missionary schemes became more denominational in the United States after 1800. The unique U.S. context allowed for a great deal of diversity, so evangelical missions experienced vibrant growth, even as some Americans opposed it on grounds similar to those articulated in Great Britain and the United Kingdom.[5]

VII, *Enlightenment, Reawakening and Revolution 1660–1815*, eds. Stewart J. Brown and Timothy Tackett (Cambridge: Cambridge University Press, 2006), 579–80; Chaney, *The Birth of Missions in America*, chaps. 4–6; Norman E. Thomas, *Missions and Unity: Lessons from History, 1792–2010*, American Society of Missiology 47 (Eugene: Cascade Books, 2010), 14–15; Charles I. Foster, *An Errand of Mercy: The Evangelical United Front, 1790–1837* (Chapel Hill: University of North Carolina Press, 1960), 121–24, 275–80; James A. De Jong, *As the Waters Cover the Sea: Millennial Expectations in the Rise of Anglo-American Missions, 1640–1810*, 2006 reprint (Kampen: J. H. Kok, 1970), chap. 6.

[5] Chaney, *The Birth of Missions in America*, chap. 5; De Jong, *As the Waters Cover the Sea*, 199–204; Wilbert R. Shenk, "Introduction," in *North American Foreign Missions, 1810–1914: Theology, Theory, and Policy*, ed. Wilbert R. Shenk, Studies in the History of Christian Missions (Grand Rapids: Eerdmans, 2004), 1–8; Thomas, *Missions and Unity*, 21; A. C. Guelzo, "New England Theology (1750–1850)," ed. Daniel G. Reid et al., *Dictionary of Christianity in America* (Downers Grove: InterVarsity Press, 1990), 810–12; R. W.

Thomas Campbell's Break from the Presbyterian Church

Thomas Campbell arrived in Philadelphia in May 1807, and immediately received a ministerial assignment with the Chartiers Presbytery in Western Pennsylvania.[6] He arrived when the Associate Synod of North America was in session. Presenting letters from his Irish presbytery and Ahorey church,[7] he was by no means an uncommon case, as Irish immigrants and their families constituted one-fourth of the white population in Pennsylvania by the 1790s. The Associate Synod of North America assigned him the Chartiers Presbytery, an area that included Washington, Pennsylvania, where a number of his friends from Ireland had settled and where he made his residence.[8]

Within months of starting his ministry, Campbell came into conflict with members of the Chartiers Presbytery. On a preaching trip in August 1807 with fellow minister William Wilson, Campbell had invited all Presbyterians to take the Lord's Supper. Wilson later charged that he heard Campbell articulate a number of controversial views in a Communion sermon, including: challenges to the divine authority of confessions, testimonies, typical practices such as fasting before administering the Lord's Supper, and the Presbyterian view of experiential faith and appropriation of Christ. Wilson reported this to John Anderson and other ministers in the presbytery, and Anderson refused to fulfill his appointment to "assist Mr. Campbel in dispensing the sacrament of the Lord's Supper at Buffaloe." Anderson could not accompany Campbell, because he believed Campbell's teachings "were inconsistent with some articles of our testimony."[9] The presbytery meeting

---

Pointer, "Plan of Union," ed. Daniel G. Reid et al., *Dictionary of Christianity in America* (Downers Grove: InterVarsity Press, 1990), 911.

[6] Ecclesial conflict, together with growing political unrest, caused Thomas Campbell to immigrate to America where he reconnected with other immigrant families. See Jason Fikes, "In a Manner Well Pleasing: The Theology and Practice of the Lord's Supper in the Stone-Campbell Movement, 1800–1875" PhD diss., Fuller Theological Seminary, 2005), 49–52.

[7] The letter from his presbytery is provided in Alexander Campbell and Thomas Campbell, *Memoirs of Elder Thomas Campbell, Together with A Brief Memoir of Mrs. Jane Campbell* (Cincinnati: H. S. Bosworth, 1861), 20–21.

[8] D. Newell Williams, Douglas A. Foster, and Paul M. Blowers, eds., *The Stone-Campbell Movement: A Global History* (St. Louis: Chalice Press, 2013), 18; William Herbert Hanna, *Thomas Campbell: Seceder and Christian Union Advocate*, reprint (Joplin: College Press, 1986), 26–30; Robert Richardson, *Memoirs of Alexander Campbell: Embracing A View of the Origin, Progress and Principles of the Religious Reformation Which He Advocated*, vol. 1 (Cincinnati: Standard Publishing Company, 1890), 1:78–86, 222–23.

[9] Both the *Records of the Associate Presbytery of Chartiers* and the *Acts and Proceedings of the Associate Synod of North America* are available at the Presbyterian Historical Society in Philadelphia, PA, MF 1353 and MF 9, respectively. Large excerpts are transcribed in Hanna, *Thomas Campbell*, chaps. 2–5; Charles

in October voted that Anderson's actions were justified, and Campbell angrily left the meeting the next day. The presbytery created a committee to investigate Campbell's teachings and submit charges in the form of a libel at the next meeting. The committee also agreed not to give Campbell any preaching appointments "on account of his disorderly behavior."[10]

In January 1808, the committee had expanded the two counts to seven libel charges against Campbell. Each of the seven charges began with, "It is erroneous and contrary to the Holy Scriptures and our subordinate standards" to assert or teach something Campbell allegedly taught. The committee offered evidence from Scripture and confessions to support its points. The presbytery gave Campbell one month to construct formal responses. In the charges, Campbell's responses, and the rulings of the presbytery, the major conflict centered on Campbell's challenge to Presbyterian authority by disregarding rules and doctrines based on his primitivist individual interpretation.

The presbytery first charged Campbell for having a wrong view of saving faith, because he maintained faith was a natural response to evidence which did not need to be proved by an emotional experience. The second charge rehearsed the common tensions between authority, primitivism, and confessions, as also reflected in the subscription controversies throughout the transatlantic. The presbytery found it erroneous to "assert that a church has no divine warrant for holding Confessions of Faith as terms of communion." Third, Campbell approved of elders praying and exhorting publicly when no minister was present, and the presbytery disapproved because this practice did not preserve distinctions between the duties of the teaching and ruling elders. The fourth claimed Campbell erroneously taught "that it is warrantable for the people of our communion to hear ministers that are in a state of opposition to our testimony." Campbell had always listened to ministers of many denominations (i.e., "occasional hearing") in Ireland, and he defended the practice in his response with a careful caveat: it was lawful if Christians had no opportunity to hear a minister of their own

---

F. Brazell, Jr., "Reluctant Restorationist: Thomas Campbell's Trial and Its Role in His Legacy" (PhD diss., The University of Texas at Arlington, 2007), chaps. 4-5. The quotes here are from *Records of the Associate Presbytery of Chartiers*, October 27, 1807, 123, in Brazell, Jr., "Reluctant Restorationist," 119-20.

[10] *Records of the Associate Presbytery of Chartiers*, October 29, 1807, 128-29, in Brazell, Jr., "Reluctant Restorationist," 122.

party. Regardless, the Chartiers Presbytery found this unacceptable. Fifth, the presbytery did not think Campbell adhered to thorough substitutionary atonement. Sixth, the committee charged that Campbell erroneously asserted that a person "is able in this life to live without sinning in thought, word, and deed." Seventh, it was against the Holy Scriptures and "the rules of presbyterial church government for a minister of our communion to preach in a congregation where any of our ministers are settled without any regular call or appointment." The charge concerned a settled minister in Canonsburg, Pennsylvania. Campbell admitted to preaching at Canonsburg, but he argued that people had called him to preach there, and that he had not preached in a congregation where a minister was settled. The presbytery found two of Campbell's responses at least partially satisfactory (charges five and six), but the others as either evasive or admitting to the charge. They voted to censure him and suspend his ministerial standing.[11]

Campbell appealed to the May 1808 Associate Synod of North America, which reversed his suspension, but continued opposition from the presbytery eventually led to division. The synod called the presbytery's handling of Campbell "irregular," which was a reason for its reversal of his suspension. Nonetheless, it still found him guilty of several of the libel charges. The synod concluded that Campbell's responses to the presbytery were evasive and equivocal, and it voted to censure Campbell with a rebuke and admonition. Campbell protested in a letter to the synod, which it read aloud. According to the synod minutes, the letter contained "grievous charges against the Synod ... of partiality and injustice," and in it Campbell declined the authority of the synod. Campbell responded to a summons and eventually yielded to the decision of the synod, but he handed in a declaration "that his submission should be understood to mean no more ... than an act of deference to the judgment of the court, that, by so doing, he might not give offence to his brethren by manifesting a refractory spirit."[12] After Campbell submitted to censure, the synod gave him preaching assignments in Philadelphia for two months, after which time he was to

---

[11] The germane *Records of the Associate Presbytery of Chartiers* and commentary are provided in Ibid., 116–40; Hanna, *Thomas Campbell*, 39–67; Lester G. McAllister, *Thomas Campbell: Man of the Book* (St. Louis: Bethany Press, 1954), 72–84.

[12] As quoted in Richardson, *Memoirs of Alexander Campbell*, 1890, 1:229.

return to Washington and preach under Chartiers Presbytery. Upon return, however, the presbytery had not given him preaching assignments. At the September meeting, Campbell and the presbytery had their final dispute, as Campbell eventually submitted a letter[13] rejecting the authority of the presbytery and the Associate Synod of North America after the presbytery refused to give him preaching assignments.[14] As historian Charles Brazell notes, Campbell reluctantly left the Seceders and Presbyterians.[15]

Campbell's break from Presbyterianism shared many similarities with that of transatlantic evangelicals who left their denominations. Authority became the key contention between Campbell, the Associate Synod of North America, and the presbytery. His primitivism led him to see his individual interpretation of the Bible as a more significant authority for his beliefs and actions than the interpretations and rulings of the presbytery or synod. When the disagreement seemed unresolvable, Campbell chose to see himself as a minister ordained by God (rather than the presbytery) under the "divine standard" of Scripture (rather than the *Testimony* or any other denominational standard). He knew these notions well from his experiences in evangelical missions and his Independent acquaintances. Like transatlantic evangelicals he knew, Campbell was the object of either informal resentment or formal libels for several beliefs and practices: open Communion and a liberality that implied latitudinarianism, disruption through itinerant preaching, valuing primitivism over subscription to denominational standards, practicing primitivism that challenged church order, erroneous beliefs, and anti-sectarianism. Evangelical missions sometimes produced ecumenism, primitivism, toleration, and at times a combination of these that led individuals out of what they perceived to be bigoted denominations and into Independent congregations and voluntary societies to accomplish their goals. Campbell eventually got pushed onto

---

[13] This letter is no longer extant. See Brazell, Jr., "Reluctant Restorationist," 147–48; Hanna, *Thomas Campbell*, 110.

[14] This paragraph relies on *Acts and Proceedings of the Associate Synod of North America*, Monday, May 23 through Friday, May 27, 1808, 170–200, as provided with commentary in Brazell, Jr., "Reluctant Restorationist," chap. 4.

[15] Ibid.; McAllister, *Thomas Campbell*, 140–44. Campbell wanted to remain with the Presbyterians, demonstrated not only by his persistence with Seceders, but by his application to the Pittsburgh Synod of the Presbyterian church in 1810. By that time, his views on biblical authority and against ecclesiastical authority were simply beyond the threshold of Presbyterian forbearance.

the path out of Presbyterianism, the same road that many of his friends and acquaintances in Great Britain, Ireland, and Scotland had traveled. The ideas and practices that got him pushed onto that path, as well as the route he took once on the path, had their origins in evangelical missions.

Thomas Campbell's Evangelical Missions Society: Christian Association of Washington

Thomas Campbell never stopped preaching during the Presbyterian trials, and it was not long before he created structures to disseminate evangelical missions around Washington, Pennsylvania. Ideals and practices of evangelical missions proved popular, as Campbell won support from new and old friends preaching in fields and houses about Christian unity upon a simple evangelical Christianity.[16] In early summer 1809, a group of diverse Christians met at Abraham Altars's house, where Campbell offered a sermon on the evils of sectarianism and the propriety of Christian cooperation and union on the basis of the simple gospel. He concluded with what became a principle of the Stone-Campbell Movement, even if it proved impossible to practice: "Where the Scriptures speak, we speak; where the Scriptures are silent, we are silent."[17] Due to the restorationist axiom and the experiences of those present, the gathering discussed the issue of infant baptism, a contentious issue among transatlantic primitivists. Although some, such as James Foster—a previous leader in John Gibson's Independent church in Rich Hill, Ireland—already concluded that infant baptism had no scriptural justification, the group left the issue open-ended, and chose to focus on forbearance for the end of their interdenominational evangelical goals.

The group met again on August 17, 1809, and chose to create an interdenominational voluntary society called the Christian Association of Washington. This followed the custom of naming evangelical societies by regional location. The group appointed twenty-one members to confer together and, with the assistance of Campbell, "to determine upon the

---

[16] For example, the Acheson brothers, who had lived in Markethill; James Foster, who was a leader at John Gibson's Independent church in Rich Hill; and others who were among his Old World friends in the area.

[17] Richardson marked this meeting and this statement as the *"formal and actual commencement of the Reformation."* Richardson, *Memoirs of Alexander Campbell*, 1890, 1:237.

proper means to carry into effect the important ends of their association."[18] In a typical method of evangelical societies, they built a log building they called the "cross-roads"[19] meetinghouse, which doubled as a common school. The committee appointed Campbell to prepare a plan and address for the Christian Association of Washington, which the committee approved for publication in September 1809 after it was read aloud at a meeting.[20]

Campbell titled the publication *Declaration and Address of the Christian Association of Washington*, and it became probably the most influential of the foundational documents of the Stone-Campbell Movement. The *Declaration and Address* consisted of fifty-six pages organized into three major parts, plus a paragraph introduction to the formation of the Christian Association of Washington at the beginning, and a two-page "Postscript" at the end. The first major part, the "Declaration," summarized the context and reasons for founding the Association, and provided its plan or constitution in nine items. An eighteen-page "Address" to "all that love our Lord Jesus Christ . . . throughout all the Churches" constituted the second part, the heart of which included thirteen propositions that summarized the imperative of Christian unity, voluntary association, and restorationism. The "Appendix" was the last, longest, and most original section. It anticipated objections which were already circulating by clarifying major points from the other sections, and defending the Association against charges of divisiveness and latitudinarianism.[21]

Traces of evangelical missions exude from nearly every page of the *Declaration and Address*. The plan of the Christian Association of Washington resembles the plans of the Evangelical Society of Ulster, London Missionary Society, Society for Propagating the Gospel at Home, and other

---

[18] Thomas Campbell, *Declaration and Address of the Christian Association of Washington* (Washington: printed by Brown & Sample, 1809), 2.

[19] They built it on the Sinclair farm at the crossing of a road to Canonsburg and another road to Washington. Richardson, *Memoirs of Alexander Campbell*, 1890, 1:241.

[20] Williams, Foster, and Blowers, *The Stone-Campbell Movement: A Global History*, 20; Richardson, *Memoirs of Alexander Campbell*, 1:234–42; McAllister, *Thomas Campbell*, 95–104; Campbell and Campbell, *Memoirs of Thomas Campbell*, 18–20.

[21] Berryhill notes about the Appendix, "The length, the complexity, indeed the very existence of this portion of the document bear witness to the depth of the wounds that he had suffered in trying to reconcile religious strife in Ireland and in America." Carisse Mickey Berryhill, "Scottish Rhetoric and the *Declaration and Address*," in *The Quest for Christian Unity, Peace, and Purity in Thomas Campbell's* Declaration and Address: *Text and Studies*, eds. Thomas H. Olbricht and Hans Rollmann, ATLA Monograph Series 46 (Lanham: Scarecrow Press, 2000), 202.

evangelical societies.[22] The first item announced that the group established the Association "for the sole purpose of promoting simple evangelical christianity, free from all mixture of human opinions and inventions of men." The Association would promote this simple evangelical Christianity by charging membership dues that would support itinerant ministers to "preach at considerable distances" and supply the poor with Bibles. The gospel itinerants the Association supported would promote "a pure evangelical reformation, by the simple preaching of the everlasting gospel, and the administration of its ordinances in an exact conformity to the Divine Standard." The plan averred it a "duty" of the Association to encourage the formation of and cooperation with similar evangelical societies. The plan noted that the Association was not a church, but a collection of "voluntary advocates for church reformation." The plan established that the officers (secretary and treasurer) and committee would be chosen annually, when the biannual meetings would take place, and it specified how funds would be collected.[23] In the Postscript, the Association informed the public of its plans—beyond sending itinerants and distributing Bibles—for two publications.[24] Every single one of these goals and methods of achieving them were typical of transatlantic evangelical societies.[25]

Like other evangelical societies, Campbell's Christian Association of Washington vehemently opposed religious division. Members of the Association were "tired and sick of the bitter jarrings and janglings of a party spirit." The "diversity and rancour of party contentions" and the "clashing of human opinions" had completely destroyed the original "unity, peace, and purity" of the primitive church. Campbell argued that division was

---

[22] Hiram J. Lester, "The Form and Function of the *Declaration and Address*," in *The Quest for Christian Unity, Peace, and Purity in Thomas Campbell's Declaration and Address: Text and Studies*, eds. Thomas H. Olbricht and Hans Rollmann, ATLA Monograph Series 46 (Lanham: Scarecrow Press, 2000), 173–92; David M. Thompson, "The Irish Background to Thomas Campbell's *Declaration and Address*," *Discipliana* 46 (1986): 23–27; David M. Thompson, "The Irish Background to Thomas Campbell's *Declaration and Address*," *Journal of the United Reformed Church History Society* 3, no. 6 (1985): 215–25.

[23] Campbell, *Declaration and Address*, 4–5.

[24] First, the *Christian Catechism* would be a "catechetical exhibition of the fullness and precision of the holy scriptures upon the entire subject of Christianity." Second, *The Christian Monitor* would be a monthly periodical "for the express purpose of detecting and exposing the various anti-christian enormities, innovations and corruptions, which infect the christian church." Ibid., 55–56.

[25] However, many societies avoided administering ordinances because denominations typically required ordained clergy for such. Although Campbell did not want the Christian Association of Washington to be a church, with its itinerants offering all the functions of settled churches (preaching, baptism, and the Lord's Supper), it took the shape of an Independent congregation.

"anti-christian" because it divided Christ's body, "anti-scriptural" because it violated God's "express command," and "anti-natural" because it encouraged Christians to condemn and oppose those who were divinely obligated to love one another as Christ loved them. Division is the "deadly enemy, that is sheathing its sword in the very bowels of [Christ's] church, rending and mangling his mystical body into pieces" and advancing Satan's kingdom.[26]

Campbell opposed division because of its deleterious effects within and without the church. Division caused reproach, backbiting, angry contentions, excommunications, persecutions, and broken congregations. Division brought the punishment of God upon Christians because they had perverted the gospel of peace—so God either withheld his "gracious influential presence from his ordinances," gave up the authors of discord to fall into scandals, "or visit[ed] them with judgments, as he did the house of Eli." Furthermore, divisions deprived people of gospel ordinances on the frontier, where "large settlements, and tracts of country, remain to this day entirely destitute of a gospel ministry; many of them in little better than a state of heathenism." This sectarianism even deprived people of the Lord's Supper, "that great ordinance of unity and love." Division obstructed the spread of the gospel not only on the frontier but also to Jews, Muslims, and pagans. Campbell related an 1805 letter from Seneca chiefs to a missionary to demonstrate how division in the church thwarted evangelism and discredited the gospel. The chiefs found nothing in the witness of bickering Christian communities that supposedly offered more than the religion they had received from their ancestors. Division precluded conversion, but unity would foster it. Campbell believed that restoring the church's "original constitutional unity and purity" would cause the church to "be exalted to the enjoyment of her promised prosperity—that the Jews may be speedily converted and the fullness of the Gentiles brought in."[27]

Christians could no longer continue in division because, Campbell explained, it went against the very design of Christianity. He believed all Christians agreed "THAT it is the grand design, and native tendency, of our holy religion, to reconcile and unite men to God, and to each other, in truth and love, to the glory of God, and their own present and eternal good."

---

[26] Campbell, *Declaration and Address*, 3, 8, 12, 17–18.
[27] Ibid., 6–7, 20, 29–30, 53–54.

Therefore, the glory of God and happiness of people correlated to the degree that "holy unity and unanimity of love is attained." Moreover, "the church of Christ upon earth is essentially, intentionally, and constitutionally one; consisting of all those in every place that profess their faith in Christ and obedience to him in all things according to the scriptures." Although the church existed in local congregations and associations, it should never be divided. Christian unity was not merely a good idea, but a Christian duty. Campbell repeatedly referred to John 17 and Jesus's prayer for the unity of his followers as clear evidence that Christ wanted believers to unite. Jesus's

> dying commands, his last and ardent prayers, for the visible unity of his professing people, will not suffer you to be indifferent in this matter. You will not, you cannot, be silent, upon a subject of such vast importance to his personal glory and the happiness of his people—consistently you cannot; for silence gives consent.

Campbell assumed that the apostolic church walked in unity and peace and that the "rubbish of the ages" had replaced that unity with bigotry. Although Campbell believed bigotry was on the decline, it would continue animating divisive Christians until a reformation focused on restoring unity began. For Campbell, to neglect unity was to neglect the design and constitution of Christianity, the "Greatest Commandments," and Christ's dying wish.[28]

Campbell urged Christians to cooperate across denominational lines through voluntary associations to spread the gospel and foster Christian unity. The cause of Christian unity, Campbell argued, was not the cause of a party or sect but the "cause of Christ and our brethren of all denominations." This unity would not happen through denominational structures, but through voluntary associations. Therefore, Campbell viewed voluntary association as a Christian duty:

> Till you associate, consult, and advise together; and in a friendly and christian manner explore the subject, nothing can be done.

---

[28] Ibid., 6–7, 11–13, 16, 19, 22–23. Campbell cited Malachi 2:1–10 (in which God cursed the people and their offspring because they did not bring glory to God's name) to argue that God would curse Christians continuing in the status quo of division and not striving for unity (13).

> We would therefore ... call the attention of our brethren to the obvious and important duty of association. Unite with us in the common cause of simple evangelical christianity—In this glorious cause we are ready to unite with you—United we shall prevail. It is the cause of Christ, and of our brethren throughout all the churches, of catholic unity, peace, and purity—a cause that must finally prosper in spite of all opposition. Let us unite to promote it.[29]

Like all evangelical missions advocates, Campbell urged Christians to associate with the Christian Association of Washington, or to start associations of their own if they were too far away, and he guaranteed that the Association would work with similar societies. Surely the power of embodied unity in worship and preaching at society meetings had not escaped him; thus he pushed for such physical encounters that had shaped evangelical missions. He was trying to set up a network like those that worked so well in Great Britain and the United Kingdom. He encouraged these voluntary associations of Christians from all denominations to meet at least once each month to pray for the Lord to end the divisions and restore the "original constitutional unity and purity" of the church.[30] Campbell believed the Christian Association of Washington and similar societies that were constituted on voluntary individual membership would foster Christian unity, as diverse Christians came together in formative prayer for evangelical causes.[31]

Campbell provided a number of justifications for the pursuit of Christian unity by the Association at that spiritually significant time and place in history. First, Campbell considered the United States a "highly favored country" in which to procure Christian unity because "the sword of the civil magistrate has not as yet learned to serve at the altar." A nation with religious freedom provided the best opportunity for the church to "resume that original unity, peace, and purity, which belongs to its constitution, and constitutes its glory." Campbell's eschatology and reading of the times influenced his understanding of the unique opportunities in the

---

[29] Ibid., 14.
[30] Ibid., 20.
[31] Ibid., 13–14.

United States, juxtaposed to the "baneful influence" of civil establishments of Christianity in Europe, which Campbell described in apocalyptic language that is not specific, without commentary, and uncertain in meaning.[32] What is clear about his language of the United States as a "highly favored country" is that he believed civil establishments of Christianity thwarted God's plans and were the objects of God's eventual wrath, from which the United States had gained an exemption due to disestablishment.[33]

Second, Campbell's embrace of the eschatological views common in transatlantic evangelical missions persuaded him that the "auspicious phenomena of the times" proved "that our dutiful and pious endeavors shall not be in vain in the Lord." Eschatologically, it was time for the Christian Association of Washington to restore New Testament unity and remove obstructions to evangelism. Among these "auspicious phenomena" were the French Revolution and the two central components of evangelical missions in the 1790s—advances in missions and Christian unity.

> Is it not the day of the Lord's vengeance upon the anti-christian world; the year of recompences for the controversy of Zion? Surely then the time to favour her is come; even the set time. And is it not said that Zion shall be built in troublous times? Have not greater efforts been made, and more done, for the promulgation of the gospel among the nations, since the commencement of the French revolution, than had been for many centuries, prior to that event? And have not the churches both in Europe and America, since that period, discovered a more than usual concern for the removal of contentions, for the healing of divisions, for the restoration of a christian and brotherly intercourse one with another, and for the promotion of each others spiritual good; as the printed documents, upon those subjects, amply testify?[34]

---

[32] For possible meanings, see Hans Rollmann, "The Eschatology of the *Declaration and Address*," in *The Quest for Christian Unity, Peace, and Purity in Thomas Campbell's* Declaration and Address: *Text and Studies*, eds. Thomas H. Olbricht and Hans Rollmann, ATLA Monograph Series 46 (Lanham: Scarecrow Press, 2000), 341–60.

[33] Campbell, *Declaration and Address*, 7–8; Rollmann, "The Eschatology of the *Declaration and Address*," 341–60.

[34] Campbell, *Declaration and Address*, 8.

Campbell believed the "troublous times" were indicative also of hopeful times, when the ecumenical missionary movement would set the stage for restoring a simple evangelical Christianity, with primitive unity at its center and conversion of the world and the millennial reign of Christ as its ends.[35]

In fact, the eschatology of evangelical missions governed Campbell's articulation of the goals of the Christian Association of Washington. Responding to opponents of the missionary movement who often claimed that the time had not yet come for missions, Campbell urged readers not to be "lulled asleep by that siren song of the slothful and reluctant professor, 'The time is not yet come—the time is not come—saith he,—the time that the Lord's house should be built.' Believe him not.—Do ye not discern the signs of the times?" Campbell provided a list of vague references to apocalyptic events that were ostensibly signs that the time had indeed come for the Christian Association of Washington and societies like it. Although it is impossible to identify exactly what Campbell had in mind for his numerous references to apocalyptic events, it is clear that all the declarations of divine judgment served primarily to demonstrate that the "troublous times" during which Zion would be built were occurring in Campbell's day.[36]

The idea that Zion would be built in these "troublous times" (Dan. 9:25 KJV) had deep roots in evangelical missions, which followed New Testament authors in using "Zion" allegorically to signify the eschatological church.[37] William Carey interpreted Zechariah 12:10-14 to "teach that when there shall be an universal conjunction in fervent prayer, and all shall esteem Zion's welfare as their own, then copious influences of the Spirit shall be shed upon the churches, which like a purifying *fountain* shall cleanse the servants of the Lord."[38] The New York Missionary Society viewed interdenominational cooperation as a "sign that the LORD is about to build up

---

[35] Ibid., 6, 8–10.

[36] Historian Hans Rollman, who provides an analysis of eschatology in the *Declaration and Address*, notes that "All the other apocalyptic signs from the Bible—the Great Earthquake, lightning, thunderings, voices, and hail—can be interpreted either as natural events of symbolic value . . . or as symbolic signifiers of historical and political events reshaping at the time the European continent and significantly affecting the ecclesiastical establishment." Rollmann, "The Eschatology of the *Declaration and Address*," 348; Frederick Doyle Kershner, *The Christian Union Overture: An Interpretation of the Declaration and Address of Thomas Campbell* (St. Louis: Bethany Press, 1923), 57–59; Brazell, Jr., "Reluctant Restorationist," 198–99.

[37] Rollman argues that "Zion" in the *Declaration and Address* means the "eschatologically triumphant church." See Rollmann, "The Eschatology of the *Declaration and Address*," 352.

[38] William Carey, *An Enquiry into the Obligations of Christians, to Use Means for the Conversion of the Heathens* (Leicester: printed and sold by Ann Ireland, 1792), 78.

Zion, and to appear in his glory."[39] George Hamilton utilized the concept in the founding sermon of the Evangelical Society of Ulster—a sermon Campbell knew very well, as he defended it before his synod one decade before he wrote the *Declaration and Address*. Hamilton preached:

> Behold, my brethren, the peculiar aspect of the present times! Does not the shaking of the nations indicate, that he is on his way to receive the heathen for his inheritance? ... Are we not told, that in troubleous times, Zion shall be built up? And are not the present times of this very description?

Hamilton quoted Cotton Mather to persuade his readers to see the signs and evangelize the world: "I am well satisfied that if men had the wisdom to discern the signs of the times, every hand would be at work to spread the name of our adorable Jesus into all the corners of the earth."[40] Evangelical missions viewed the world through eschatological lenses, which envisioned the events of the late eighteenth century—especially unity, missions, and revolutions—as "auspicious." Therefore, Campbell's use of Zion twelve times in the *Declaration and Address*, in ways exactly like Hamilton and transatlantic evangelicals used the name, is no surprise.[41] Campbell wrote that it was not time "to sit still in our corruptions and divisions," but time to work for Christian unity and the spread of simple evangelical Christianity: "Awake, awake; put on thy strength, O Zion, put on thy beautiful garments, O Jerusalem, the holy city. ... Shake thyself from the dust, O Jerusalem; arise, loose thyself from the bands of thy neck, O captive daughter of Zion."[42]

---

[39] New-York Missionary Society, *The Address and Constitution of the New-York Missionary Society* (New York: printed by T. and J. Swords, 1796), 10.

[40] George Hamilton, *The Great Necessity of Itinerant Preaching: A Sermon Delivered in Armagh at the Formation of the Evangelical Society of Ulster, on Wednesday, 10th of Oct. 1798. With a Short Introductory Memorial, Respecting the Establishment and First Attempt of the Society* (Armagh: printed and sold by T. Stevenson, and by each Member of the Committee, 1799), 27, 34–35.

[41] Christopher Hutson explains Campbell's use of Scripture in the *Declaration and Address*: "He makes use of oracles about the restoration of Jerusalem to anticipate a glorious outcome for the enterprise he is undertaking. For this purpose, he reads the prophets eschatologically, applying their language about Jerusalem to the church in the end times, which he identifies with his own day." Christopher R. Hutson, "Thomas Campbell's Use of Scripture in the *Declaration and Address*," in *The Quest for Christian Unity, Peace, and Purity in Thomas Campbell's* Declaration and Address: Text and Studies, eds. Thomas H. Olbricht and Hans Rollmann, ATLA Monograph Series 46 (Lanham: Scarecrow Press, 2000), 213.

[42] Campbell, *Declaration and Address*, 14.

Evangelical missions provided Campbell an eschatological motive and interdenominational cooperation for the cause.

Campbell provided a more detailed method of identifying and restoring "simple evangelical Christianity" than many of his evangelical counterparts. In fact, whereas most of the advocates for evangelical missions promoted a pragmatic ecumenism for the sake of cooperating in voluntary societies for missionary endeavors, Campbell focused on achieving Christian unity through restoring a New Testament church that had no division, because it preceded the human traditions (e.g., creeds, confessions, catechisms, disciplines, courts) that had divided Christianity. The church should "resume that original unity, peace, and purity, which belongs to its constitution, and constitutes its glory."[43] Campbell's "simple evangelical Christianity" was actually a proposal for Christian communion based on agreement of only the clear beliefs and practices in the New Testament. His restoration hermeneutic was indebted to the Reformed tradition and the intellectual milieu of the Scottish Enlightenment, and he assumed it was something upon which every Christian on the planet could unite.

Campbell's restorationism began with the typical assumption of interdenominational missions that historical Christian traditions had added to the New Testament, though he explained these precisely as additions to the "express" (simple or clear) "doctrine, worship, discipline, and government" of the "original" (primitive or apostolic) church. His restoration agenda partly offered a response to his experience with presbyteries and synods that made historical "standards" (confessions, creeds, and disciplines) "terms of communion." Campbell was not opposed to confessions and testimonies as aids in understanding Scripture—he called them "highly expedient." Instead, he opposed using them as terms of communion because they were full of "human opinions." Campbell believed using historical standards as terms of communion created the opposite effect of their intentions, because they decisively and permanently divided the church with confessions full of what Campbell perceived to be human opinions. His solution to the division was to require only the clear statements of the New Testament, rather than human opinions, as terms of communion. He believed two things

---

[43] Ibid., 10.

had caused the divisions in the church: "a partial neglect of the expressly revealed will of God" and "an assumed authority for making the approbation of human opinions, and human inventions, a term of communion, by introducing them into the constitution, faith, or worship, of the church." These two things "are, and have been, the immediate, obvious, and universally acknowledged causes, of all the corruptions and divisions that ever have taken place in the church of God."[44] For Campbell, as for many evangelicals in early missions, the force of the argument that Christians should unite on the apostolic gospel, and not later traditions, seemed irrefutable.

Campbell's restoration hermeneutic relied on the idea of "express" statements in Scripture—some form of the word "express" appears over one hundred times in the *Declaration and Address*, usually in conjunction with commands or terms in Scripture. "Express commands," or things expressly declared in Scripture, were the hinge of Campbell's entire restoration and unity programs. The word "expressly" means clearly, explicitly, directly, definitely, or positively.[45] He used the word in the sense of clarity—a command or declaration in the New Testament that is universal and irrefutable and, therefore, the basis of apostolic unity is one that is "express." Campbell was firmly within Reformed interpretive guidelines up to this point—he adhered to the Reformed principle that Scripture regulates beliefs and practices, as codified in the *Westminster Confession of Faith* 1.6[46] and 21.1,[47] particularly in regard to things "expressly set down."[48] However, Campbell opposed using "good and necessary" deductions (e.g., "inferences" and "human opinions" in Campbell's thinking) as authoritative—this is where he parted company with Westminster hermeneutics, as noted in 1.6 and 21.1 above. Campbell saw good and necessary deductions or inferences

---

[44] Ibid., 17–18, 38–39.

[45] See "expressly, *adv.*," in *Oxford English Dictionary*.

[46] "The whole counsel of God concerning all things necessary for His own glory, man's salvation, faith and life, is either *expressly set down* in Scripture, or *by good and necessary consequence may be deduced* from Scripture: unto which nothing at any time is to be added, whether by new revelations of the Spirit, or traditions of men. Nevertheless, we acknowledge the inward illumination of the Spirit of God to be necessary for the saving understanding of such things as are revealed in the Word" (italics mine).

[47] "The acceptable way of worshipping the true God is instituted by Himself, and so limited by His own revealed will, that He may not be worshipped according to the imaginations and devices of men, or the suggestions of Satan, under any visible representation, or *any other way not prescribed in the holy Scripture*" (italics mine).

[48] Casey, "The Origins of the Hermeneutics of the Churches of Christ, 2 Pts," January 1, 1989, 75–91; Casey, "The Origins of the Hermeneutics of the Churches of Christ, 2 Pts," January 1, 1989, 193–206.

as expedient or useful, but he felt that they should not be made terms of communion due to their lack of certainty. Express commands were clearly understood by all, but inferences were not. Beyond things "expressly set down," Campbell added the category of "approved precedents" or "apostolic examples," which had origins in early Protestant traditions of interpretation.[49] Therefore, Campbell's restorationism depended upon the hermeneutical device of "express commands" and "approved precedents." His unity program assumed all could agree on these express commands and precedents, and that all would be willing to practice forbearance in regard to inferences or deductions which were not expressly set down in the New Testament. The holy precepts and "approved and imitable examples, would unite the Christian church in a holy sameness of profession and practice, throughout the whole world."[50]

Campbell's hermeneutical proposal for restoring an apostolic church and primitive unity utilized the Reformed tradition of interpretation, but modified it based on British empiricism. Campbell argued that inferences should not be made terms of communion, which was a departure from Westminster hermeneutics and theology. Historian Michael Casey argues that John Locke's empiricism, which undergirded British toleration, partly explains Campbell's rejection of necessary inferences as authoritative. John Locke proposed Christian unity based on clear commands in the Bible in *A Letter Concerning Toleration* (1689):

> *Schism* then, for the same reasons that have already been alledged, is nothing else but a Separation made in the Communion of the Church, upon account of something in Divine Worship, or Ecclesiastical Discipline, that is not any necessary part of it. Now nothing in Worship or Discipline can be necessary to Christian Communion, but what Christ our

---

[49] Thomas H. Olbricht, "Hermeneutics and the *Declaration and Address*," in *The Quest for Christian Unity, Peace, and Purity in Thomas Campbell's* Declaration and Address: *Text and Studies*, eds. Thomas H. Olbricht and Hans Rollmann, ATLA Monograph Series 46 (Lanham: Scarecrow Press, 2000), 246-47; Thomas H. Olbricht, "Hermeneutics," ed. Douglas A. Foster et al., *The Encyclopedia of the Stone-Campbell Movement* (Grand Rapids: Eerdmans, 2004), 387.

[50] Campbell, *Declaration and Address*, 36.

Legislator, or the Apostles, by Inspiration of the Holy Spirit, have commanded in express words.⁵¹

If a truth required logical argumentation because it was not expressly stated, it occupied secondary status for Locke. Campbell's proposal in the *Declaration and Address* is basically that of Locke, except he added "approved precedents." Casey also points to Scottish Common Sense philosophers Thomas Reid and George Jardine (Campbell's teacher) as another key source for Campbell's rejection of "necessary inference" as authoritative. Reid argued that necessary inference came from Aristotelian syllogism,⁵² and Jardine followed Reid in viewing Baconian induction as a more effectual method of reasoning. Therefore, when Christians made inferences into terms of communion, they violated individual liberty of opinion in interpretation, the Christian virtues of forbearance and charity, and inductive reasoning.⁵³ These violations led to the evil divisions in the church. In contrast, agreement upon the "solid basis of universally acknowledged, and self-evident truths, must have the happiest tendency to enlighten and conciliate."⁵⁴ Thus the *Westminster Confession* and British empiricism, especially as manifested in Scottish Common Sense Philosophy, constituted the hermeneutical and intellectual foundations of Campbell's view of Christian unity upon a simple or "clear" New Testament.⁵⁵ These intellectual foundations animated many transatlantic evangelical leaders on both unity and restoration.

Campbell's optimism in the ability of human common sense to acquire, and for people to agree on, the clear statements in Scripture and thereby "exhibit a complete conformity to the Apostolick church" was exceeded only by his optimism in the ability of the New Testament to deliver a monolithic, fixed, certain, and perfect standard for doctrine, worship, discipline, and

---

[51] John Locke, *A Letter Concerning Toleration* (London: printed for Awnsham Churchill, at the Black Swan at Amen-Corner, 1689), 61.

[52] That is, two premises lead logically to a necessarily inferred conclusion.

[53] Campbell saw inferences and opinions in confessions as "expedients," useful for unpacking complex ideas, but not authorities that should determine who was in and out of the Christian fold.

[54] Campbell, *Declaration and Address*, 12.

[55] Michael W. Casey, "The Theory of Logic and Inference in the *Declaration and Address*," in *The Quest for Christian Unity, Peace, and Purity in Thomas Campbell's Declaration and Address: Text and Studies*, eds. Thomas H. Olbricht and Hans Rollmann, ATLA Monograph Series 46 (Lanham: Scarecrow Press, 2000), 223–42.

government of the modern church. "Truth is something certain and definite," Campbell averred, and "this [defining truth] we suppose God has sufficiently done already in his Holy Word." Campbell believed the New Testament was "a fixed and certain standard of divine original" in which the wisdom of God revealed and determined everything in a "perfect constitution" for the doctrine, worship, discipline, and government of the church. The New Testament was a "divinely inspired rule" and "original pattern" which, if restored, would create primitive unity. Campbell knew he was assuming that the New Testament had a perfect original pattern, but he believed all "rational professors" had to agree the New Testament was all-sufficient in all these areas—the only other option for him was to say Scripture was insufficient. Following the New Testament "pattern" would "infallibly" lead the church to eradication of division, establishment of primitive unity, and removal of obstructions to evangelization.[56] This optimism had roots in Scottish intellectual traditions. Campbell posited, "it is high time for us not only to think, but also to act for ourselves; to see with our own eyes, and to take all our measures directly and immediately from the Divine Standard." He thought that when people read the Bible, they received the "impressions" that the Bible "must necessarily produce upon the receptive mind."[57] As scholar Carisse Berryhill notes:

> An 'impression' in Scottish psychology is the imprint of a stimulus on an appropriate receptor. The analogy is of pressure, as in printing, or as in pressing a seal into wax. So when TC says they intend to 'take all our measures directly and immediately from the Divine Standard,' he means that reading the Bible will stamp into the reader's mind a replica of the idea signified. His word 'immediate' carries the force similar to our 'unmediated.' This unmediated interaction with the text is his best hope for an exact duplication of the original community of the church.[58]

Campbell believed the Bible impressed its truths on all people in all places at all times because it spoke in plain and obvious ways, presenting obvious

---

[56] Campbell, *Declaration and Address*, 10–11, 19, 46–50.
[57] Ibid., 3, 37.
[58] Berryhill, "Scottish Rhetoric and the *Declaration and Address*," 200.

truths and facts to the common sense of the reader.⁵⁹ Campbell's Reformed Protestant tradition told him that Scripture provided a rule for doctrine, worship, discipline, and government, while his intellectual inheritance from the Scottish Enlightenment gave him great confidence in the ability of individuals to receive the impressions of clear Scripture statements without the mediation of church authorities. Although he periodically reminded readers that the whole process required guidance from the Holy Spirit, Campbell believed that individuals would receive the same objective impressions of the express statements in Scripture; agree on "simple evangelical Christianity"; produce primitive unity upon New Testament doctrine, worship, discipline, and government; and remove obstacles to world evangelization.

Campbell's Enlightenment training not only funded his hermeneutic but fostered his seemingly liberal program for unity. Opponents sensed "New Light" latitudinarianism in Campbell's disregard for "inferences" and church traditions as authorities and tests of communion, as well as his individualistic and liberal basis for Christian unity. Campbell spent a great deal of time at the 1799 Antiburgher Synod in Ireland explaining the Evangelical Society of Ulster documents, but the synod concluded that the principles of the Society were "completely Latitudinarian whereby the truth of the Gospel is in Danger of Being Destroyed & the practice of Godliness overthrown."⁶⁰ Again, a decade later, Campbell spent a significant portion of the Appendix defending the Christian Association of Washington against those who "impeach us with the vague charge of Latitudinarianism (let none be startled at this gigantic term)." If latitudinarianism meant "we take no greater latitude than the divine law allows, either in judging of persons, or doctrines—either in profession, or practice," then the church needed more of it. But if the word meant something bad, "it better belongs to those that brandish it so unmercifully at their neighbors; especially if they take a greater latitude than their neighbours do; or than the divine law allows." In this way, Campbell reversed the charge. The

---

⁵⁹ Ibid., 203.
⁶⁰ *Minutes of the Associate (Antiburgher) Synod of Ireland* (1799), 117–18.

> truly latitudinarian principle and practice, which is the bitter root of almost all our divisions ... [is] the imposing of our private opinions upon each other, as articles of faith or duty; introducing them into the public profession and practice of the church, and acting upon them, as if they were the express law of Christ, by judging and rejecting our brethren that differ with us in those things.

Campbell defended the Christian Association of Washington against latitudinarianism, and deflected the charge at his opponents for allowing too much latitude (e.g., inference and human opinion) in running the church—rather than "simple evangelical Christianity," they practiced a convoluted confessional Christianity.[61]

Campbell's Christian Association of Washington and *Declaration and Address* shared many similarities with typical transatlantic evangelical missionary societies and sermons, and they provide an excellent cultural context for understanding the origins of the Campbell Movement. One obvious similarity included the structure of a voluntary society designed not to promote a party or a church, but to promote interdenominational cooperation. Also similar were the goals of the Society to practice "simple evangelical Christianity" through sending itinerant preachers to distant places with a primitive gospel that all Christians could agree upon, and through distributing Bibles. Itinerancy and Bible distribution were the two most common functions of the early evangelical and missionary societies. The plan and address of the Christian Association of Washington's were written and published in typical evangelical format, although the Appendix was a unique feature.[62] Campbell's critique of sectarian bigotry or party zeal, and his desire for Christian cooperation upon a simple, primitive, evangelical gospel were the most prominent characteristics of early evangelical missions. Campbell shared with evangelical missions the assumption that the practices and beliefs in the New Testament provided an earlier and more pristine version of Christianity than what one found in the later Protestant

---

[61] Campbell, *Declaration and Address*, 30–35. A form of latitude or latitudinarian occurs twenty times in the *Declaration and Address* Appendix.

[62] Defense against objections to missions culture had been a common part of publications, though they were not typically included in plans and sermon pamphlets.

confessional traditions. The intellectual milieu of the Enlightenment provided diverse resources that transatlantic people utilized for divergent agendas, and evangelicals found much that they liked. Campbell's experience in the Scottish intellectual world at the University of Glasgow provided the framework for his appropriation of evangelical missions, especially how he understood unity and restoration in the *Declaration and Address*. He shared the idea that events such as revolutions and developments in Christianity, particularly interdenominational cooperation and missionary endeavors, constituted "signs of the times." His postmillennial eschatology was similar to transatlantic evangelical missions advocates in the eighteenth and nineteenth centuries—they saw interdenominational prayer, Christian unity, and the missionary movement as precursors to conversion of Jews and Gentiles and as sure signs that they were experiencing the latter days. Transatlantic evangelical missions efforts provide historians a comprehensive and transnational context for understanding the historical origins of Thomas Campbell's *Declaration and Address* and the Christian Association of Washington.

Campbell emphasized certain reform proposals in the *Declaration and Address* in unique ways and from a distinct perspective. His experiences with Seceder Presbyterianism in Ireland and especially in the United States led him to see Christian unity as more than a pragmatic means to evangelism; rather, unity was both a goal and a means to an end. He held to the idea that a united Christianity would lead to conversion of the "heathen." However, he focused as much on division precluding expansion as he did on unity fostering it. Campbell assumed that the New Testament church walked united without division, and to restore that primitive unity to the modern church was a worthy goal in itself. Although Campbell explicitly said that this unity would serve an evangelistic end, his focus throughout the *Declaration and Address* was more on restoring an ostensible apostolic unity through restoration than on attaining pragmatic unity for the sake of missions. Furthermore, his framing of divisions as evil and against the very design of Christianity waged war on sectarianism in more vehement ways than many other missionary advocates. To be sure, the missions culture produced fiery opponents of sectarianism, such as Rowland Hill, who itinerated in Ireland numerous times when Campbell lived there. However,

Campbell set up Christian unity as not only a better option to sectarian bigotry, but also as an end in itself, because the church was essentially and constitutionally one. Campbell's restorationism also set a different ecclesiological course than that which had supported evangelical cooperation for missions since the early eighteenth century. Pietists and their evangelical heirs constructed ecclesiological unity based on experiential new birth—those who were born again made up the invisible and spiritual church which reached beyond historical and concrete denominations. Regarding the basis of invisible unity across denominations, Campbell replaced experiential new birth with visible unity in congregations and between congregations based on a restored New Testament church. These distinguished the Christian Association of Washington and its address from some other missionary and evangelical societies and their founding addresses. It also set a trajectory for many in the Campbell Movement to see restoration not only of New Testament unity, but also of New Testament doctrine and practice as an end goal.

This restoration trajectory was similar to that of the Haldanes, Alexander Carson, and John Walker—Christians who were, like Campbell, indelibly influenced by evangelical missions, but who eventually focused less on unity and more on restoration of New Testament doctrine, worship, discipline, and government. This emphasis runs throughout the *Declaration and Address*, though always with an end goal of primitive unity for the glory of God, the happiness of Christians, and the evangelization of the world. Campbell offered a constructive hermeneutical proposal for restoring the New Testament church. No one read the *Declaration and Address* without understanding that the plan for unity was Christian communion and cooperation based upon the beliefs and practices of the New Testament, as found in either express terms or approved precedents. Although much was left unsaid, Campbell provided a clearer restoration hermeneutic than typical missions advocates. Typically, "simple evangelical gospel" was not specifically defined, and was used mostly as a justification of Reformed-leaning denominations working together despite their different polities. Missions advocates in the 1790s certainly believed it meant more than that, both eschatologically and ecclesiologically, but it was practically a means of Congregationalists, Presbyterians, Baptists, and Anglicans working together for missions. Even the proposal from the Christian Association of Washington for a monthly periodical, *The Christian Monitor*, exposed the restorationism that would eventually become sectarian rather than ecumenical. Although it was common for missionary societies to establish their own periodicals, *The Christian Monitor* was meant to be more of a restoration watchdog, calling out people who used creeds and confessions as terms of communion more than performing the typical tasks of evangelical missions magazines, which usually focused on reports concerning missions, interdenominational meetings and sermons, itinerant preaching tours, and Bible and tract distribution, and included some doctrinal articles. The *Declaration and Address* defined "simple evangelical Christianity" as express New Testament beliefs and practices, and it laid out a hermeneutic for restoring them.[63] That restoration project eventually looked more like the work of the Haldanes or Walker than that of the London Missionary Society, though all were permanently influenced by the motives and practices of 1790s evangelical missions.

Getting the Story of the Christian Association of Washington Straight

In 1809, the *Declaration and Address* came off the press at the same time the Campbell family finally arrived from Scotland, and Alexander immediately embraced the goals of the *Declaration and Address*, resolving "to consecrate his life to the advocacy of the principles which it presented."[64] Alexander turned down a generous offer to run a nearby school because he wanted to devote all his efforts to the Christian Association of Washington and its proposed reformation. Pleased with his son's decision, Thomas arranged for Alexander to devote at least six months to intensive study of the New Testament. His daily studies included Greek, Latin, Hebrew, church history, the Bible with Henry and Scott's notes on practical observations, and Scripture memorization. From 1810 to 1811, he read books by John Walker, Robert Sandeman, the Haldane brothers, and many more.[65] In July 1810,

---

[63] This is why Mark Noll calls the document an "early manifesto of American Restorationism." See Mark A. Noll, *America's God: From Jonathan Edwards to Abraham Lincoln* (Oxford: Oxford University Press, 2002), 380.

[64] Richardson, *Memoirs of Alexander Campbell*, 1890, 1:274–75.

[65] Ibid., 1:278–79, 442–43.

Alexander preached his first sermon at a preaching stand in a grove. He delivered more than one hundred sermons in his first year of ministry for the Christian Association of Washington, preaching in private houses, in outdoor preaching stands, at the "cross-roads" meetinghouse, and at a second meetinghouse in the valley of Brush Run. Both Campbells were active itinerants for the Christian Association of Washington, preaching not just the gospel, but about evangelical missions in their unique Washington manifestation.[66]

Motivated by requests from Presbyterians and worried that the Christian Association of Washington was becoming a new "party,"[67] Thomas applied for "christian and ministerial communion" to the Presbyterian Synod of Pittsburgh in in October 1810.[68] The minutes describe Campbell as formerly in connection with the Associate Synod, but now "representing himself as in some relation to a society called the Christian Society of Washington." After hearing Campbell "at length," the synod explained its rejection of the Association and similar societies:

> The Synod unanimously resolved, that however specious the plan of that christian association, and however seducing its professions, as experience of the effects of similar projects, in other parts, has evinced their baneful tendency, and destructive operations on the whole interests of religion, by promoting division, instead of union, by degrading the ministerial characters, by providing free admission to any errors in doctrine, and to any corruption in discipline, whilst a nominal approbation of the scriptures as the only standard of truth may be professed, the Synod are constrained, by the most solemn considerations to disapprove the plan and its native effects.

---

[66] Ibid., 1:274–80, 311–24.

[67] Like the Haldanes had explicitly said in the plan of their Society for Propagating the Gospel at Home, Campbell also expressly stated that he did not want his society to become a "party" and thereby contribute to denominationalism. Campbell wanted his voluntary society to bring individuals from denominations together in unity for evangelistic purposes. He was not creating a church or a denomination (i.e., "party").

[68] According to Richardson, Thomas applied to the Synod of Pittsburgh for two reasons. First, the Christian Association of Washington, under the ministration of both Campbells, began to take on the characteristics of a distinct religious body, and Thomas did not want to form another "party." Second, Presbyterians had solicited him to take such action, believing the synod would embrace him and the Christian Association of Washington. See Richardson, *Memoirs of Alexander Campbell*, 1890, 1:324–27.

And farther, for the above and many other important reasons, it was resolved that Mr. Campbell's request to be received into christian and ministerial communion can not be granted.[69]

The synod knew of evangelical societies like the Christian Association of Washington, and found them destructive for their alleged deception and divisiveness. Beyond that, the synod had established itself as the Western Missionary Society at its founding meeting in 1802, and therefore already had means for missions. The object of this synodical missionary society was "to diffuse the knowledge of the Gospel among the inhabitants of the new settlements, the Indian Tribes, and if need be, among some of the interior inhabitants, where they are not able to support the gospel."[70] The Western Missionary Society appointed a person to preach an annual missionary sermon at the synod meeting, which in 1810 raised considerable funds for missions. Therefore, the Presbyterian Synod had already created denominational structures that fulfilled one of the major tasks for which the Christian Association of Washington and societies like it existed: itinerant missions. Campbell requested an explanation of the "many other important reasons" for its rejection of receiving him into communion, which the synod eventually provided and to which Campbell responded.[71] The proposal from the Association for an interdenominational evangelical missionary endeavor, founded on the simple New Testament gospel, was no more acceptable to the Presbyterian church than it was to the Associate synods in the United States or the United Kingdom.[72]

Alexander responded to the charges from the synod, and defended evangelical missions in a sermon at the Christian Association of Washington

---

[69] Synod of Pittsburgh, *Records of the Synod of Pittsburgh: From Its First Organization, September 29, 1802 to October 1832 Inclusive* (Pittsburgh: published by Luke Loomis, Agent, 1852), 71–72.

[70] Ibid., 11; Chaney, *The Birth of Missions in America*, 173–74.

[71] The synod rejected Campbell's teachings that the *Westminster Confession* included opinions not found in the Bible, the New Testament did not have precept or example supporting infant baptism which made it a matter of indifference, encouraging his son to preach the gospel without "regular authority," "for opposing creeds and confessions as injurious to the interest of religion," and simply because the Presbyterian church did not regulate the formation of connections with ministers, churches, or associations. Synod of Pittsburgh, *Records of the Synod of Pittsburgh*, 75.

[72] Richardson, *Memoirs of Alexander Campbell*, 1890, 1:324–34; McAllister, *Thomas Campbell*, 140–44; Williams, Foster, and Blowers, *The Stone-Campbell Movement: A Global History*, 21–22.

semiannual meeting in November 1810.[73] He publicized the meeting in *The Reporter* (local newspaper in Washington), inviting all to hear his discourse, which would illustrate the "principles and design" of the Association, and respond to "certain mistakes and objections which ignorance or willful opposition has attached to the humble and well-meant attempts of the Society to promote a scriptural reformation, as testified in their address to the friends and lovers of peace and truth throughout all the Churches."[74]

Alexander took Isaiah 57:14[75] and 62:10[76] as his sermon texts on the cause of Zion, as represented in the Christian Association of Washington and similar evangelical societies. Campbell argued that the glorious day when the "'heathen' shall be given to King Jesus 'for his inheritance,' and 'the uttermost parts of the earth for his possession;' when the 'Gentiles shall see Zion's righteousness'" was not far-off because of the "many noble exertions that have been made, and are at this day making, for the conversion of the heathen. Rapid progress is making in the translation of the Scriptures into every language under heaven." In this late 1810 sermon, Campbell explicitly described the Christian Association of Washington as a recent attempt of the transatlantic evangelical missionary endeavor for Zion.[77]

Campbell's creative Bible interpretation argued that the Christian Association of Washington had performed the duties that were allegorically instructed in the Isaiah texts. He said the texts instructed the church to separate from Babylon in order to "go through the gates" to Zion. The church needed to "prepare the way" for a permanent reformation by taking the "stumbling block out of the road of my people." This stumbling block was analogous to "human opinions and inventions of men" that had replaced Scripture. In order to "cast up the highway," the church needed

---

[73] This section relies on the sermon text as provided in Richardson, *Memoirs of Alexander Campbell*, 1890, 1:335–47. The first part of the sermon is available in T. W. Phillips Memorial Library, Bethany College, Bethany, WV, Archives and Special Collections, Campbell Papers, Part 14—Manuscripts, *Manuscript C* transcription from microfilm, "Sermon Propounded at the Semiannual Meeting of the Christian Association, 1810 Nov. 1," 66–68. Unfortunately, this tiny portion of the sermon constitutes only the introduction of his biblical texts.

[74] Quoted in Ibid., 1:335.

[75] "Cast ye up, cast ye up, prepare the way, take up the stumbling block out of the road of my people." This is Alexander Campbell's rendering of the text in *Manuscript C*, 66. The KJV has "way" instead of "road."

[76] "Go through the gates, go through the gates; prepare the way of the people; cast up, cast up the highway; gather out the stones; lift up a standard for the people" (as in Campbell, *Manuscript C*, 66).

[77] Alexander Campbell, "Sermon Propounded at the Semiannual Meeting of the Christian Association, 1810 Nov. 1," in Richardson, *Memoirs of Alexander Campbell*, 1890, 1:336–38.

to "'disencumber the Scriptures from the traditions of men, and exhibit them in a simple and perspicuous manner,' as they are the only authorized highway from Babylon to Zion, or from this world to heaven." Therefore, to "lift up a standard for the people" meant lifting up the true standard, which was the testimony of Jesus Christ in Scripture. According to Campbell, the Christian Association of Washington had fulfilled the duties suggested in the Old Testament text:

1. By endeavoring to remove the stumbling block of making the private opinions of men a term of communion.
2. By gathering out of the way the stumbling stones of human invention.
3. By pointing to the good old way, and maintaining that it is perfect, infallible, and sufficient.
4. By lifting up as our standard and maintaining that the New Testament is as perfect a constitution for the worship, discipline, and government of the New Testament Church, and as perfect a rule for the particular duties of its members, as the Old Testament was for its members.[78]

Campbell believed the proposed reformation by the Christian Association of Washington offered solutions for the church that were analogous to Isaiah's directions for the Old Testament "church."

The rest of Campbell's sermon at the Christian Association of Washington meeting offered rebuttals to each specific charge from the Synod of Pittsburgh and other charges as well, referring to various sections of the *Declaration and Address* to justify each rebuttal. To the charge that the Association increased division and would create a new party, he said it could be a new party "only in the same sense that the primitive Christians became a new party." The synod charged that the Association tended to "degrade the ministerial character." Campbell pointed to the fifth resolution of the address, which made the New Testament the standard for its ministerial principles; if New Testament principles degraded something, then it needed to be degraded. Campbell flatly denied the charge that the plan of

---

[78] Alexander Campbell, "Sermon Propounded at the Semiannual Meeting of the Christian Association, 1810 Nov. 1," in Richardson, *Memoirs of Alexander Campbell*, 1:341.

the Christian Association of Washington opened the door to corruption in discipline, citing several passages from the *Declaration and Address*. On the charge that the principles of the Association excluded infant baptism, he explained that its actual position was that this should be a matter of forbearance, analogous to Paul's policy on circumcision, since there was no express precept or example for the practice of infant baptism in the New Testament. On the charge that the plan of the Association tended to establish independent church government, Campbell agreed the church was independent under the "government of her glorious Head," ruled by "elders and deacons." Local churches were independent, but should be in "brotherly relation to each other," yet the Christian Association of Washington found no evidence in Scripture that the churches at Corinth, Antioch, and Pisidia were "governed by their rulers *in conjunction with one another*" or by votes in "*superior* and *inferior* courts"; thus, the members of the Association were "*scriptural* Presbyterians." On lay preaching, Campbell appealed to resolution twelve of the address, which stated that the ministers of the Association were "duly and scripturally qualified"—if lay preachers were those "duly and scripturally qualified," then "let us have a number of them."[79] This portion of the sermon demonstrates that by the end of 1810, the Campbells and the Christian Association of Washington had publicly articulated views that limited its prospective membership. Unlike the London Missionary Society, which consistently attempted not to discuss polity in order to maintain cooperation among Independents, Baptists, Presbyterians, and Anglicans, Alexander's sermon, in the wake of public condemnation by the Synod of Pittsburgh of the Christian Association of Washington and his father, excluded all but congregational polity as scriptural.

The next extant evidence of Christian Association of Washington activity comes from Alexander's itinerant preaching tour for the Association in Ohio, beginning on May 16, 1811, which he narrated in "Account of My Circuit on My First Mission over the Ohio—1811." On this mission, he engaged numerous people in debate on the "principles which we advocate," and preached in churches, a courthouse, and in houses before Presbyterians, Methodists, and others. Among his sermon texts were a favorite missions

---

[79] Alexander Campbell, "Sermon Propounded at the Semiannual Meeting of the Christian Association, 1810 Nov. 1," in Richardson, *Memoirs of Alexander Campbell*, 1:341–47.

text (Mark 16:15–16) and a text suggesting the all-sufficiency of Scripture (John 5:39). He also preached on Isaiah 57:14 and 62:10, probably making the same points noted above when he preached these texts at the Christian Association of Washington meeting in November 1810 (in the context of evangelical missions, he placed the Association as one of the auspicious endeavors of the "times"). His itinerancy lasted about three weeks, during which he preached about a dozen times.[80]

Also in the summer of 1811, the Christian Association of Washington formed an Independent congregation. According to Robert Richardson, Thomas decided to do this "on account of the continued hostility of the different parties." The Association "should assume the character of an independent Church, in order to the enjoyment of those privileges and the performance of those duties which belong to the Church relation."[81] Thomas was appointed elder, four deacons were chosen, and Alexander was licensed to preach the gospel. Their first meeting as a church was on May 5, 1811, when they held their first Communion. After several did not participate because they had never been baptized, Thomas performed the first three immersions.[82] The Independent congregation met alternately at the two Christian Association of Washington buildings—cross-roads and Brush Run.

Despite the typical historical narrative,[83] the Christian Association of Washington did not disband when it formed an Independent congregation, nor was it then called the Brush Run Church. Rather, the Independent congregation, sometimes identified as the "first Church" of the Christian Association of Washington, continued meeting at both the cross-roads and Brush Run log buildings—one church in two Association locations. For example, there is a document dated January 29, 1812 in Alexander's *Manuscript 332* and titled "3 Questions proposed for [illegible word] respecting the principles practices and progress of the Christian Association of Washington." In it, Campbell used passages from Scripture

---

[80] The "Account" I have ends abruptly on his third Sunday out, at which point he had been itinerating eighteen days and had preached eleven times. See Alexander Campbell, "Account of My Circuit on My First Mission over the Ohio—1811," in *Manuscript C*, 72–73. Richardson notes that he returned home, preaching twice more on the way. See Richardson, *Memoirs of Alexander Campbell*, 1:371.

[81] Ibid., 1:366–67.

[82] Alexander Campbell and Thomas Campbell, "3 Questions proposed for [illegible word] respecting the principles practices and progress of the Christian Association of Washington," in *Manuscript 332*, 156–59.

[83] That is, the Christian Association of Washington disbanded and became the Brush Run Church.

and the *Declaration and Address* to affirm the principles and practices of the Association, demonstrating that the Campbells still worked under the name of the Christian Association of Washington in early 1812, long after they had established an Independent congregation. In another example, when the Independent congregation ordained Alexander on January 1, 1812,[84] Thomas signed Alexander's ordination certificate on September 21, 1812, as "Thomas Campbell, Senior Minr. of the first Church of the Christian association of Washington meeting at Crossroads & Brushrun Washington County, Pensylvania [sic]" along with signatures of four "Deacons of the said Church."[85] Despite the fact that the congregation adopted believer's immersion in June 1812, three months later it still identified as a congregation of the Christian Association of Washington. That is, as late as September 1812, the Campbells' Independent congregation is more accurately described as the "First Church of the Christian Association of Washington" than the "Brush Run Church," as historical narratives usually have it.

To recap, the Christian Association of Washington was an evangelical missions society that provided a central framework for the self-understanding of the Campbells and the emergence of their Movement, or "reformation" as they called it. Although the typical narrative of the Association in historical surveys of the Stone-Campbell Movement is mostly limited to analysis of the *Declaration and Address*, with little on the Society other than its "failure," it was the Society under whose name the Campbell Movement emerged and operated from 1809 through late 1812. And although the ideals in the *Declaration and Address* became the most influential aspect of the Christian Association of Washington for the development of the Stone-Campbell Movement, members involved in its founding and early history certainly did not foresee that conclusion. In their minds, the Society itself was a manifestation of the missionary endeavor that people viewed as a "sign of the times"—Thomas recognized this in his *Declaration and Address*, as did Alexander in his sermons on Isaiah in 1810 and 1811. Some of the Association members had seen internationally famous itinerant preachers

---

[84] For Alexander's beliefs and thoughts about ordination, see his "A Review of Religious Principles," Jan. 1, 1812, in *Manuscript 332*, 114–17.

[85] This ordination certificate provided to Brooke County is available in T. W. Phillips Memorial Library, Bethany College, Bethany, WV, Archives and Special Collections, Campbell Papers, Part 18—Ordination, no. 1. Deed Book E, 123.

in Ireland, witnessed thousands receive Bibles, and knew of people who received Christian education through the work of regional evangelical societies that were organized exactly like their Association. Their Society would provide the means of Christian cooperation for spreading the gospel locally. The Campbells defended the principles of the Christian Association of Washington to the Synod of Pittsburgh and to numerous religious people on their itinerant journeys. Their Independent congregation was called the "First Church of the Christian Association of Washington" until at least September 1812. The Association and *Declaration and Address* were manifestations of transatlantic evangelical missions that the Campbells encountered in the United Kingdom. Their self-understanding as Christians and their identity as reformers in the earliest years was inextricably tied to transatlantic evangelical missions.

For a number of reasons, the Christian Association of Washington did not experience success comparable to the Evangelical Society of Ulster or General Evangelical Society in Ireland, or the Society for Propagating the Gospel at Home or Edinburgh Missionary Society in Scotland. September 1812 is the last reference I have found to the Campbells identifying with the Christian Association of Washington. Its proposed publications never materialized, and no sister associations were formed. A number of factors help explain its relatively brief, though influential, existence. First, a sparsely settled frontier with long distances between settlements with small populations, unlike the United Kingdom, created a more difficult context for success. Second, the Christian Association of Washington was in the heart of Presbyterian settlements in the United States—Presbyterians often opposed voluntary evangelical societies, which could undermine parish and clerical order. Beyond the practical concept of itinerant preachers, the idea that Association adherents would "administer the ordinances according to the Divine Standard" went further in subverting the functions of settled congregations, which made membership in the Society less tenable for those in non-Congregational denominations (this official stance had to severely limit the draw of the Association, more so than societies whose itinerants only preached). Third, the Association had no magazine with a readership from which they could draw support. Fourth, some denominations already had means for missionary involvement on the frontier, nullifying the contextual need that made the Evangelical Society of Ulster, General Evangelical Society, London Missionary Society, and Society for Propagating the Gospel at Home so necessary and then successful. Finally, the Campbells' acceptance of believer's baptism in 1812, discussed in the next chapter, limited their sphere of influence to the Baptist community.

CONCLUSION

The Campbell Movement emerged in the United States by leaving the Presbyterian church and following the path of evangelical missions advocates in the transatlantic region. Thomas Campbell's interdenominational cooperation, influenced by evangelical missions, proved too latitudinarian for Presbyterians in both Ireland and the United States. When his relationship with Presbyterians finally ended, he started the Christian Association of Washington, a voluntary evangelical missionary society almost exactly like the one he cofounded in Ireland. After a nine-month mentorship in Glasgow with Greville Ewing, one of the most influential transatlantic evangelical missions leaders in Scotland, Alexander fully devoted himself to the goals of the Christian Association of Washington. Both Campbells perceived the Association to be one of the many eschatologically significant evangelical efforts for united missions founded on a simple primitive gospel. These interdenominational voluntary associations seemed to harbinger the coming conversion of the world and imminent return of Christ.

Transatlantic evangelical missions provide historians a comprehensive and transnational context for understanding the origins of Thomas Campbell's *Declaration and Address* and the Christian Association of Washington. Viewed from this context, all of Thomas Campbell's ideas and practices cohere in a vision of Christianity shared by a specific historical movement. Viewing Campbellite origins in transatlantic evangelical missions offers a more historically aware and holistic reading of the early documents, which roots the Campbells in a vibrant missionary movement that captured the imagination of evangelicals all over the transatlantic in the 1790s and early 1800s.

The earliest documents and actions of the Campbell Movement reveal its roots in evangelical missions, but the Movement eventually aligned less with pragmatic primitivism for the end of ecumenical cooperation and more with patternist primitivism[86] aimed at restoring New Testament faith and practice.

---

[86] Patternist primitivism refers to the view that that New Testament contains a "pattern" for worship. This primitivism focuses on identifying, extracting, and applying that primitive pattern in modern times. The pattern is associated with God's desire for the worship of the church. Therefore, it is typically sectarian in nature, separating from those who either ignore or misunderstand the pattern. Patternist primitivism contrasts with pragmatic patternism, which simply used the Bible generically (rather than a legalistically defined pattern) as a shared foundation on which denominations could unite for "simple evangelical gospel" missions.

Chapter Seven

A BAPTIST AND ANTI-MISSIONARY VIEWPOINT, 1812–1830

ALTHOUGH THE CAMPBELL MOVEMENT EMERGED FROM THE transatlantic evangelical missionary movement, by 1823, Alexander Campbell vehemently rejected the legitimacy of missionary and other evangelical societies in his new periodical, *The Christian Baptist*. In 1825, Alexander lucidly explained his patternist primitivism:

> it belongs to every individual and to every congregation of individuals to discard from their faith and their practice every thing that is not found written in the New Testament ... and to believe and practice whatever is there enjoined. This done, and every thing is done which ought to be done.[1]

Here and elsewhere, Alexander, though not always consistently, argued that the silence of the New Testament on a practice or a belief meant churches should prohibit it. Among those practices that Campbell vehemently opposed as unscriptural, and therefore unauthorized due to their absence

---

[1] Alexander Campbell, "A Restoration of the Ancient Order of Things—No. II," *The Christian Baptist* 2, no. 8 (March 7, 1825): 133; Michael W Casey, *The Battle Over Hermeneutics in the Stone-Campbell Movement, 1800–1870* (Lewiston: E. Mellen Press, 1998), 51–96; Bill J. Humble, "The Missionary Society Controversy in the Restoration Movement (1823–1875)" (PhD diss., University of Iowa, 1964), 27–33.

in the New Testament, was participation in missionary societies.[2] Given the previous chapters of this book, Campbell's intense opposition to missionary societies should come as a surprise. In fact, his scathing critique, which began in 1823, has led almost all historians of Stone-Campbell Movement missions to begin their analyses at that point, which has led to neglect of earlier missions influences on the Campbells. A more appropriate question, given what we know now about Campbell origins is: How and why did the Campbells make a 180-degree turn in the early 1820s to oppose missionary societies? Along with answering that question, this chapter narrates the Campbells' career from 1812 to 1830, a period during which the Campbell Movement associated with Baptists and developed their hermeneutic in sectarian patternist directions.

The Campbells and Missions During the Early Baptist Years (1812–1823)

The Campbells naturally began considering affiliation with Baptists in 1812, after they concluded believer's immersion was an express and positive divine command in the New Testament. Alexander married Margaret Brown in 1811, and they had their first child in March 1812, which precipitated a careful study of infant baptism and believer's immersion. The Campbells were well aware of the views of evangelical missions advocates such as the Haldanes, Alexander Carson, and others who adopted believer's baptism and became Baptists after embracing a more patternist primitivism. They concluded similarly, and in June 1812, had a local Baptist, Matthias Luce, baptize five members of the Campbell family and two members of the Christian Association of Washington's Independent church. In the subsequent meetings of the congregation, most of the others were either baptized or left the Association. The public stance on believers' immersion proved polarizing, because it was a move from the Association's previous position of forbearance on an unclear New Testament practice (which fostered cooperation among Presbyterians, Independents, and Baptists) to its new

---

[2] Casey, *The Battle Over Hermeneutics*, 263–64; Alexander Campbell, "The Christian Religion," *The Christian Baptist* 1, no. 1 (August 3, 1823): 5–8; Alexander Campbell, "To Mr. Robert Cautious," *The Christian Baptist* 1, no. 8 (March 1, 1824): 53–54.

position that it was a positive divine ordinance (which caused those who believed in infant baptism to leave).[3]

From 1812 to 1830, the Campbells retained some type of acquaintance or association with Baptists. On December 28, 1812, a certificate from Brooke County for Alexander to celebrate the rites of matrimony said he "produced credentials of his ordination, and also of his being in regular communion with the Regular Baptist Church of Brush Run."[4] From as early as December 1812, then, Campbell was apparently willing to identify as Baptist. After numerous conversations with local Baptists, the Independent congregation that became known as Brush Run Church joined the Redstone Baptist Association in 1815 "on the ground that no terms of union or communion other than the Holy Scriptures should be required."[5] However, the Campbells' view of unity and restoration of New Testament Christianity created the problems of, on the one hand, aversion to becoming a new party and, on the other hand, opposition to the seeming divisiveness of joining a denomination. In December 1815, in a letter to his uncle in Ireland, Alexander reported his drastic religious changes and some of his major influences:

> In the first place, I became a Scotch Independent next a Sandemanian then a Separatist with John Walker. Then a Baptist and am now an Independent in church government, a Sandemanian in faith or rather if there is any difference of that faith and view of the gospel exhibited in John Walker of letters to Alexander Knox, and a Baptist in so far as respects

---

[3] Richardson, *Memoirs of Alexander Campbell*, 1890, 1:395–405.

[4] T. W. Phillips Memorial Library, Bethany College, Bethany, WV, Archives and Special Collections, Campbell Papers, Part 18—Ordination, no. 2. Certificate to Celebrate the Rites of Matrimony, Brooke County.

[5] Many historians take 1813 as the date Brush Run joined the Redstone Baptist Association, because Alexander misremembered that date as early as 1825 and continued to do so thereafter, but the Redstone Baptist Association minutes record the entry of the Brush Run Church in 1815. See Gary L. Lee, "Background to *The Christian Baptist*," in *The Christian Baptist* (Joplin: College Press, 1983), 5, n15; Alexander Campbell, "An Address to the Public," *The Christian Baptist* 2, no. 2 (September 6, 1824): 92; the Redstone Baptist Association, *Minutes of the Redstone Baptist Association, Held by Appointment, At Big Redstone, Fayette County, Penn.: September 1st, 2d, and 3d, 1815* (Pittsburgh: printed by S. Engles, 1815), 5. Redstone Baptist Association minutes are quoted from *Minutes of the Redstone Baptist Association, 1804–1836* (n.p.: M. F. Cottrell, 1964) and the much fuller personal collections of Dale Broadhurst, to whom I am grateful for sending me images of the original minutes in good condition. I am also indebted to Carisse Berryhill and her staff at Abilene Christian University, Brown Library, Center for Restoration Studies, for providing me a copy of the Redstone Baptist Association minutes as published by M. F. Cottrell.

> Baptism. . . . But yet notwithstanding I am in Connexion with
> the Regular Baptist Church in this country, and am now on
> a tour preaching in all the Baptist churches in the cities of
> Philadelphia New York—Baltimore Washington &c.[6]

Despite the uneasy connection, the Campbells remained active in the Redstone Baptist Association and other Baptist associations until 1830, when the tenuous relationship ended.[7]

Baptists were pioneers of the great missionary societies of the nineteenth century, and the leaders of the Redstone Baptist Association were exhilarated by the missionary efforts taking place around the globe and in their own territory.[8] Therefore, the Baptist Board of Foreign Missions was founded in 1814.[9] As a result, zeal for missions escalated around the time the Brush Run Church joined the Redstone Baptist Association in 1815. In the 1815 Association meeting, just a few moments after the admittance of the Brush Run Church, Article 10 recorded:

> This association resolves itself into a Missionary Society, auxiliary to the Baptist Board of Foreign Missions; and for the future, the society shall consist of the Elders and Messengers of every church, who shall collect and forward to the Treasurer of this society annually, at least five dollars.[10]

During those years, Baptist associations often either became missionary societies or substantially supported missions.[11] The Redstone Baptist

---

[6] Alexander Campbell to Archibald Campbell, December 28, 1815, 2, T. W. Phillips Memorial Library, Bethany College, Bethany, WV, Archives and Special Collections, Campbell Papers, Part 01. I quote from Jeanne Cobb's March 13, 2003 transcription, available in the same folder.

[7] The rocky relationship finally ended between 1829 and 1830, when the distinctions between traditional Baptist theology and the Campbells' theology warranted a division that was enacted through the printing of charges and censures of the associations. Errett Gates, *The Early Relation and Separation of Baptists and Disciples* (Chicago: R. R. Donnelley & Sons Company, 1904); James L. Gorman, "From Burning to Blessing: Baptist Reception of Alexander Campbell's New Translation," *Stone-Campbell Journal* 16, no. 2 (2013): 179–89; Anthony J. Springer, "Baptists," *Encyclopedia of the Stone-Campbell Movement* (Grand Rapids: Eerdmans, 2004), 67–69.

[8] Charles L. Chaney, *The Birth of Missions in America* (Pasadena: William Carey Library, 1976), 163, 196–99.

[9] Ibid., 196–99; C. Douglas Weaver, *In Search of the New Testament Church: The Baptist Story*, 1st ed. (Macon: Mercer University Press, 2008), 90–92; American Baptist Foreign Mission Society, *Proceedings of the Baptist Convention for Missionary Purposes—Held in Philadelphia, in May, 1814* (Philadelphia: printed for the Convention by Ann Coles, 1814).

[10] The Redstone Baptist Association, *Minutes (1815)*, 5.

[11] Chaney, *The Birth of Missions in America*, 170–72.

Association recommended the Massachusetts Baptist missionary magazine "to the churches as a valuable source of missionary and other religious information." The following year opened with a sermon on the missionary text of Mark 16:15, and the Association revised Article 10 from the previous year, resolving instead:

> That all the churches in this Association consider it their duty and privilege to contribute annually to propagate the gospel among the heathen, and that the churches henceforth forward their contributions by their messengers, and mention the sum in their letter to the Association. The amount received from each church shall be published in the minutes and the moderator shall forward the contributions to the Baptist Board of Foreign Missions, and produce a receipt of the next Association.[12]

Historian of missions Charles Chaney notes that by the late 1810s, "the missionary cause had become the great passion of the American churches."[13] Clearly, this was true of the Redstone Baptist Association.[14]

Through their association with the Baptists, the Campbells continued supporting the missionary movement until at least 1821. From 1816 to 1821, the Brush Run Church gave approximately eighty dollars to the Baptist Board of Foreign Missions, a larger sum than the average contribution of most member churches.[15] In 1820, the circular letter from the Redstone

---

[12] The Redstone Baptist Association, *Minutes of the Redstone Baptist Association, Held by Appointment, At Cross-Creek, Brooke County, VA.: August 30th, 31st, and Sept, 1st, 1816* (Washington: printed by William Sample, 1816), 3, 6.

[13] Chaney, *The Birth of Missions in America*, 174, 192.

[14] For information on Baptist associationalism and Alexander's discussions about it, see H. Leon McBeth, *The Baptist Heritage* (Nashville: Broadman, 1987), 239–46; Walter B. Shurden, "The Authority of a Baptist Association," *Baptist History and Heritage* 40, no. 1 (2005): 6–7; Hugh Wamble, "Beginning of Associationalism Among English Baptists," *Review & Expositor* 54, no. 4 (October 1957): 544–59; Alexander Campbell, "Remarks on the Communion of Churches," *The Christian Baptist* 4, no. 1 (August 7, 1826): 261–63; Alexander Campbell, "Ecclesiastical Tyranny," *The Christian Baptist* 4, no. 3 (October 2, 1826): 275–77; Alexander Campbell, "A New Association," *The Christian Baptist* 4, no. 3 (October 2, 1826): 277–78.

[15] The Redstone Baptist Association, *Minutes (1816)*, 7; the Redstone Baptist Association, *Minutes of the Redstone Baptist Association, Held by Appointment, At Peter's Creek, Washington County, (Pa.): September 2d, 3d & 4th, 1817* (Washington, PA: printed by William Sample, 1817), 6; the Redstone Baptist Association, *Minutes of the Redstone Baptist Association, Held at Connelsville, Fayette County, (Pa.): September 1st, 2d & 3d, 1818* (Washington: printed by William Sample, 1818), 5; the Redstone Baptist Association, *Minutes of the Redstone Baptist Association, Held at the Horseshoe, Washington County, (Pa.): September 3d. 4th. & 5th. 1819* (Washington: printed by Samuel Workman, 1819), 5; the Redstone Baptist Association, *Minutes of the Redstone Baptist Association, Held at Plum Run, Washington County, (Pa.):*

Baptist Association to its congregations urged churches to contribute to the worthy causes of Bible translation, missions to the "heathen," and the societies that supported such activity.[16] This was possibly a response to the decline of giving in 1819 and 1820.[17] If so, it did not work—member-church giving in the Redstone Baptist Association plummeted in 1821 to thirty-eight dollars, ten dollars of which the Brush Run Church gave. The 1821 "Corresponding Letter" from the Association to other associations assured readers that the low collection that year for foreign missions was "owing to the pecuniary embarrassments of the country and not to a disregard to that great and important object."[18] During the 1821 Redstone Baptist Association meeting, Alexander preached on Matthew 28:18–20, a passage stressing missions to all nations. The 1822 minutes did not list the missionary fund, but included a short note on "Missionary Business" which formed a committee of five people, including Alexander, "to settle with all persons on that subject."[19] The 1822 "Corresponding Letter" noted excitement at the recent activity of U.S. Baptist churches in foreign and domestic missions, but said nothing more.[20] The Association collected forty dollars in 1822, but the minutes do not indicate which churches gave the money.[21] The 1823 minutes said nothing of missions giving that year, and the Campbells' relationship with the Redstone Baptist Association came to an end in 1824. The main point to take from this information is that the Campbells financially supported the Baptist missionary society until at least 1821.

A contributing factor leading to Alexander's 1823 great reversal on missionary societies comes from 1820 to 1822, when he wrote a series of articles in *The Reporter* that opposed the moral society of West Middletown, one of many moral societies during this period whose purpose was to enforce

---

September 1, 2, & 3, 1820 (n.p.: n.p., 1820), 4; the Redstone Baptist Association, *Minutes of the Redstone Baptist Association, Held at Ruff's Creek, Greene County, Pa.: August 31 and September 1st and 2nd, 1821* (n.p.: n.p., 1821), 3; Lee, "Background to *The Christian Baptist*," 28–29.

[16] The Redstone Baptist Association, *Minutes (1820)*, 5–7.

[17] 1816—$288; 1817—$245; 1818—$222; 1819—$124; 1820—$112.

[18] The Redstone Baptist Association, *Minutes (1821)*, 8.

[19] The Redstone Baptist Association, *Minutes of the Redstone Baptist Association, Held at Washington, Washington County, Pa.: August 31, and September 1 and 2, 1822* (n.p.: n.p., 1822), 4.

[20] Ibid., 12.

[21] The Redstone Baptist Association, *Minutes of the Redstone Baptist Association, Held at Pittsburgh, Allegheny County, Pa.: September 5th, 6th, and 7th, 1823* (n.p.: n.p., 1823), 3; the Redstone Baptist Association, *Minutes (1821)*, 3.

morality and keep the Christian Sabbath (Sunday) holy.[22] In the tradition of William Wilberforce's society for suppressing vice and promoting good morals,[23] moral societies were an outgrowth of evangelical activism through voluntary societies intended to Christianize culture.[24] In Pennsylvania, moral societies enforced legislation such as "An Act for the Prevention of Vice and Immorality, and of Unlawful Gaming, and to Restrain Disorderly Sports and Dissipation" (1794). This Pennsylvania Act outlawed "worldly employment," "unlawful game, hunting, shooting, sport or diversion whatsoever" on "the Lord's day, commonly called Sunday."[25] Keeping Sunday holy meant that even if people did not attend church, they would revere the "Sabbath" and appease God by following Christian laws.[26] In Pennsylvania, the fines for violation of Sunday rules and other laws enforcing morality included fines and imprisonment.[27] According to Robert Richardson, the moral society Campbell opposed had formed in 1815 "for the suppression of vice and immorality," especially on the Sabbath.[28]

Under the pen name "Candidus," Alexander rejected the propriety of the moral societies and the Act of 1794 in thirty-one articles published in *The Reporter* from April 1820 to February 1822.[29] Campbell argued that the moral societies were "anti-evangelical" and "anti-constitutional"; a moral

---

[22] I rely on Keith Huey's transcriptions of *The Reporter* articles and his introduction, available online: Alexander Campbell and Keith B. Huey, *The Candidus Essays By Alexander Campbell: First Published in* The Reporter, *Washington, Pa., 1820–1822*, ed. Keith B. Huey (n.p.: Keith B. Huey, 2001), http://web.archive.org/web/20120114230913/http://www.mun.ca/rels/restmov/texts/acampbell/ce/CE00A.HTM.

[23] Charles I. Foster, *An Errand of Mercy: The Evangelical United Front, 1790–1837* (Chapel Hill: University of North Carolina Press, 1960), 133.

[24] On the evangelical impulse to Christianize culture, as inherited from the magisterial reformations, see Richard T. Hughes, "Why Restorationists Don't Fit the Evangelical Mold; Why Churches of Christ Increasingly Do," in *Re-Forming the Center: American Protestantism, 1900 to the Present*, eds. Douglas Jacobsen and William Vance Trollinger (Grand Rapids: Eerdmans, 1998), 194–213.

[25] James Tyndale Mitchell et al., eds., "An Act for the Prevention of Vice and Immorality, and of Unlawful Gaming, and to Restrain Disorderly Sports and Dissipation," in *The Statutes at Large of Pennsylvania from 1682 to 1801*, vol. 15 (Harrisburg: Clarence M. Busch, State Printer of Pennsylvania, 1911), 110; Campbell and Huey, *The Candidus Essays*, Introduction.

[26] Campbell and Huey, *The Candidus Essays*, Introduction.

[27] Mitchell et al., "An Act for the Prevention of Vice and Immorality," 110–18.

[28] Richardson provides portions of what he calls the "Washington Moral Society" founding documents and goals, in Richardson, *Memoirs of Alexander Campbell*, 1890, 1:516–17. In the Candidus articles, Campbell opposed the moral societies in general and the one in West Middletown in particular. I am uncertain if Richardson had the West Middletown Constitution or another of the apparent several moral societies in the county, since he quoted it as the "Washington Moral Society." In its "Constitution" and its "Address," it encouraged the formation of similar associations, and assumed all agreed on the correctness of its goals.

[29] Campbell and Huey, *The Candidus Essays*, Introduction.

evil, they were "subversive of the principles of true religion and civil liberty."[30] Campbell's "first principle," the "pole star of [his] course," was that the Bible provided the only system of morality, and "consequently it must point out the only sure and efficient means of encouraging and promoting it. To suppose the contrary, would be a reproach to its author."[31] Therefore, moral societies were anti-evangelical (i.e., anti-scriptural), because no such societies existed in the Old Testament or New Testament—that made them modern inventions.[32] He used passages in Scripture to argue that the biblical ideal precluded the imposition of Christian morality upon broader society—Sabbath observance was not a civil or moral matter, but a religious matter and thus a matter of conscience.[33] For Campbell, the moral societies were unconstitutional because they violated liberty of conscience and religious liberty. Campbell distinguished between what he saw as "moral positives," which should govern the church, and "moral natural precepts," which should govern all society. The church and society were two distinct institutions, and one should not control members of the other.[34] Campbell, as "Candidus," engaged several opponents in *The Reporter* on this issue.

In the moral societies, Campbell experienced an unpalatable aspect of the benevolent empire that was closely related to evangelical missions, and this experience influenced his forthcoming opposition to missionary societies. In the moral societies, evangelicals attempted to Christianize culture, and Campbell's religio-political philosophy made this perspective untenable. More importantly, he articulated opposition to moral societies on grounds that they had no example in the New Testament—he later opposed missionary societies on the same grounds. While the two kinds of societies (moral and missions) were different, he would eventually see hegemonic tendencies in both. The fact that he said moral societies lacked support in Scripture, while simultaneously giving money to the national

---

[30] Candidus, "For the Reporter. No. I," *The Reporter*, April 17, 1820, 1; Candidus, "For the Reporter. No. II," *The Reporter*, May 22, 1820, 1–2.

[31] Candidus, "For the Reporter. No. IV," *The Reporter*, June 19, 1820, 1.

[32] Candidus, "For the Reporter. No. II," 1–2.

[33] For example, Campbell argued that "no precept was ever more definite, more authoritative, or more perspicuous than" that in 1 Corinthians 5:12, which he interpreted to mean that Christians should judge Christians, but not people outside the church. See Candidus, "For the Reporter. No. III." *The Reporter*, June 5, 1820, 1.

[34] Candidus, "For the Reporter. No. VI," *The Reporter*, August 21, 1820, 1; Candidus, "For the Reporter. No. 10," *The Reporter*, March 19, 1821, 1.

Baptist missionary society, demonstrates that he had not yet worked out a complete theory on societies. The "Candidus" essays were one of Campbell's first written protests against political and religious practices, and they were not his last.

The Anti-Missionary Society Years (1823-1830)

Religious journalism in the United States became more interesting in 1823, when Alexander started a monthly periodical called *The Christian Baptist*, in which his position on missionary societies completely changed.[35] The purpose of *The Christian Baptist* was "the eviction of truth and the exposing of error in doctrine and practice."[36] Its character was satirical, iconoclastic, lively, and blunt. Campbell's most vitriolic attacks of confessional Christianity, clergy, and societies (missionary, Bible, etc.) appeared in the earliest issues of *The Christian Baptist*. This anti-missionary society "Campbell" is typically viewed as the "first Campbell," juxtaposed to the "second Campbell," who became president of the Stone-Campbell Movement's national missionary society in 1849. The previous chapters demonstrate there was an earlier Campbell—the earliest Campbell who, with his father, supported missionary societies for two decades; a "second" who opposed them in *The Christian Baptist*; and a "third" who eventually affirmed them. This section is concerned with explaining the transition from the Campbells of evangelical missions to the anti-missionary society phase of the "second" Alexander.

From the earliest issues of *The Christian Baptist*, Alexander spilled a great deal of ink in vehemently critiquing missionary societies and enumerating the abuses that pricked his conscience.[37] Campbell's opposition

---

[35] For general information on the *Christian Baptist*, see Lee Snyder, "Christian Baptist, The," ed. Douglas A. Foster et al., *The Encyclopedia of the Stone-Campbell Movement* (Grand Rapids: Eerdmans, 2004); Lee, "Background to *The Christian Baptist*," 1–36; Richardson, *Memoirs of Alexander Campbell*, 1890, 2:43–51. We do not know the exact number of subscribers, but by Robert Richardson's calculation, Alexander issued no fewer than forty-six thousand volumes of his own works during the life of *The Christian Baptist*, from 1823 to 1830, and Gary Lee notes that the income for the final year was $1,200.

[36] Alexander Campbell, "PROSPECTUS OF THE CHRISTIAN BAPTIST," *The Christian Baptist* 1, no. 1 (July 4, 1823): iv. This quote comes from the first edition (PRINTED AND PUBLISHED BY A. CAMPBELL, AT THE BUFFALOE PRINTING-OFFICE, 1827). Unless otherwise noted, *The Christian Baptist* quotations in this paper are from Alexander Campbell and D. S. Burnet, eds., *The Christian Baptist*, 15th ed. (St. Louis: Christian Publishing Company, 1889).

[37] Richardson, *Memoirs of Alexander Campbell*, 1890, 2:49–68; Humble, "The Missionary Society Controversy in the Restoration Movement (1823–1875)," 33–43; William J. Richardson, "Alexander

to missionary societies coincided with the larger antimissions movement among Baptists in the United States and the United Kingdom.[38] Eventually called "primitive" or "hard-shell" Baptists, representative individuals of this group, such as John Taylor and Daniel Parker, critiqued the growing missionary enterprise—often associated with denominational centralization—from the 1810s based on grounds of greed, hegemonic authority, sectionalism, and theology. Historian Douglas Weaver notes that Taylor's *Thoughts on Missions* (1819) critiqued famous missionaries such as Luther Rice and Adoniram Judson, claiming they were motivated by money, power, and prestige. Campbell later used invective similar to Taylor's assault on missionaries from the Eastern United States, which Taylor derisively styled the "*New England Rat*."[39] Constant appeals for money caused some churches and associations to shut their doors to missions preachers.[40] Some Baptists also took issue with regional and national hierarchical organizations that undergirded the missionary endeavor. A primitivist impulse partly animated this ecclesiological critique, as some Baptists opposed "extra-church" efforts on the grounds that they were "inventions of men," and had no basis from New Testament examples.[41] The sectional critique came from Western suspicion of the educated elite on the East Coast and what seemed to be imperial sectional elitism. Some Easterners viewed Western frontier people as uneducated, inferior, and in need of Eastern aid. Some Westerners perceived the missionary societies as supporting Eastern elitism and challenging Western democratic populism of the frontier. Furthermore, Easterners sometimes looked west and south to acquire new areas of influence to replace what they were losing in their recently disestablished areas.[42] Finally, some Baptists

---

Campbell's Conception of Mission," in *Unto the Uttermost: Missions in the Christian Churches/Churches of Christ*, ed. Doug Priest (Pasadena: William Carey Library, 1984), 95–115.

[38] Weaver, *In Search of the New Testament Church*, 89–96; David W. Bebbington, *Baptists Through the Centuries: A History of A Global People* (Waco: Baylor University Press, 2010), 87–91; McBeth, *The Baptist Heritage*, 371–77.

[39] Weaver, *In Search of the New Testament Church*, 93; John Taylor, *Thoughts on Missions* (Franklin County, Kentucky: n. p., 1819), 4, http://baptiststudiesonline.com/wp-content/uploads/2007/02/thoughts-on-missions.pdf.

[40] Bebbington, *Baptists Through the Centuries: A History of A Global People*, 87–88.

[41] McBeth, *The Baptist Heritage*, 374; Weaver, *In Search of the New Testament Church*, 93–95; Bebbington, *Baptists Through the Centuries: A History of A Global People*, 90.

[42] James R Mathis, *The Making of the Primitive Baptists: A Cultural and Intellectual History of the Antimission Movement, 1800–1840* (New York: Routledge, 2004), 9.

opposed the moderate Calvinism that propelled Reformed missions. The Baptist antimissions movement certainly influenced the Campbells.

Campbell articulated many of the same arguments against the missionary, Bible, and other societies that his fellow Baptists had expressed in the 1810s, when Campbell's Brush Run Church was still supporting the national Baptist missionary society. Nonetheless, in one of the first issues of *The Christian Baptist*, Campbell published his opposition to Eastern missionary societies, listing their choice of missionaries with elite theological training, their focus on foreign rather than home missions, the substantial funds raised for these missionary endeavors, and their failure to follow the New Testament example for missions. After a report of a Baptist missionary meeting and a satirical account of how the meeting was not like the New Testament examples, Campbell pleaded, "It is much to be desired that the Baptists in the western country will not imitate these precedents of pompous vanity, so consecrated to the east."[43]

One of Campbell's major critiques concerned the wealth and mentality of the missionary societies. In 1824 he reminded readers, "I did contribute my mite and my efforts to the popular missionary cause, until my conscience forbade me from an acquaintance with the abuses of the principle."[44] He told stories of the large sums of money missionaries made, like one who came to Pittsburgh and collected forty dollars for preaching four sermons.[45] He also disliked the large expense of the missionary enterprise. He frequently printed the annual income of societies, and noted what he believed to be a disproportionate number of converts.[46] For an example of how quickly evangelical missions grew into a "benevolent empire," Charles Foster notes that U.S. government expenditures for internal improvements from 1789 to 1828 totaled $3,585,534, while during the same period the thirteen largest benevolent societies had revenues of $2,813,550.[47] The Baptist Board of

---

[43] Alexander Campbell, "Note by the Editor [about 'Missionaries to Burma']," *The Christian Baptist* 1, no. 2 (September 1, 1823): 17.

[44] ["the Bishop of a Respectable Church"], "[Letter to the Editor]," *The Christian Baptist* 1, no. 11 (June 7, 1824): 69–70; Alexander Campbell, "[Reply To 'the Bishop of a Respectable Church']," *The Christian Baptist* 1, no. 11 (June 7, 1824): 70–72.

[45] Campbell, "To Mr. Robert Cautious," 53–54.

[46] For general information on the enormity of the enterprise, see Foster, *An Errand of Mercy*; Wilbert R. Shenk, "Introduction," in *North American Foreign Missions, 1810–1914: Theology, Theory, and Policy*, ed. Wilbert R. Shenk, Studies in the History of Christian Missions (Grand Rapids: Eerdmans, 2004), 4, n8.

[47] Foster, *An Errand of Mercy*, 121, 275–79.

Foreign Missions had the eighth highest income of the benevolent societies for the fiscal year 1826–1827.[48] In 1826, Alexander said the popular mentality about missions was

> that if the church had the bank of the United States, that of London, and Paris, it could, in twenty years, convert the whole world. . . . While such is the spirit breathed from the pulpit and from the press, there exist ten thousand good reasons for lifting up our voices like a trumpet, crying aloud, and sparing not.[49]

Like his Baptist counterparts, Campbell opposed missionary societies because they were not "authorized" in the New Testament. Historian Michael Casey traced the development of the Campbells' hermeneutic as they worked out the restoration implications of the *Declaration and Address*. As Alexander developed his patternist hermeneutic during his 1820 and 1823 debates and his publication of the *Christian Baptist* (1823 on), he focused on a restoration of only those beliefs and practices found in the New Testament.[50] Although the *Declaration and Address* did suggest silence in the New Testament was prohibitive, it was a minor emphasis.[51] In *The Christian Baptist*, Campbell usually (though not always) argued that silence in Scripture on a practice meant it should be prohibited.[52] As he concluded for moral societies by 1820, he eventually also concluded that the absence of missionary societies in the New Testament meant they were

---

[48] Ibid., 121–22.

[49] Alexander Campbell, "A Restoration of the Ancient Order of Things—No. XII. The Bishop's Office—No. I," *The Christian Baptist* 3, no. 9 (April 3, 1826): 232.

[50] Casey, *The Battle Over Hermeneutics*, 263–64. Alexander reprinted an article that argued, "[the primitive Christians'] example is as the law to Christians of all ages; for they acted under the eye and instruction of the apostles, to whom the Lord Jesus said, 'He that hears you hears me.'" "Abuses of Christianity," *The Christian Baptist* 1, no. 4 (November 3, 1823): 28.

[51] Thomas Campbell, *Declaration and Address of the Christian Association of Washington* (Washington: printed by Brown & Sample, 1809), 16–17; Thomas H. Olbricht, "Hermeneutics and the *Declaration and Address*," in *The Quest for Christian Unity, Peace, and Purity in Thomas Campbell's Declaration and Address: Text and Studies*, eds. Thomas H. Olbricht and Hans Rollmann, ATLA Monograph Series 46 (Lanham: Scarecrow Press, 2000), 248.

[52] Casey, *The Battle Over Hermeneutics*, 51–96; Humble, "The Missionary Society Controversy in the Restoration Movement (1823–1875)," 27–33. In 1825, Alexander wrote, "it belongs to every individual and to every congregation of individuals to discard from their faith and their practice every thing that is not found written in the New Testament . . . and to believe and practice whatever is there enjoined. This done, and every thing is done which ought to be done." See Campbell, "A Restoration of the Ancient Order of Things—No. II," 133.

unauthorized for the church.⁵³ Campbell's development in hermeneutics goes a long way in explaining his change from approbation to disapproval of missionary societies.

Among the most persistent of Alexander's contentions with missionary societies was his belief that they perpetuated sectarianism, and subsequently hindered Christian unity and the conversion of the world. Like many evangelical missions writings, Thomas's *Declaration and Address* argued that divisions among Christians were evil, and that they hindered the witness of Christianity to the world.⁵⁴ As already noted about the *Declaration and Address*, the Campbells envisioned something like a three-piece domino effect: restore primitive Christianity, Christian unity would ensue, and then the conversion of the world would follow.⁵⁵ Alexander believed this simple system was clear in John 17:20–21:

> 'Neither pray I for these (the Apostles) alone, but for them also which shall believe on me through their word, that they may be one; as you, Father, are in me and I to you, that they also may be one in us, that the world may believe that you have sent me.' *John* xvii. 20, 21[.] This is God's plan for union and for the conversion of the world. . . . We are constantly praying and laboring for the conversion of sinners among us, and for the conversion of the heathen; but as long as we retain our sectarian divisions, God is bound to his Son, as far as these divisions are concerned, not to hear our prayers nor bless our exertions. . . . Should our prayers and exertions be heard, and blessed, in the present state of division and disunion . . . the Lord Jesus Christ would be dishonored, his truth would fail.⁵⁶

Campbell interpreted John 17 to mean that God's plan—the only valid plan—for the conversion of the world was Christian unity. Missionary societies worked against Christian unity because they were

---

⁵³ Casey, *The Battle Over Hermeneutics*, 263–64; Campbell, "The Christian Religion"; Campbell, "To Mr. Robert Cautious," 53–54.
⁵⁴ Campbell, *Declaration and Address*, 53–54.
⁵⁵ Richard T. Hughes and C. Leonard Allen, *Illusions of Innocence: Protestant Primitivism in America, 1630–1875* (Abilene, TX: Abilene Christian University Press, 2008), 109; Hiram Van Kirk, *A History of the Theology of the Disciples of Christ* (St. Louis: Christian Publishing Company, 1907), 109–24.
⁵⁶ Christian Union, "Christian Union–No. II," *The Christian Baptist* 3, no. 1 (August 1, 1825): 173.

spreading denominationalism, rather than working toward Christian unity.[57] Consequently, the missionary societies and their advocates were opposed to the Lord's plan for the conversion of the world, and their attempts to evangelize the world were futile.[58] The shift away from interdenominational societies such as the London Missionary Society, Evangelical Society of Ulster, and Christian Association of Washington to predominately denominational missionary societies took place across the transatlantic in the 1820s and 1830s—the Campbells encountered these denominational societies in the 1810s and 1820s, and Alexander concluded they were means to sectarian division, rather than to unity.

Although the Campbells stressed that Christian unity was the means for conversion of the world, Alexander did offer a patternist proposal for foreign missions. The proper way to spread the gospel to the world, Campbell argued, was through the local church, as it was "the only institution of God left on earth to illuminate and reform the world."[59] He suggested that if a church of twenty people immigrated to a "heathen" land,

> where they would support themselves like the natives, wear the same garb, adopt the country as their own . . . ; should such a society sit down and hold forth in word and deed the saving truth, not deriding the gods nor the religion of the natives, but allowing their own works and example to speak for their religion . . . ; we are persuaded that, in process of time a more solid foundation for the conversion of the natives would be laid, and more actual success resulting, than from all the missionaries employed for twenty-five years. Such a course would have some

---

[57] It is important to note here that, according to Foster, only four of the top fourteen benevolent societies at this time were under denominational control. The ten that were not associated with a denomination accounted for 91 percent of the total revenues of the top fourteen—so the interdenominational voluntary society continued in popularity at this time, even if denominations took over the missionary wing of Protestantism. See Foster, *An Errand of Mercy*, 122.

[58] Alexander Campbell, "The Conversion of the World," *The Christian Baptist* 1, no. 6 (January 5, 1824): 42; Campbell, "A Restoration of the Ancient Order of Things—No. II," 135.

[59] Alexander Campbell, "Remarks on Missionaries," *The Christian Baptist* 1, no. 2 (September 1, 1823): 13–17. This conclusion of Alexander's was based on a long line of reasoning about cessation of miraculous gifts: (1) biblical missionaries had miraculous gifts that accredited their mission as of divine origin; (2) those gifts ceased and were no longer necessary because the gospel was preached to the whole world by the end of the apostolic age; (3) modern missionaries were unauthorized because they lacked miracles and success; (4) the local church is "the only institution of God left on earth to illuminate and reform the world."

warrant from scripture; but the present has proved itself to be all human.[60]

Campbell thought Christianity was a social religion and, therefore, pagan cultures were unlikely to accept it through the missionary model of sending one or two people. Rather, when the pagans saw the congregational church in their midst, then they would more likely understand and accept Christianity. But Campbell was not always consistent on this point. For example, just four months after this proposal of congregational missions, he published a short article that implied individual missionaries could be legitimate, that they were called by God so long as they were successful and did not ask for permission or financial support from any board of missions.[61] He was susceptible to such inconsistencies in a short span of time because his writings were situational, rather than systematic. Regardless of inconsistencies, Campbell made clear his distaste for the missionary enterprise in numerous *Christian Baptist* articles from 1823 to 1827.

In 1827, the Campbell-led Mahoning Baptist Association made its most important contribution to missions practices when it hired Walter Scott as an itinerant preacher. The Campbells had been acquainted with leaders of the Mahoning Baptist Association since at least 1821. Therefore, when Alexander had a falling out with the Redstone Baptist Association in 1824, the church where he ministered in Wellsburg, West Virginia, joined the Mahoning Association.[62] Walter Scott was a good friend of the Campbells, and was a leader of the Campbell Movement in Pittsburgh and Ohio. At the 1827 Mahoning meeting, one of the churches made a typical request that the Association consider employing "an evangelical preacher . . . to travel and teach among the churches."[63] The Association chose Walter Scott for the job, and requested for member churches to make "voluntary and

---

[60] Ibid., 16–17; Alexander Campbell, "[Reply to Mr. Robert Cautious]," *The Christian Baptist* 1, no. 5 (December 1, 1823): 34. In the latter article, Campbell suggested the same thing for distributing Bibles—it should be done by local churches rather than associations of churches, because only the local church could illumine the world.

[61] Alexander Campbell, "Queries," *The Christian Baptist* 1, no. 8 (March 1, 1824): 54.

[62] *Minutes of the Mahoning Baptist Association* in Mary Agnes Monroe Smith, "A History of the Mahoning Baptist Association" (master's thesis, West Virginia University, 1943), Appendix C, 24.

[63] Ibid., Appendix C, 37.

liberal contributions ... for creating a fund for his support."[64] Alexander reported the news in the *Christian Baptist*:

> The Mahoning Regular Baptist Association ... agreed to support ... a messenger of the churches, who is to labor every day for one entire year ... in the word and doctrine, amongst the churches in the Association. He is to proclaim the word to those without, and to teach those within to walk in the Lord. Brother Walter Scott, who is now in the field, accepted of the appointment.[65]

Scott's identity in Campbell's mind as an itinerant home missionary "in the field" becomes clearer later in the same article. Campbell critiqued the amount of resources used on foreign missions "while millions at home demand more energies than all now employed to ameliorate their condition."[66] Scott was a home missionary proclaiming "the word to those without" the church. The Mahoning Baptist Association minutes reveal that Alexander was a primary leader of the Association by 1827, and the above *Christian Baptist* article discloses his support of the Association's action. Yet, Campbell had come to see an "evangelist" as a New Testament officer supported by one or more congregations to preach the gospel, baptize converts, organize congregations, and teach assembled Christians until they could elect elders.[67] Although hiring Scott as a frontier "messenger" employed by the Association was normal for Baptist associational missions,[68] it was a significant step toward extra-congregational missionary efforts in the Campbell Movement.

Scott's evangelistic tool, the five-finger exercise, was influential on missions practices, overall expansion, and soteriology in the Campbell

---

[64] Ibid., Appendix C, 38–39.

[65] Alexander Campbell, "Miscellaneous Letters—No. I," *The Christian Baptist* 5, no. 3 (October 1, 1827): 382.

[66] Ibid.

[67] D. Newell Williams, Douglas A. Foster, and Paul M. Blowers, eds., *The Stone-Campbell Movement: A Global History* (St. Louis: Chalice Press, 2013), 24; Campbell, "A Restoration of the Ancient Order of Things, No. XII. The Bishop's Office, No. 1," 231–33; Alexander Campbell, "A Restoration of the Ancient Order of Things, No. XIX. The Deacon's Office," *The Christian Baptist* 4, no. 10 (May 7, 1827): 335–36; Alexander Campbell, "A Restoration of the Ancient Order of Things, No. XXXII. Official Names and Titles." *The Christian Baptist* 7, no. 2 (September 7, 1829): 585–86.

[68] Chaney, *The Birth of Missions in America*, 170–72.

Movement. Scott is credited with packaging the Campbells' ideas about faith as rational belief in testimony and baptism for the remission of sins into a memorable "plan of salvation" or, as it came to be known, the five-finger exercise: have faith, repent, be baptized, receive remission of sins, and receive the gift of the Holy Spirit and eternal life.[69] Scott's concise formula for conversion was well-received by frontier people looking for assurance of salvation through their own personal decisions. The Campbells' view of faith and conversion and their sacramental view of baptism distanced them from the evangelical new birth experience they had earlier embraced and experienced.[70] Scott baptized around one thousand people that first year as an evangelist. He continued such industrious evangelism throughout his life, and the Campbell Movement expanded rapidly thereafter.[71]

In the 1820s, the Campbells made a 180-degree turn from their earlier interdenominational approach of evangelical missions to an anti-denominational approach of *The Christian Baptist*. The Campbells' take on Christian unity made proselytization of Christians in denominations a prominent feature of their evangelization. If conversion of the world depended on Christians assenting to the Campbells' New Testament pattern of Christianity, persuading other Christians to join them was crucial. Baptists became one of the primary targets, as the Campbells had made many friends among Baptists in Pittsburgh, Philadelphia, New Jersey, New York, and all over the western frontier.[72] But whether Baptists, Methodists,

---

[69] Peter M. Morgan, "Five Finger Exercise," ed. Douglas A. Foster et al., *The Encyclopedia of the Stone-Campbell Movement* (Grand Rapids: Eerdmans, 2004), 338–39; M. Eugene Boring, *Disciples and the Bible: A History of Disciples Biblical Interpretation in North America* (St. Louis: Chalice Press, 1997), 41.

[70] The focus of the Campbell Movement on faith and baptism was another reason later historians have missed the evangelical missionary movement origins. In the 1820s, when Alexander began debating in public and publishing the *Christian Baptist*, he had moved far away from both evangelicalism and its missionary movement. It is little wonder Alexander forgot the influence, and misdirected later historians as well.

[71] Williams, Foster, and Blowers, *The Stone-Campbell Movement: A Global History*, 25; Thomas H. Olbricht, "Missions and Evangelization Prior to 1848," *Discipliana* 58, no. 3 (Fall 1998): 77; A. S. Hayden, *Early History of the Disciples in the Western Reserve, Ohio; with Biographical Sketches of the Principal Agents in Their Religious Movement* (Cincinnati: Chase & Hall Publishers, 1875), 72–87; Richardson, *Memoirs of Alexander Campbell*, 1890, 2:173–76.

[72] The Campbell Movement and Stone's "Christians" probably made proselytes of at least ten thousand Baptists before 1830. For example, they stole John Rogers from the Baptists, and by 1828, Rogers had "capsized" 1,500 more Baptists and continued proselytizing them. Bill Humble claims that by 1830, the Campbell "movement had churches scattered over several states with 12,000 to 20,000 members, most of them ex-Baptists." See Humble, "The Missionary Society Controversy in the Restoration Movement (1823–1875)," 16; Thomas Campbell, "Constitution of a Congregation in Ohio," *The Christian Baptist* 5, no. 12 (July 7, 1828): 457; Lee, "Background to *The Christian Baptist*," 15–21; Mark G. Toulouse, "Christian

Presbyterians, or other denominations, the Campbells and their followers proselytized anyone willing to listen to what they saw as an irrefutable system of Christianity based only on the New Testament. Scott's packaging of the gospel in five fingers and its subsequent success was unprecedented in the Campbell Movement. To members of this Movement, the accomplishments were a sign of God's blessing on these new ideas and practices. But those ideas and practices had transformed into something far different from their beginnings in transatlantic evangelical missions.

A number of religious, political, and economic issues help explain the Campbells' rejection of missionary societies in the 1820s. The Campbells were one part of a larger antimissions movement that was concentrated among Baptists.[73] The development of the Campbells' restoration hermeneutic took center stage following the Christian Association of Washington years. As the Campbells moved in a patternist direction like some of their earlier evangelical acquaintances had done, they usually viewed silence as prohibitive. Therefore, they eventually rejected missionary societies because they were not authorized in the New Testament. Furthermore, Alexander's public writing to promote a New Testament reformation in the genre of *The Christian Baptist* pushed his message in an iconoclastic and critical direction. As the missionary enterprise became enormous and promoted the spread of denominational Christianity rather than New Testament Christianity, the vitriolic pages of *The Christian Baptist* were destined to attack it.

Other important influences and developments that led the Campbells to change their position on missionary societies included

- the "anti-evangelical" and "anti-constitutional" moral societies;
- the large amount of money being raised by the missionary societies and their seemingly disproportionate numerical success;
- the mentality that more money was the answer to successful missions;
- the focus on foreign missions to the neglect of home needs;
- alleged irresponsible behavior of home and foreign missionaries;

Century, The," ed. Douglas A. Foster et al., *The Encyclopedia of the Stone-Campbell Movement* (Grand Rapids: Eerdmans, 2004).

[73] For the antimission movement, see James R. Mathis, *The Making of the Primitive Baptists: A Cultural and Intellectual History of the Antimission Movement, 1800–1840* (New York: Routledge, 2004).

- missionary societies, perpetuating of denominational sectarian division and thus opposing of unity; and
- the Campbells' belief that the conversion of the world would be a direct result of Christian unity.

The Campbells consistently promoted what Thomas articulated in the *Declaration and Address*: if Christians united, then the witness of the church as a united body would stimulate the conversion of the world. They arrived at this conclusion from the influence of evangelical missions and their interpretation of Jesus's prayer in John 17:20–21. About these verses, Alexander said, "This is God's plan for union and for the conversion of the world." The Campbells concluded that the missionary societies worked against Christian unity because they perpetuated sectarianism and, therefore, obstructed the Lord's plan for converting the world.

However, the Campbells started their journey back toward supporting missionary societies in 1827, and set the stage for a historiography of omitting the early evangelical missions influence on them. The need for ministers on the frontier led the Campbells and the Mahoning Baptist Association to hire Scott as a home missionary, and Scott's success made adherents believe that New Testament Christianity was the means to Christian unity and the conversion of the world. This success in extra-congregational cooperation led Alexander to write at length in the 1830s and 1840s about the legitimacy of extra-congregational cooperation, which he seemed to oppose in *The Christian Baptist*. The Campbells' missions ideas oscillated from their early support of missionary societies to Alexander's rejection of them and back to circumspect support of cooperative home missions, making the Campbells' missions history in the United States a history of ambivalence. As irony, pragmatism, and ambivalence would have it, in 1849 Alexander became the president of the American Christian Missionary Society, the Stone-Campbell Movement's own national missionary society for world evangelization. The American Christian Missionary Society eventually became one of the major causes of the first division in the Stone-Campbell Movement—some adherents looked to *The Christian Baptist* opposition to "unauthorized" missionary societies, while others pointed to Campbell as president of the American Christian Missionary Society and viewed missionary societies as expedient. Due to this scenario, which led to a significant division in the Movement, missions historians sought to explain why Campbell moved from anti-missionary society in 1823 to pro-missionary society later. This emphasis led to a neglect of the previous two decades of significant Stone-Campbell Movement missions history, which roots the very origins of the Campbell Movement in evangelical missions.[74]

CONCLUSION

The Campbells supported missions into the early 1820s, but numerous factors led them to reject missionary societies for a period of time, beginning in 1823. Alexander rejected missionary societies in *The Christian Baptist*, explaining that he changed his position because he encountered abuses of what had become an enormous system running on the assumption that money, rather than unity, would lead to world conversion. Furthermore, a hermeneutic that authorized only those beliefs and practices for which there were New Testament commands or examples, coupled with silence in the New Testament as prohibitive, led Alexander to oppose moral societies by 1820 and missionary and other societies by 1823. The Campbells believed John 17:20-21 provided God's plan for Christian unity as the prerequisite to the conversion of the world. As denominations took over the transatlantic missionary societies in the 1820s, the Campbells argued that they disseminated denominational sectarianism, rather than pure and united New Testament Christianity.

---

[74] Doug Priest, "Missionary Societies, Controversy Over," ed. Douglas A. Foster et al., *The Encyclopedia of the Stone-Campbell Movement* (Grand Rapids: Eerdmans, 2004), 534–36; Dennis W. Helsabeck, "Societies," ibid., 691–92; William J. Nottingham, "American Christian Missionary Society," ibid., 24–26; Paul Allen Williams, "Missions, Missiology," ibid., 537–42.

Chapter Eight

CONCLUSION: THE CAMPBELL MOVEMENT'S ROOTS IN TRANSATLANTIC EVANGELICAL MISSIONS

THIS BOOK HAS DEMONSTRATED THAT THE CAMPBELL MOVEMENT emerged from the transatlantic evangelical missionary movement. That is, the Campbells' early ideals and practices, as expressed in 1809, were not unique among transatlantic evangelicals of the era. Common features included

- a simple evangelical Christianity, devoid of "partyism," that served as a primitive basis for interdenominational cooperation;
- interdenominational cooperation in voluntary societies for evangelization;
- evangelization through itinerant preaching, education, and distribution of Bibles and tracts; and
- a millennial view of the times, which served as further motive for missions.

Both Campbells experienced their religious formation in the transatlantic evangelicalism that flourished around them. Thomas's Christian Association of Washington and its *Declaration and Address* were reproductions of other evangelical missionary society charters, plans, organizations, ideals, and means of evangelization.

Interdenominational cooperation among Christians in various denominations was a major feature from the beginning of the Protestant missionary movement, and missions advocates were able to work together for a number of reasons. The novelty of early Protestant missions created an exciting atmosphere that was charged with eschatological meaning and featured a tightknit community of mission-minded people. Furthermore, many came to view interdenominational missions as the primary goal of Christian activism in a world that needed a simple gospel shorn of denominational bigotry. The common viewing of the indigenous as "heathen" and of other world religions as evil provided powerful motivation for the missionary movement. Postmillennial eschatology directly connected Christian unity, world missions, pity for the "heathen," and the eschaton. United missions to the "heathen" were obvious signs that participants lived in the last days. Early missions advocates utilized Protestant agreement on the idea that Scripture was superior to later traditions, which provided space for Christians affiliated with diverse Protestant traditions to cooperate for the spread of a primitive evangelical gospel. Missionary advocates did not always agree on what this primitive core was, and some did not define it. Some evangelicals utilized the primitive gospel ideal to endorse a pragmatic ecumenism for missions, whereas others—such as John Walker, the Haldanes, and the Campbells—developed missions primitivism into a patternist restorationism. The latter group often became Independents (i.e., Congregationalists) or Baptists, though each individual and group developed primitivism in different ways, depending on innumerable contextual variables in each case.

The evangelical revival, inextricably connected to the rise of the Protestant missionary movement, provided another rallying point and justification for cooperation based on the idea of new birth experience as the fundamental marker of a "real" Christian and of primitive Christianity. Evangelicals also created the interdenominational concerts of prayer for missions, a structure that ignited missions fervor and provided formative, embodied, ritual experiences that shaped the conscious and subconscious of individuals and groups. Finally, many drew on Enlightenment thinkers' ideas of toleration as grounds for cooperation on the primitive gospel. New economic models and Enlightenment thinkers provided the justification for the voluntary society, which became the structure through which evangelicals across denominations cooperated to transform Christianity and transatlantic culture through its "united front" or "benevolent empire" in the nineteenth century. One or some combination of these grounds for interdenominational cooperation, all of which permeated evangelical missions, made cooperation legitimate for many people; Thomas Campbell even argued in 1809 that cooperation was a Christian duty.

Thomas and Alexander Campbell founded an evangelical missionary society in the United States, the Christian Association of Washington, based on the evangelical societies and advocates that influenced them in Ireland and Scotland. Prior, they participated in the creation and perpetuation of evangelical missions in the nearby areas of Armagh and Rich Hill, Ireland, which were centers of interdenominational missions. Thomas cofounded one of the most influential interdenominational evangelical voluntary societies in Ireland during the 1790s, the Evangelical Society of Ulster, and defended its legitimacy before the Antiburgher Presbyterian Synod. Thomas and Alexander heard famous evangelicals preach in Ireland and Scotland, and held private conversations with some of them. Thomas founded the Christian Association of Washington in 1809 on the model and with the goals of evangelical societies, and he planted this organization in the unique frontier and democratic context of Western Pennsylvania. Alexander eagerly joined in the Association's mission after spending more than half a year under the mentorship of Greville Ewing, one of the leading evangelical missions advocates in Scotland, and he acquired from the University of Glasgow the scholarly tools that aided his work as an itinerant for the Christian Association of Washington and in later leadership of the Campbell Movement.

From the 1790s to the 1820s, the missions culture and some of its major advocates influenced the development of the Campbell Movement in patternist restoration directions. Many restorationists in missions were key influences on Alexander's attempts to flesh out the patternist restorationism articulated in the *Declaration and Address*. He drew especially on John

Walker, the Haldanes, and other Scottish sources that the missionary schools of Greville Ewing and the Haldanes utilized, such as Robert Sandeman and John Glas. All these influences, planted in the context of the Pennsylvania frontier, led the Campbells to associate eventually with Baptists, following a path similar to other evangelical missions advocates. The Campbells' restorationism led them to accept believer's baptism by immersion and to associate with Baptists for a turbulent period from 1812 to 1830. The Campbells continued supporting missions until at least 1821, but similar to a number of Baptists at the time, Alexander launched vigorous opposition to missionary societies in 1823.

Transatlantic evangelical missions provide a clear context for understanding the emergence of the Campbell Movement in 1809, as manifested in the Christian Association of Washington and its *Declaration and Address*. It not only illuminates historical explanations for both, but also brings together the various historiographical tributaries of Campbell Movement origins into one contextual river. The focus of the Christian Association of Washington on unity, anti-sectarianism, restoration, mission, millennialism, Enlightenment tolerance, individual interpretation, itinerant preaching, Bible distribution, and voluntary societies were key parts of the evangelical missions culture. Both Campbells absorbed a particular historical and contextual version of evangelical Christianity in Ireland and Scotland, and they planted it in the United States. This transatlantic perspective need not diminish the importance of the frontier and democratic context in which the Campbells planted their evangelical missionary movement heritage, nor does it need to dictate the development of the Campbell Movement in that context. Instead, evangelical missions illuminate the vision of the world and of Christianity with which the Campbell Movement began in the United States. The Presbyterian conflicts, the frontier, and democratic contexts of Western Pennsylvania in the early nineteenth century proved immeasurably important in the early shaping of the Campbell Movement. Nonetheless, when the Campbell Movement began in earnest, with the founding of the Christian Association of Washington and publication of the *Declaration and Address*, the Movement was a child of transatlantic evangelical missions. The Campbells' early writings evince that they were at least partly aware of this heritage.

Conclusion: The Campbell Movement's Roots in Transatlantic Evangelical Missions

This book strives to push historiography of the Stone-Campbell Movement and U.S. religious history to take stock of these influences in the future, depicting the Campbell tradition as emerging from transatlantic evangelical missions that eventually developed in (rather than being created by) a unique context on the U.S. frontier, influenced by the democratic milieu of the early national period. Transatlantic evangelical missions provide a comprehensive and transnational context for understanding the origins of the Campbell Movement. This historical perspective of the Campbells shows that their vision of Christianity and proposals for unity and restoration were shared by a group of evangelicals in a specific historical missionary movement. As I have argued elsewhere:

> This view of origins moves historiography away from compartmentalized or one-sided focus on either Scottish restoration, Lockean unity, or over-emphasis on the frontier or democratization as the key influences or contexts that created the Campbells. It pushes beyond historical inquiry restricted to one nation-state or one denomination. It also critiques triumphalist versions of the Campbells which depict them as unique in their earliest ideas and inaccurately portray Campbell's *Declaration and Address* as a new development for Christian unity and restoration. In fact, Campbell's *Declaration and Address* appeared over a decade after the first transatlantic publications of its kind; and the ideas at the foundation of Campbell's document emanated from an evangelical missions culture that had existed for more than one hundred years.[1]

This historiographical revision offers a more globally aware and holistic reading of the early Campbell documents. The Campbells, with all the people who were part of the interdenominational missionary movement that arose throughout the eighteenth century and exploded in the 1790s, were riding a wave of eschatological missionary enthusiasm that led them to attempt to minimize differences so they could cooperate to spread a primitive and simple evangelical gospel at home and abroad.

---

[1] James L. Gorman, "The Omission of Missions: Transatlantic Evangelical Missions Culture and the Historiography of the Campbell Movement's Origins," *Stone-Campbell Journal, forthcoming.*

When we read the sources relevant to the early Campbell Movement with transatlantic evangelical missions in mind, it becomes clear that historians have not fully understood the context and influences animating the Campbells' earliest ideas and actions. Two decades of Campbell support of the missionary enterprise (before the anti-missionary writings of 1823) have been almost entirely omitted from previous historical narratives. Exploring those two decades in light of the missionary movement illustrates the sway of transatlantic evangelical missions upon the early Campbell Movement. Accounting for the extraordinary shift in Alexander Campbell's view on missionary societies by the 1820s demonstrates how substantially and swiftly the new Campbell hermeneutic, public reformation program, and U.S. contextual variables shaped the religious thought and reform practices of the Campbell tradition. The Campbell hermeneutic and reformation program had, by the 1820s, become fixated on restoring the "pattern" of Christian beliefs and practices found in the New Testament, and on questioning authorities that threatened individual liberty of interpretation. This move, which in interdenominational missions transformed pragmatic primitivism for the result of ecumenical cooperation into a sectarian primitivism for the result of a restored New Testament church, happened in many cases; several of the Campbells' acquaintances and influences made similar journeys from pragmatic primitivism to sectarian primitivism. That is, although the U.S. context enormously influenced what the Campbell Movement became by the 1820s, a transatlantic purview and attention to earliest years demonstrates that the first ideas and practices of the Campbell Movement emerged from transatlantic evangelical missions and not from anything uniquely American.

Postscript

VIEWING CAMPBELL MOVEMENT CHURCHES THROUGH A NEW LENS

THIS STUDY REVEALS A TROUBLING IRONY: BICKERING OVER cooperation in missionary societies has been one of the central themes of the Stone-Campbell Movement, a tradition which emerged from a missionary movement focused on unity. The three major streams of the Movement today all look to the Campbell Movement as foundational to their respective traditions, yet one of the major reasons these three streams exist, instead of only one, is division over opinions on missionary societies. The first division in the Stone-Campbell Movement had the missionary society of 1849 at its heart, though differing hermeneutical views and sectional conflict drove the disagreements. And the proper level of cooperation with other denominations in the worldwide missionary endeavor was at the center of the second division in the twentieth century, though the Fundamentalist-Modernist Controversy also influenced that division. Ironically, twice the Stone-Campbell Movement has divided at least in part because of disagreements on missions, whereas the Campbell tradition emerged from a missionary movement grounded in Christian cooperation among all denominations, based on a simple evangelical gospel.

Churches in the Stone-Campbell Movement today ought to question how significantly its history, along with the history of their own congregations, would be different if the historical origins of the Campbell Movement had not been lost for so long. Certainly, the narrative that has driven almost all the history of missions in the Stone-Campbell Movement would have been very different. According to that narrative, a "first" Alexander Campbell opposed missionary societies in the 1820s, and then a "second" Campbell came to accept missionary societies, and became the first president of the American Christian Missionary societies in 1849. Historians have asked, "How and why did this shift happen?" Furthermore, congregations and Stone-Campbell Movement adherents have constructed entire traditions based upon one or the other of these Campbells. One segment, the Churches of Christ, found a usable history in the "first" Campbell, who was right to oppose missionary societies because they represented extra-congregational cooperation that was unbiblical in origin and denominational in direction. Another stream, the Independent Christian Churches, liked the "second" Campbell, but came to oppose a centralized structure for missions when it meant they were going to accept as full members those who had not been immersed. Of course, the earliest Campbell Movement not only advocated cooperation among all denominations who would accept the New Testament as the only term of communion, but its adherents had also not been immersed. The Christian Church (Disciples of Christ) largely left these issues in the past, as it embraced an open and inclusive ecumenical missionary model.

All the Stone-Campbell Movement streams have something to learn from the history told in the preceding pages. At the very root of the Movement was a belief that Christians have a duty to cooperate with Christians in other denominations for missions. This prods those segments of the Movement who have completely rejected cooperation with other denominations, or even with other Stone-Campbell Movement congregations, to reconsider their own historical development and how they got to a place so different from anything Thomas Campbell envisioned at the beginning of the Movement. For those segments of the Movement who have attempted to cling only to restoration or only to unity, this history is instructive. Although tensions between these two ideals of unity and restoration were natural, the culture from which the Campbells emerged held the two ideals of primitivism and Christian unity as mutually dependent—neither could survive without the other. And for those segments who practice congregationally autonomous missions and refuse to cooperate with other Christians, the earliest impetus of the Movement is worth considering.

In 1809, Thomas Campbell argued that cooperation with Christians in other denominations was a Christian duty. The historical development of the early Campbell Movement led it away from its ecumenical roots in evangelical missions into a sectarian restorationism in the 1820s, and back into something more cooperative by the 1840s. At the very least, the history produced here provides a corrective to the traditional narrative of the "first" anti-missionary society Alexander Campbell of the 1820s—that was, in fact, the "second" Campbell. The "first" Campbell(s) and the earliest articulations of the Campbell Movement were products of the interdenominational evangelical missionary movement, characterized by cooperation and interdenominationalism, that captivated many Protestants in the transatlantic for three decades (1790s to 1820s). These vibrant roots provide a corrective to old narratives, ones that embraced exclusion and sectarianism, as the original vision of the Campbells; they also provide the riches of a usable Christian past for Stone-Campbell Movement adherents.

BIBLIOGRAPHY

I. Primary Sources

I. A. Primary Sources: Periodicals
The Christian Baptist
The Evangelical Magazine
The Millennial Harbinger
The Missionary Magazine

I. B. Primary Sources: Manuscripts, Books, and Articles
An Account of the London Missionary Society, Extracted from Dr. Rippon's Baptist Annual Register. Philadelphia: printed by Lang & Ustick, 1796.
Acts and Proceedings of the Associate Synod of North America. Associate Synod of North America Minutes, 1801–1821. Call Number MF 9. Philadelphia: Presbyterian Historical Society.
American Baptist Foreign Mission Society. *Proceedings of the Baptist Convention for Missionary Purposes–Held in Philadelphia, in May, 1814*. Philadelphia: printed for the Convention by Ann Coles, 1814.
Bible Christian Book Committee. *A Collection of Hymns, For the Use of the People Called Bible Christians*. 2nd ed. Plymouth: printed by S. Thorne, 1863.
Bogue, David. "Objections Against A Mission to the Heathen, Stated and Considered." In *Sermons, Preached in London, at the Formation of the Missionary Society, September 22, 23, 24, 1795; To Which Are Prefixed, Memorials, Respecting the Establishment and First Attempts of That Society*, 120–158. London: printed and sold by T. Chapman, 1795.
Campbell, Alexander. "Disciples of Christ," edited by J. Newton Brown. *Encyclopedia of Religious Knowledge*. Brattleboro: Brattleboro' Typographic Company, 1838. Accessed August 11, 2015. http://web.archive.org/web/20111208232724/http://www.mun.ca/rels/restmov/texts/acampbell/doc-erk.htm.
Campbell, Alexander, and Thomas Campbell. *Memoirs of Elder Thomas Campbell, Together with A Brief Memoir of Mrs. Jane Campbell*. Cincinnati: H. S. Bosworth, 1861.

Campbell, Alexander, and Keith B. Huey. *The Candidus Essays By Alexander Campbell: First Published in* The Reporter, *Washington, Pa., 1820–1822*, edited by Keith B. Huey. n.p.: Keith B. Huey, 2001. Accessed July 29, 2015. http://web.archive.org/web/20120114230913/http://www.mun.ca/rels/restmov/texts/acampbell/ce/ce00a.htm.

Campbell, Alexander, and Lester G. McAllister. *Alexander Campbell at the University of Glasgow 1808–1809*. Nashville: Disciples of Christ Historical Society, 1971.

Campbell, Thomas. *Declaration and Address of the Christian Association of Washington*. Washington: printed by Brown & Sample, 1809.

Campbell Papers. T. W. Phillips Memorial Library Archives and Special Collections. Bethany: Bethany College.

Carey, William. *An Enquiry into the Obligations of Christians, to Use Means for the Conversion of the Heathens*. Leicester: printed and sold by Ann Ireland, 1792.

Centinel of Freedom. "[Last Tuesday]." *Centinel of Freedom* News/Opinion section. Newark: November 9, 1796.

Coke, Thomas. *An Address to the Pious and Benevolent, Proposing an Annual Subscription for the Support of Missionaries in the Highlands and Adjacent Islands of Scotland, the Isles of Jersey, Guernsey, and Newfoundland, the West Indies, and the Provinces of Nova Scotia and Quebec*. London: n.p., 1786.

Cooper, William. *Daniel's Seventy Weeks. A Second Sermon Preached at Sion-Chapel, on Sunday Afternoon, September 18, 1796, to the Jews*. London: printed by T. Chapman, 1796.

———. "Documentary Notices of the Dublin and Ulster Evangelical Societies." In *The Irish Congregational Record*, 1:224–231. Dublin: John Robertson and Company, 1834.

———. *The Flying Angel: A Sermon, Delivered in the New Meeting House Armagh, Ireland, before the Committee of the Evangelical Society of Ulster, on Monday, the 27th of May, 1799*. London: printed by S. Rousseau for T. Chapman, 1799.

———. *The Promised Seed. A Sermon, Preached to God's Ancient Israel the Jews, at Sion-Chapel, Whitechapel, on Sunday Afternoon, August 28, 1796*. London: printed by T. Chapman, 1796.

Edwards, Jonathan. *A History of the Work of Redemption: Containing the Outlines of a Body of Divinity in a Method Entirely New*. Boston: reprinted by Draper and Folsom, 1782.

———. *An Humble Attempt to Promote Explicit Agreement and Visible Union of God's People in Extraordinary Prayer for the Revival of Religion and the Advancement of Christ's Kingdom on Earth, Pursuant to Scripture-Promises and Prophecies Concerning the Last Time*. Boston: printed for D. Henchman in Cornhill, 1747.

———. "Sinners in the Hands of an Angry God." In *Jonathan Edwards's* Sinners in the Hands of an Angry God: *A Casebook*, edited by Wilson H. Kimnach,

Caleb J. D. Maskell, and Kenneth P. Minkema. New Haven: Yale University Press, 2010.

Ewing, Greville. *A Defence of Itinerant and Field Preaching: A Sermon, Preached before the Society for Gratis Sabbath Schools, on the 24th of December 1797, in Lady Glenorchy's Chapel, Edinburgh*. Edinburgh: printed by J. Ritchie, 1799.

———. *A Defence of Missions from Christian Societies to the Heathen World: A Sermon, Preached before the Edinburgh Missionary Society, on Thursday, Feb. 2, 1797*. Edinburgh: printed by J. Ritchie, 1797.

Ewing, Greville, and Robert Haldane. *Facts and Documents Respecting the Connections Which Have Subsisted between Robert Haldane, Esq. and Greville Ewing, Laid before the Public, in Consequence of Letters Which the Former Has Addressed to the Latter, Respecting the Tabernacle at Glasgow*. Glasgow: printed by James Hedderwick, 1809.

Foster, Jacob Kirkman. *The Life and Times of Selina, Countess of Huntingdon*. 2 vols. London: W. E. Painter, 1839.

General Assembly of the Church of Scotland. *The Principal Acts of the General Assembly of the Church of Scotland, Convened at Edinburgh, the 23d Day of May 1799: Collected and Extracted from the Records by the Clerk Thereof*. Edinburgh: printed by James Dickson, 1799.

General Synod of Ulster. *Records of the General Synod of Ulster: From 1691 to 1820*. Vol. 3. Belfast: General Assembly of the Presbyterian Church in Ireland, 1898.

Gregory, William. *Visible Display of Divine Providence, Or, The Journal of a Captured Missionary Designated to the Southern Pacific Ocean, in the Second Voyage of the Ship Duff*. London: printed by T. Gillet, 1800.

———. *Visible Display of Divine Providence, Or, The Journal of a Captured Missionary Designated to the Southern Pacific Ocean, in the Second Voyage of the Ship Duff*. 2nd ed. London: printed by J. Skirven, 1801.

Griffin, Edward Dorr. *The Kingdom of Christ: A Missionary Sermon Preached before the General Assembly of the Presbyterian Church in Philadelphia, May 23, 1805*. Philadelphia: printed by Jane Aitken, 1805.

Haldane, James Alexander. *A View of the Social Worship and Ordinances Observed by the First Christians: Drawn from the Sacred Scriptures Alone, Being an Attempt to Enforce Their Divine Obligation and to Represent the Guilt and Evil Consequences of Neglecting Them*. Edinburgh: printed by J. Ritchie, 1805.

———. *Journal of a Tour through the Northern Counties of Scotland and the Orkney Isles, in Autumn 1797: Undertaken with a View to Promote the Knowledge of the Gospel of Jesus Christ*. Edinburgh: printed by J. Ritchie, 1798.

———. *Reasons of a Change of Sentiment and Practice on the Subject of Baptism: Containing A Plain View of the Signification of the Word, and of the Persons for Whom the Ordinance Is Appointed; Together with a Full Consideration of the Covenant Made with Abraham, and Its Supposed Connexion with Baptism.* Edinburgh: printed by J. Ritchie, 1809.

Haldane, Robert. *Address to the Public, Concerning Political Opinions, and Plans Lately Adopted to Promote Religion in Scotland.* Edinburgh: printed by J. Ritchie, 1800.

Hamilton, George. *The Great Necessity of Itinerant Preaching: A Sermon Delivered in Armagh at the Formation of the Evangelical Society of Ulster, on Wednesday, 10th of Oct. 1798. With a Short Introductory Memorial, Respecting the Establishment and First Attempt of the Society.* Armagh: printed and sold by T. Stevenson, and by each member of the committee, 1799.

Hardy, Thomas. *The Progress of the Christian Religion: A Sermon, Preached before the Society in Scotland for Propagating Christian Knowledge, at Their Anniversary Meeting in the High Church of Edinburgh, Thursday, May 30, 1793.* Edinburgh: printed by John Patterson, 1794.

Haweis, Thomas et al. *Sermons, Preached in London, at the Formation of the Missionary Society, September 22, 23, 24, 1795; To Which Are Prefixed, Memorials, Respecting the Establishment and First Attempts of That Society.* London: printed and sold by T. Chapman, 1795.

Hibernian Society. *Report of a Deputation from the Hibernian Society, Respecting the Religious State of Ireland: To Which Is Annexed a Plan of the Society, Together with a List of Its Officers.* London: printed for the benefit of the Society by T. Rutt, 1807.

Hill, Rowland. *A Plea for Union and for a Free Propagation of the Gospel: Being an Answer to Dr. Jamieson's Remarks on the Late Tour of the Rev. R. Hill, Addressed to the Scots' Society for Propagating the Gospel at Home.* London: Printed by A. Paris, 1800.

———. *A Sermon, Preached by the Rev. Mr. Rowland Hill, on His Laying the First Stone of His Chapel, in St. George's Fields, June 24, 1782.* London: printed for M. Folingsby, 1782.

———. *Journal of a Tour through the North of England and Parts of Scotland: With Remarks on the Present State of the Established Church of Scotland and the Different Secessions Therefrom. Together with Reflections on Some Party Distinctions in England; Shewing the Origin of These Disputes, and the Causes of Their Separation. Designed to Promote Brotherly Love and Forbearance among Christians of All Denominations.* London: printed by T. Gillet, 1799.

Hiram Lester Papers. T. W. Phillips Memorial Library Archives and Special Collections. Bethany: Bethany College.

Hopkins, Samuel. *A Discourse upon the Slave-Trade, and the Slavery of the Africans.* Providence: J. Carter, 1793.

———. *An Inquiry into the Nature of True Holiness.* Newport: Solomon Southwick, 1773.

———. *A Treatise on the Millennium.* Boston: Isaiah Thomas and Ebenezer T. Andrews, 1793.

Horne, Melville. *Letters on Missions: Addressed to the Protestant Ministers of the British Churches*. Bristol: printed by Bulgin and Rosser, 1794.

Jamieson, John. *Remarks on the Rev. Rowland Hill's Journal, In a Letter to the Author, Including Reflections on Itinerant and Lay Preaching*. Edinburgh: printed for J. Ogle, 1799.

Locke, John. *A Letter Concerning Toleration*. London: printed for Awnsham Churchill, at the Black Swan at Amen-Corner, 1689.

———. *The Reasonableness of Christianity, As Delivered in the Scriptures*. 2nd ed. London: printed for Awnsham and John Churchill, at the Black Swan in Pater-Noster-Row, 1696.

MacWhorter, Alexander. *The Blessedness of the Liberal: A Sermon, Preached in the Middle Dutch Church, before the New-York Missionary Society, at Their First Institution, November 1, 1796*. New York: printed by T. and J. Swords, 1796.

Mather, Cotton. *Blessed Unions. An Union with the Son of God by Faith. And, An Union in the Church of God by Love, Importunately Pressed; In A Discourse Which Makes Divers Offers, for Those Unions; Together with a Copy of Those Articles, Where-upon A Most Happy Union, Has Been Lately Made between Those Two Eminent Parties in England, Which Have Now Changed the Names of Presbyterians, and Congregationals, for that of United Brethren*. Boston: printed by B. Green, 1692.

———. *The Heavenly Conversation*. Boston: printed by Barth Green, for Eleazar Phillips, 1710.

———. *India Christiana: A Discourse, Delivered unto the Commissioners, for the Propagation of the Gospel among the American Indians Which Is Accompanied with Several Instruments Relating to the Glorious Design of Propagating Our Holy Religion, in the Eastern as Well as the Western, Indies, An Entertainment Which They That Are Waiting for the Kingdom of God Will Receive as Good News from A Far Country*. Boston: printed by B. Green, 1721.

———. *Selected Letters of Cotton Mather*, edited by Kenneth Silverman. Baton Rouge: Louisiana State University Press, 1971.

———. *The Stone Cut Out of the Mountain, And the Kingdom of God, in Those Maxims of It, That Cannot Be Shaken*. Boston: n.p., 1716.

———. *The Triumphs of the Reformed Religion, in America: The Life of the Renowned John Eliot*. Boston: printed by Benjamin Harris & John Allen, for Joseph Brunning, 1691.

Millar, Robert. *The History of the Propagation of Christianity and Overthrow of Paganism*. 3rd ed. 2 vols. London: printed for A. Miller, 1731.

Minutes of the Associate (Antiburgher) Synod of Ireland. Hiram Lester Papers. T. W. Phillips Memorial Library Archives and Special Collections. Bethany: Bethany College.

Minutes of the Associate (Burgher) Synod of Ireland. Hiram Lester Papers. T. W. Phillips Memorial Library Archives and Special Collections. Bethany: Bethany College.

Missionary Society. *Four Sermons, Preached in London at the Second General Meeting of the Missionary Society, May 11, 12, 13, 1796 . . . To Which Are Prefixed, The Proceedings of the Meeting*. London: sold by T. Chapman, 1796.

———. *Four Sermons, Preached in London at the Fourth General Meeting of the Missionary Society, May 9, 10, 11, 1798 . . . To Which Are Prefixed, The Proceedings of the Meeting, and the Report of the Directors; Also Are Added, A List of Subscribers*. London: printed for T. Chapman, 1798.

———. *Four Sermons, Preached in London at the Third General Meeting of the Missionary Society, May 10, 11, 12, 1797 . . . To Which Are Prefixed, The Proceedings of the Meeting, and the Report of the Directors*, xv–xxix. London: sold by T. Chapman, 1797.

Mitchell, James Tyndale et al., eds. *The Statutes at Large of Pennsylvania from 1682 to 1801*. Vol. 15. Harrisburg: Clarence M. Busch, State Printer of Pennsylvania, 1911.

New-York Missionary Society. *The Address and Constitution of the New-York Missionary Society*. New York: printed by T. and J. Swords, 1796.

Northern Missionary Society. *The Constitution of the Northern Missionary Society in the State of New-York: To Which Is Annexed the Address of the Society to the Public*. Schenectady: printed by C. P. Wyckoff, 1797.

Outlines of a Plan for the Formation of an Evangelical Academy. n.p.: n.p., n.d. Accessed May 20, 2014. Eighteenth Century Collection Online, Range 14564.

Records of the Associate Presbytery of Chartiers. Associate Presbyterian Church of North America. Presbytery of Chartiers. Presbyter minutes, 1801–1858. Call Number MF 1353. Philadelphia: Presbyterian Historical Society.

Redstone Baptist Association. *Minutes of the Redstone Baptist Association, 1804–1836*. N.p.: M. F. Cottrell, 1964.

———. *Minutes of the Redstone Baptist Association*. Dale Broadhurst Personal Collections. Email Contact, dbroadhu@hawaiiantel.net.

———. *Minutes of the Redstone Baptist Association, Held at Connelsville, Fayette County, (Pa.): September 1st, 2d & 3d, 1818*. Washington: printed by William Sample, 1818.

———. *Minutes of the Redstone Baptist Association, Held at the Horseshoe, Washington County, (Pa.): September 3d. 4th. & 5th. 1819*. Washington: printed by Samuel Workman, 1819.

———. *Minutes of the Redstone Baptist Association, Held at Pittsburgh, Allegheny County, (Pa.): September 5th, 6th, and 7th, 1823*. n.p.: n.p., 1823

———. *Minutes of the Redstone Baptist Association, Held at Plum Run, Washington County, (Pa.): September 1, 2, & 3, 1820*. n.p.: n.p., 1820.

———. *Minutes of the Redstone Baptist Association, Held at Ruff's Creek, Greene County, (Pa.): August 31 and September 1st and 2nd, 1821*. n.p.: n.p., 1821.

———. *Minutes of the Redstone Baptist Association, Held at Washington, Washington County, Pa.: August 31, and September 1 and 2, 1822.* n.p.: n.p., 1822.

———. *Minutes of the Redstone Baptist Association, Held by Appointment, At Big Redstone, Fayette County, Penn.: September 1st, 2d, and 3d, 1815.* Pittsburgh: printed by S. Engles, 1815.

———. *Minutes of the Redstone Baptist Association, Held by Appointment, At Cross-Creek, Brooke County, VA.: August 30th, 31st, and Sept, 1st, 1816.* Washington: printed by William Sample, 1816.

———. *Minutes of the Redstone Baptist Association, Held by Appointment, At Peter's Creek, Washington County, (Pa.): September 2d, 3d & 4th, 1817.* Washington: printed by William Sample, 1817.

Society for Propagating the Gospel at Home. *An Account of the Proceedings of the Society for Propagating the Gospel at Home, From Their Commencement, December 28, 1798, to May 16, 1799.* Edinburgh: J. Ritchie, 1799.

Spener, Philip Jacob. *Pia Desideria.* Translated by Theodore G. Tappert. Eugene: Wipf and Stock, 2002.

Synod of Pittsburgh. *Records of the Synod of Pittsburgh: From Its First Organization, September 29, 1802 to October 1832 Inclusive.* Pittsburgh: published by Luke Loomis, Agent, 1852.

Taylor, John. *Thoughts on Missions.* Franklin County, Kentucky: n.p., 1819. http://baptiststudiesonline.com/wp-content/uploads/2007/02/thoughts-on-missions.pdf.

Walker, John, and Alexander Knox. *An Expostulatory Address to the Members of the Methodist Society in Ireland: Together with a Series of Letters to Alexander Knox, Esq. M.R.I.A.* 4th ed. Edinburgh: J. Ritchie, 1806.

Wesley, John. *A Collection of Hymns: For the Use of the People Called Methodists.* London: Wesleyan Conference Office, 1877.

———. *Hymns and Spiritual Songs, Intended for the Use of Real Christians of All Denominations.* 1st ed. London: printed by William Strahan, 1753.

———. *The Journal of the Reverend John Wesley, A.M., Sometime Fellow of Lincoln College, Oxford.* 2 vols. New York: Carlton & Phillips, 1855.

———. *A Sermon on the Death of the Rev. Mr. George Whitefield. Preached at the Chapel in Tottenham-Court-Road, and at the Tabernacle near Moorfields, on Sunday, November 18, 1770.* London: printed by J. and W. Oliver, 1770.

———. "Sermon XXXIX: Catholic Spirit." In *Sermons on Several Occasions by the Rev. John Wesley, M.A., Late Fellow of Lincoln College, Oxford*, 515–28. New edition. Leeds: printed by Edward Baines, 1799.

Whitefield, George. *The Nature and Necessity of Our New Birth in Christ Jesus, in Order to Salvation. A Sermon Preached in the Church of St. Mary Radcliffe, in Bristol.* 2nd ed. London: printed for C. Rivington in St. Paul's Church-yard, 1737.

Worcester, Samuel. "Sermon to the Massachusetts Missionary Society, May 1809." In *The Life and Labors of Rev. Samuel Worcester, D.D.*, edited by Samuel Melancthon Worcester, 2:71–79. Boston: Crocker and Brewster, 1852.

Zinzendorf, Count Nicholas Ludwig von. "Brotherly Union and Agreement at Herrnhut (1727)." In *Pietism: Selected Writings*, edited by Peter C. Erb, 325–30. The Classics of Western Spirituality. New York: Paulist Press, 1983.

———. "Concerning Saving Faith (1746)." In *Pietism: Selected Writings*, edited by Peter C. Erb, 304–10. The Classics of Western Spirituality. New York: Paulist Press, 1983.

———. "On the Essential Character and Circumstances of the Life of a Christian (1746)." In *Pietism: Selected Writings*, edited by Peter C. Erb, 311–24. The Classics of Western Spirituality. New York: Paulist Press, 1983.

———. "Thoughts for the Learned and Yet Good-Willed Students of Truth (1732)." In *Pietism: Selected Writings*, edited by Peter C. Erb, 291–95. The Classics of Western Spirituality. New York: Paulist Press, 1983.

II. Secondary Sources

Allen, C. Leonard, and Richard T. Hughes. *Discovering Our Roots: The Ancestry of Churches of Christ*. Abilene, TX: Abilene Christian University Press, 1988.

Arnold, David, and Robert A. Bickers. "Introduction." In *Missionary Encounters: Sources and Issues*, edited by Robert A. Bickers and Rosemary E. Seton. Richmond: Curzon Press, 1996.

Ayabe, John A. "Evangelicals and the Antimission Crisis: A Study of Religious Identity in the Central Mississippi Valley, 1820–1840." PhD diss., Saint Louis University, 2007.

Barkley, John M. *A Short History of the Presbyterian Church in Ireland*. Belfast: Publications Board, Presbyterian Church in Ireland, 1959.

Beaver, R. Pierce. "The Concert for Prayer for Missions: An Early Venture in Ecumenical Action." *Ecumenical Review* 10, no. 4 (1958): 420–27.

———. *Pioneers in Mission: The Early Missionary Ordination Sermons, Charges, and Instructions*. Grand Rapids: Eerdmans, 1966.

Bebbington, David W. *Baptists Through the Centuries: A History of a Global People*. Waco: Baylor University Press, 2010.

———. *The Dominance of Evangelicalism: The Age of Spurgeon and Moody*. A History of Evangelicalism 3. Downers Grove: InterVarsity Press, 2005.

———. *Evangelicalism in Modern Britain: A History from the 1730s to the 1980s*. London: Routledge, 1989.

———. "The Growth of Voluntary Religion." In *The Cambridge History of Christianity: Volume VIII, World Christianities, c.1815–c.1914*, edited by Sheridan Gilley and Brian Stanley, 53–69. Cambridge: Cambridge University Press, 2006.

———. "Revival and Enlightenment in Eighteenth-Century England." In *Modern Christian Revivals*, edited by Edith Waldvogel Blumhofer and Randall Herbert Balmer, 17–41. Urbana: University of Illinois Press, 1993.

Bender, Thomas, ed. *Rethinking American History in a Global Age*. Berkeley: University of California Press, 2002.

Benz, Ernst. "Ecumenical Relations between Boston Puritanism and German Pietism: Cotton Mather and August Hermann Francke." *The Harvard Theological Review* 54, no. 3 (July 1961): 159–93.

———. "Pietist and Puritan Sources of Early Protestant World Missions (Cotton Mather and A. H. Francke)." *Church History* 20, no. 2 (1951): 28–55.

Berryhill, Carisse Mickey. "A Descriptive Guide to Eight Early Alexander Campbell Manuscripts." Research Paper. Memphis, 2000. Accessed June 29, 2015. http://web.archive.org/web/20120114232220/http://www.mun.ca/rels/restmov/texts/acampbell/acm/ACM00A.HTM.

———. "Scottish Rhetoric and the *Declaration and Address*." In *The Quest for Christian Unity, Peace, and Purity in Thomas Campbell's* Declaration and Address: *Text and Studies*, edited by Thomas H. Olbricht and Hans Rollmann, 193–210. ATLA Monograph Series 46. Lanham: Scarecrow Press, 2000.

Boring, M. Eugene. *Disciples and the Bible: A History of Disciples Biblical Interpretation in North America*. St. Louis: Chalice Press, 1997.

Bosch, David J. *Transforming Mission: Paradigm Shifts in Theology of Mission*. American Society of Missiology Series 16. Maryknoll: Orbis Books, 1991.

Bozeman, Theodore Dwight. *Protestants in an Age of Science: The Baconian Ideal and Antebellum American Religious Thought*. Chapel Hill: University of North Carolina Press, 1977.

Bradley, James E. "Toleration and Movements of Christian Reunion, 1660–1789." In *The Cambridge History of Christianity: Volume VII, Enlightenment, Reawakening and Revolution 1660–1815*, edited by Stewart J. Brown and Timothy Tackett, 348–70. Cambridge: Cambridge University Press, 2006.

Brazell, Jr., Charles F. "Reluctant Restorationist: Thomas Campbell's Trial and Its Role in His Legacy." PhD diss., The University of Texas at Arlington, 2007.

Breitenbach, Esther. "The Impact of the Victorian Empire." In *The Oxford Handbook of Modern Scottish History*, edited by T. M. Devine and Jenny Wormald. Oxford Handbooks. Oxford: Oxford University Press, 2012. Accessed April 4, 2014. oxfordhandbooks.com.

Brown, Dorothy Eugenia Sherman. "Evangelicals and Education in Eighteenth-Century Britain: A Study of Trevecca College, 1768–1792." PhD diss., The University of Wisconsin-Madison, 1992.

Brown, Stewart J. "Movements of Christian Awakening in Revolutionary Europe, 1790–1815." In *The Cambridge History of Christianity: Volume VII, Enlightenment, Reawakening and Revolution 1660–1815*, edited by Stewart J. Brown and Timothy Tackett, 575–595. Cambridge: Cambridge University Press, 2006.

———. "Religion and Society to c.1900." In *The Oxford Handbook of Modern Scottish History*, edited by T. M. Devine and Jenny Wormald. Oxford Handbooks. Oxford: Oxford University Press, 2012. Accessed April 4, 2014. oxfordhandbooks.com.

Brown, William. *History of the Propagation of Christianity Among the Heathen Since the Reformation.* 3rd ed. 3 vols. London: T. Baker, 1854.

Burleigh, John H. S. *A Church History of Scotland.* London: Oxford University Press, 1960.

Burnet, David S. *The Jerusalem Mission under the Direction of the American Christian Missionary Society.* New York: Arno Press, 1977.

Butler, Jon. "The Future of American Religious History: Prospectus, Agenda, Transatlantic *Problématique*." *William and Mary Quarterly* 42, no. 2 (1985): 167–83.

Cameron, Nigel M. de S., ed. *Dictionary of Scottish Church History & Theology.* Downers Grove: InterVarsity Press, 1993.

Canny, Nicholas, and Phillip Morgan. "Introduction: The Making and Unmaking of an Atlantic World." In *The Oxford Handbook of the Atlantic World: 1450–1850*, edited by Nicholas Canny and Phillip Morgan. Online. Oxford: Oxford University Press, 2012.

Carroll, Bret E. *The Routledge Historical Atlas of Religion in America.* New York: Routledge, 2000.

Carwardine, Richard. *Transatlantic Revivalism: Popular Evangelicalism in Britain and America, 1790–1865.* Westport: Greenwood Press, 1978.

Casey, Michael W. *The Battle Over Hermeneutics in the Stone-Campbell Movement, 1800–1870.* Lewiston: E. Mellen Press, 1998.

———. "The Origins of the Hermeneutics of the Churches of Christ Part One: The Reformed Tradition." *Restoration Quarterly* 31, no. 2 (January 1, 1989): 75–91.

———. "The Origins of the Hermeneutics of the Churches of Christ Part Two: The Philosophical Background." *Restoration Quarterly* 31, no. 4 (January 1, 1989): 193–206.

———. "The Theory of Logic and Inference in the *Declaration and Address*." In *The Quest for Christian Unity, Peace, and Purity in Thomas Campbell's Declaration and Address: Text and Studies*, edited by Thomas H. Olbricht and Hans Rollmann, 223–42. ATLA Monograph Series 46. Lanham: Scarecrow Press, 2000.

Casey, Michael W., and Douglas A. Foster. "Introduction: The Renaissance of Stone-Campbell Studies: An Assessment and New Directions." In *The Stone-Campbell Movement: An International Religious Tradition*, edited by Michael W. Casey and Douglas A. Foster, 1–65. Knoxville: University of Tennessee Press, 2002.

Chaney, Charles L. *The Birth of Missions in America.* Pasadena: William Carey Library, 1976.

Clark, J. C. D. "Great Britain and Ireland." In *The Cambridge History of Christianity: Volume VII, Enlightenment, Reawakening and Revolution 1660–1815*, edited by Stewart J. Brown and Timothy Tackett, 54–71. Cambridge: Cambridge University Press, 2006.

Clark, Martin Bailey. "The Missionary Position of the Movement of Disciples of Christ in the Early Years of the Nineteenth Century Reformation." Master's thesis, Butler University, 1949.
Conforti, Joseph. "Jonathan Edwards's Most Popular Work: 'The Life of David Brainerd' and 19th Century Evangelical Culture." *Church History* 54, no. 2 (1985): 188–201.
Conkin, Paul Keith. *American Originals: Homemade Varieties of Christianity*. Chapel Hill: University of North Carolina Press, 1997.
Coohill, Joseph. *Ireland: A Short History*. 4th ed. London: Oneworld, 2014.
Daughrity, Dyron. "Glasite Versus Haldanite: Scottish Divergence on the Question of Missions." *Restoration Quarterly* 53, no. 2 (2011): 65–79.
Davies, Ronald E. "Jonathan Edwards: Missionary Biographer, Theologian, Strategist, Administrator, Advocate—and Missionary." *International Bulletin of Missionary Research* 21, no. 2 (April 1997): 60–67.
———. "Robert Millar: An Eighteenth-Century Scottish Latourette." *Evangelical Quarterly* 62 (1990): 143–56.
Davis, Morrison Meade. *How the Disciples Began and Grew: A Short History of the Christian Church*. Cincinnati: Standard Publishing Company, 1915.
Dean, Camille K. "British Backgrounds of Millennialism in the Campbell Tradition." *Discipliana* 60, no. 3 (2000): 67–77.
———. "Evangelicals or Restorationists? The Careers of Robert and James Haldane in Cultural and Political Context." PhD diss., Texas Christian University, 1999.
———. "Robert and James Alexander Haldane in Scotland: Evangelicals or Restorationists?" *Restoration Quarterly* 42, no. 2 (2000): 99–111.
Dunnavant, Anthony L. *Restructure: Four Historical Ideals in the Campbell-Stone Movement and the Development of the Polity of the Christian Church (Disciples of Christ)*. New York: P. Lang, 1993.
———. "Restructure: Four Historical Ideals in the Campbell-Stone Movement and the Development of the Polity of the Christian Church (Disciples of Christ)." PhD diss., Vanderbilt University, 1984.
Elkins, Phillip Wayne. *Church-Sponsored Missions: An Evaluation of Churches of Christ*. Austin: Firm Foundation Publishing House, 1974.
Erb, Peter C. "Introduction." In *Pietism: Selected Writings*, edited by Peter C. Erb, 1–27. The Classics of Western Spirituality. New York: Paulist Press, 1983.
Filbeck, David. *The First Fifty Years: A Brief History of the Direct-Support Missionary Movement*. Joplin: College Press, 1980.
Fitzgerald, Patrick. "The Seventeenth-Century Irish Connection." In *The Oxford Handbook of Modern Scottish History*, edited by T. M. Devine and Jenny Wormald. Oxford Handbooks. Oxford: Oxford University Press, 2012. Accessed June 11, 2014. www.oxfordhandbooks.com.
Foster, Charles I. *An Errand of Mercy: The Evangelical United Front, 1790–1837*. Chapel Hill: University of North Carolina Press, 1960.

Foster, Douglas A. et al., eds. *The Encyclopedia of the Stone-Campbell Movement.* Grand Rapids: Eerdmans, 2004.

Foster, John. "A Scottish Contributor to the Missionary Awakening: Robert Millar of Paisley." *International Review of Missions* 37 (1948): 138–45.

Garrison, Winfred Ernest. *Alexander Campbell's Theology: Its Sources and Historical Setting.* St. Louis: Christian Publishing Company, 1900.

———. *Religion Follows the Frontier: A History of the Disciples of Christ.* New York: Harper & Brothers Publishers, 1931.

Garrison, Winfred Ernest, and Alfred T. DeGroot. *The Disciples of Christ: A History.* Rev. ed. 1948; reprint. St. Louis: Christian Board of Publication, 1964.

Gates, Errett. *The Early Relation and Separation of Baptists and Disciples.* Chicago: R. R. Donnelley & Sons Company, 1904.

Gaustad, Edwin Scott, and Philip L. Barlow, eds. *New Historical Atlas of Religion in America.* 3rd ed. New York: Oxford University Press, 2001.

Geertz, Clifford. "Religion as a Cultural System." In *The Interpretation of Cultures: Selected Essays,* 87–125. New York: Basic Books, 2000.

———. "Thick Description: Toward an Interpretive Theory of Culture." In *The Interpretation of Cultures: Selected Essays,* 3–30. New York: Basic Books, 2000.

Gilmore, Peter. "Rebels and Revivals: Ulster Immigrants, Western Pennsylvania Presbyterianism and the Formation of Scotch-Irish Identity, 1780–1830." PhD diss., Carnegie Mellon University, 2009.

Gorman, James L. "European Roots of Thomas Campbell's *Declaration and Address*: The Evangelical Society of Ulster." *Restoration Quarterly* 51, no. 3 (2009): 129–37.

———. "From Burning to Blessing: Baptist Reception of Alexander Campbell's New Translation." *Stone-Campbell Journal* 16, no. 2 (2013): 177–91.

Green, F. M. Francis Marion. *Christian Missions, and Historical Sketches of Missionary Societies Among the Disciples of Christ: With Historical and Statistical Tables.* St. Louis: J. Burns Pub. Co., 1884.

Hackett, Rosalind I. J. "Anthropology of Religion." In *The Routledge Companion to the Study of Religion,* edited by John Hinnells, 165–85. 2nd ed. New York: Routledge, 2010.

Haldane, Alexander. *Memoirs of the Lives of Robert Haldane of Airthrey, and of His Brother, James Alexander Haldane.* London: Hamilton, Adams, and Co., 1852.

Hanna, William Herbert. *Thomas Campbell: Seceder and Christian Union Advocate.* Reprint. Joplin: College Press, 1986.

Hatch, Nathan O. "The Christian Movement and the Demand for a Theology of the People." *Journal of American History* 67, no. 3 (1980): 545–67.

———. *The Democratization of American Christianity.* New Haven: Yale University Press, 1989.

Hayden, A. S. *Early History of the Disciples in the Western Reserve, Ohio; with Biographical Sketches of the Principal Agents in Their Religious Movement.* Cincinnati: Chase & Hall Publishers, 1875.

Heitzenrater, Richard P. *Wesley and the People Called Methodists.* Nashville: Abingdon, 1995.

Helsabeck Jr., W. Dennis. "The American Frontier." *Leaven* 7, no. 4 (1999): 177–80.

Hempton, David. "Evangelicalism in English and Irish Society, 1780–1840." In *Evangelicalism: Comparative Studies of Popular Protestantism in North America, the British Isles, and Beyond 1700–1900*, edited by Mark A. Noll, D. W. Bebbington, and George A. Rawlyk, 156–76. New York: Oxford University Press, 1994.

Hempton, David, and Myrtle Hill. *Evangelical Protestantism in Ulster Society, 1740–1890.* London: Routledge, 1992.

Hicks, John Mark. "The Gracious Separatist: Moral and Positive Law in the Theology of James A. Harding." *Restoration Quarterly* 42, no. 3 (2000): 129–47.

———. "Locke, John (1632–1704)," edited by Douglas A. Foster et al. *The Encyclopedia of the Stone-Campbell Movement.* Grand Rapids: Eerdmans, 2004.

Holmes, Andrew R. "The Shaping of Irish Presbyterian Attitudes to Mission, 1790–1840." *Journal of Ecclesiastical History* 57, no. 4 (2006): 711–37.

———. *The Shaping of Ulster Presbyterian Belief and Practice, 1770–1840.* Oxford: Oxford University Press, 2006.

Howell, Brian M., and Jenell Williams Paris. *Introducing Cultural Anthropology: A Christian Perspective.* Grand Rapids: Baker Academic, 2011.

Hughes, Richard T. "The Apocalyptic Origins of Churches of Christ and the Triumph of Modernism." *Religion and American Culture: A Journal of Interpretation* 2, no. 2 (1992): 181–214.

———. *Reviving the Ancient Faith: The Story of Churches of Christ in America.* Grand Rapids: Eerdmans, 1996.

———. "Twenty-Five Years of Restoration Scholarship: The Churches of Christ, Part I." *Restoration Quarterly* 25, no. 4 (1982): 233–56.

———. "Twenty-Five Years of Restoration Scholarship: The Churches of Christ, Part II." *Restoration Quarterly* 26, no. 1 (1983): 39–62.

———. "Two Restoration Traditions: Mormons and Churches of Christ in the Nineteenth Century." *Journal of Mormon History* 19, no. 1 (1993): 34–51.

———. "Why Restorationists Don't Fit the Evangelical Mold; Why Churches of Christ Increasingly Do." In *Re-Forming the Center: American Protestantism, 1900 to the Present*, edited by Douglas Jacobsen and William Vance Trollinger, 194–213. Grand Rapids: Eerdmans, 1998.

Hughes, Richard T., and C. Leonard Allen. *Illusions of Innocence: Protestant Primitivism in America, 1630–1875.* Chicago: University of Chicago Press, 1988.

———. *Illusions of Innocence: Protestant Primitivism in America, 1630–1875.* Abilene, TX: Abilene Christian University Press, 2008.

Hughes, Richard T. et al. *American Origins of the Churches of Christ: Three Essays on Restoration History.* Abilene, TX: Abilene Christian University Press, 2000.

Humble, Bill J. "The Missionary Society Controversy in the Restoration Movement (1823–1875)." PhD diss., University of Iowa, 1964.

Hutchinson, Mark, and John Wolffe. *A Short History of Global Evangelicalism.* Cambridge: Cambridge University Press, 2012.

Hutchinson, William R. *Errand to the World: American Protestant Thought and Foreign Missions.* Chicago: University of Chicago Press, 1987.

Hutson, Christopher R. "Thomas Campbell's Use of Scripture in the *Declaration and Address*." In *The Quest for Christian Unity, Peace, and Purity in Thomas Campbell's* Declaration and Address: *Text and Studies*, edited by Thomas H. Olbricht and Hans Rollmann, 211–222. ATLA Monograph Series 46. Lanham: Scarecrow Press, 2000.

Jennings, Walter Wilson. *Origin and Early History of the Disciples of Christ: With Special Reference to the Period Between 1809 and 1835.* Cincinnati: The Standard Publishing Company, 1919.

De Jong, James A. *As the Waters Cover the Sea: Millennial Expectations in the Rise of Anglo-American Missions, 1640–1810.* 2006 Reprint. Kampen: J. H. Kok, 1970.

Kaufman, Will, and Heidi Slettedahl Macpherson. "Introduction." In *New Perspectives in Transatlantic Studies*, xi–xxv. Lanham: University Press of America, 2002.

Kelly, James. "Inter-Denominational Relations and Religious Toleration in Late Eighteenth-Century Ireland: The 'Paper War' of 1786–88." *Eighteenth-Century Ireland / Iris an dá chultúr* 3 (January 1, 1988): 39–67.

Kershner, Frederick Doyle. *The Christian Union Overture: An Interpretation of the Declaration and Address of Thomas Campbell.* St. Louis: Bethany Press, 1923.

Kidd, Thomas S. *American Christians and Islam: Evangelical Culture and Muslims from the Colonial Period to the Age of Terrorism.* Princeton: Princeton University Press, 2009.

———. *George Whitefield: America's Spiritual Founding Father.* New Haven: Yale University Press, 2014.

———. *The Great Awakening: The Roots of Evangelical Christianity in Colonial America.* New Haven: Yale University Press, 2007.

Kirk, Hiram Van. *A History of the Theology of the Disciples of Christ.* St. Louis: Christian Publishing Company, 1907.

Kresel, George. "Alexander Campbell's Theology of Missions." PhD diss., Boston University, 1961.

Larsen, Timothy. "Defining and Locating Evangelicalism." In *The Cambridge Companion to Evangelical Theology*, edited by Timothy Larsen and Daniel J. Treier, 1–14. Cambridge: Cambridge University Press, 2007.

Larsen, Timothy, D. W. Bebbington, and Mark A. Noll, eds. *Biographical Dictionary of Evangelicals*. Leicester: Inter-Varsity Press, 2003.

Lewis, Donald M., ed. *Dictionary of Evangelical Biography, 1730–1860*. 2 vols. Peabody: Hendrickson, 2004.

Lee, Gary L. "Background to *The Christian Baptist*." In *The Christian Baptist*, 1–36. Joplin: College Press, 1983.

Lester, Hiram J. "Alexander Campbell's Early Baptism in Ecumenicity and Sectarianism." *Restoration Quarterly* 30 (1988): 85–101.

———. "The Case Against Sectarianism." *The Disciple* 17, no. 3 (1990): 10–12.

———. "The Form and Function of the *Declaration and Address*." In *The Quest for Christian Unity, Peace, and Purity in Thomas Campbell's* Declaration and Address*: Text and Studies*, edited by Thomas H. Olbricht and Hans Rollmann, 173–92. ATLA Monograph Series 46. Lanham: Scarecrow Press, 2000.

———. "An Irish Precursor for Thomas Campbell's Declaration and Address." *Encounter* 50, no. 3 (1989): 247–67.

Lovegrove, Deryck W. "Unity and Separation: Contrasting Elements in the Thought and Practice of Robert and James Alexander Haldane." In *Protestant Evangelicalism: Britain, Ireland, Germany and America c 1750–c 1950: Essays in Honour of W. R. Ward*, 153–77. Oxford: Basil Blackwell, 1990.

———. "Unity and Separation: Contrasting Elements in the Thought and Practice of Robert and James Alexander Haldane." In *The Stone-Campbell Movement: An International Religious Tradition*, edited by Michael W. Casey and Douglas A. Foster, 520–43. Knoxville: University of Tennessee Press, 2002.

Lovelace, Richard F. *The American Pietism of Cotton Mather: Origins of American Evangelicalism*. Grand Rapids: Christian University Press, 1979.

Lovett, Richard. *The History of the London Missionary Society, 1795–1895*. 2 vols. London: Henry Frowde, 1899.

Mahaffey, Jerome Dean. *The Accidental Revolutionary: George Whitefield and the Creation of America*. Waco: Baylor University Press, 2011.

———. *Preaching Politics: The Religious Rhetoric of George Whitefield and the Founding of a New Nation*. Studies in Rhetoric and Religion 3. Waco: Baylor University Press, 2007.

Marsden, George M. *Jonathan Edwards: A Life*. New Haven: Yale University Press, 2004.

Martin, Roger H. *Evangelicals United: Ecumenical Stirrings in Pre-Victorian Britain, 1795–1830*. Metuchen: Scarecrow Press, 1983.

Mason, J. C. S. *The Moravian Church and the Missionary Awakening in England, 1760-1800*. Woodbridge: Royal Historical Society/Boydell Press, 2001.

Matheson, J. J. *A Memoir of Greville Ewing, Minister of the Gospel, Glasgow*. London: John Snow, Paternoster Row, 1843.

Mathis, James Rhett. "'Can Two Walk Together Unless They Be Agreed?': The Origins of the Primitive Baptists, 1800-1840." PhD diss., University of Florida, 1997.

———. *The Making of the Primitive Baptists: A Cultural and Intellectual History of the Antimission Movement, 1800-1840*. New York: Routledge, 2004.

Maxfield, Charles. "The 'Reflex Influence' of Missions: The Domestic Operations of the American Board of Commissioners for Foreign Missions, 1810-1850." PhD diss., Union Theological Seminary, 1995.

Maxwell, Ian Douglas. "Civilization or Christianity? The Scottish Debate on Mission Methods, 1750-1835." In *Christian Missions and the Enlightenment*, edited by Brian Stanley, 123-40. Grand Rapids: Eerdmans, 2001.

Mayberry, Lori Shannon Phillips. "Robert and James Alexander Haldane in Scotland: An Evangelistic Effort That Failed to Germinate." *Restoration Quarterly* 39, no. 4 (1997): 203-14.

McAllister, Lester G. *Thomas Campbell: Man of the Book*. St. Louis: Bethany Press, 1954.

McBeth, H. Leon. *The Baptist Heritage*. Nashville: Broadman, 1987.

McBride, Ian R. *Scripture Politics: Ulster Presbyterians and Irish Radicalism in the Late Eighteenth Century*. Oxford: Clarendon Press, 1998.

———. "'When Ulster Joined Ireland': Anti-Popery, Presbyterian Radicalism and Irish Republicanism in the 1790s." *Past & Present*, no. 157 (1997): 63-93.

McLeod, Hugh. *Religion and the People of Western Europe 1789-1989*. 2nd ed. Oxford: Oxford University Press, 1997.

McMillon, Lynn A. *Restoration Roots*. Dallas: Gospel Teachers Publications, 1983.

———. "The Quest for the Apostolic Church: A Study of Scottish Origins of American Restorationism." PhD diss., Baylor University, 1972.

Miller, Hugh. "The Debate on Missions." In *The Headship of Christ, and the Rights of the Christian People: A Collection of Essays, Historical and Descriptive Sketches, and Personal Portaitures*, 144-99. Boston: Gould and Lincoln, 1870.

Mills, Sr., Frederick V. "The Society in Scotland for Propagating Christian Knowledge in British North America, 1730-1775." *Church History* 63, no. 1 (1994): 15-30.

Mitchell, Christopher W. "Jonathan Edwards's Scottish Connection." In *Jonathan Edwards at Home and Abroad: Historical Memories, Cultural Movements, Global Horizons*, edited by David William Kling and Douglas A. Sweeney, 222-47. Columbia: University of South Carolina Press, 2003.

Moore, George C. *The Life of Alexander Carson*. New York: Edward H. Fletcher, 1851.
Morgan, Philip D., and Jack P. Greene. *Atlantic History: A Critical Appraisal. Reinterpreting History*. Oxford: Oxford University Press, 2009.
Morison, John. *The Fathers and Founders of the London Missionary Society: A Jubilee Memorial, Including a Sketch of the Origin and Progress of the Institution*. London: Fisher, Son & Co., 1844.
Mullin, Robert Bruce, and Russell E. Richey, eds. *Reimagining Denominationalism: Interpretive Essays*. Religion in America Series. New York: Oxford University Press, 1994.
Murch, James Deforest. *Christians Only: A History of the Restoration Movement*. Cincinnati: Standard Publishing Company, 1962.
Murdoch, Steve, and Esther Mijers. "Migrant Destinations, 1500–1750." In *The Oxford Handbook of Modern Scottish History*, edited by T. M. Devine and Jenny Wormald. Oxford Handbooks. Oxford: Oxford University Press, 2012. Accessed June 11, 2014. www.oxfordhandbooks.com.
Neill, Stephen. *A History of Christian Missions*. 2nd ed. The Penguin History of the Church 6. London: Penguin Books, 1986.
Noll, Mark A. *America's God: From Jonathan Edwards to Abraham Lincoln*. Oxford: Oxford University Press, 2002.
———. *A History of Christianity in the United States and Canada*. Grand Rapids: Eerdmans, 1992.
———. *The Rise of Evangelicalism: The Age of Edwards, Whitefield, and the Wesleys*. A History of Evangelicalism 1. Downers Grove: InterVarsity Press, 2003.
Noll, Mark A., D. W. Bebbington, and George A. Rawlyk, eds. *Evangelicalism: Comparative Studies of Popular Protestantism in North America, the British Isles, and Beyond 1700–1900*. New York: Oxford University Press, 1994.
O'Brien, Susan. "Eighteenth-Century Publishing Networks in the First Years of Transatlantic Evangelicalism." In *Evangelicalism: Comparative Studies of Popular Protestantism in North America, the British Isles, and Beyond 1700–1990*, edited by Mark A. Noll, D. W. Bebbington, and George A. Rawlyk, 38–57. New York: Oxford University Press, 1994.
———. "Study of the First Evangelical Magazines, 1740–1748." *Journal of Ecclesiastical History* 27, no. 3 (1976): 255–75.
———. "A Transatlantic Community of Saints: The Great Awakening and the First Evangelical Network, 1735–1755." *The American Historical Review* 91, no. 4 (1986): 811–32.
Olbricht, Thomas H. "Hermeneutics and the *Declaration and Address*." In *The Quest for Christian Unity, Peace, and Purity in Thomas Campbell's Declaration and Address: Text and Studies*, edited by Thomas H. Olbricht and Hans Rollmann, 243–267. ATLA Monograph Series 46. Lanham: Scarecrow Press, 2000.

———. "Missions and Evangelization Prior to 1848." *Discipliana* 58, no. 3 (Fall 1998): 67-79.

Orchard, Stephen. "Evangelical Eschatology and the Missionary Awakening." *Journal of Religious History* 22, no. 2 (1998): 132-51.

Pals, Daniel L. *Seven Theories of Religion.* New York: Oxford University Press, 1996.

Philip, Robert. *The Life, Times, and Missionary Enterprises of the Rev. John Campbell.* London: John Snow, 1841.

Phillips, Richard. "Thomas Campbell: A Reappraisal Based on Backgrounds." *Restoration Quarterly* 49, no. 2 (2007): 75-102.

Piggin, Stuart. "The Expanding Knowledge of God: Jonathan Edwards's Influence on Missionary Thinking and Promotion." In *Jonathan Edwards at Home and Abroad: Historical Memories, Cultural Movements, Global Horizons,* edited by David William Kling and Douglas A. Sweeney, 266-96. Columbia: University of South Carolina Press, 2003.

Porter, Andrew. "Church History, History of Christianity, Religious History: Some Reflections on British Missionary Enterprise since the Late Eighteenth Century." *Church History* 71, no. 3 (2002): 555-84.

Priest, Doug. *Unto the Uttermost: Missions in the Christian Churches/Churches of Christ.* Pasadena: William Carey Library, 1984.

Ranelagh, John O'Beirne. *A Short History of Ireland.* 3rd ed. Cambridge: Cambridge University Press, 2012.

Reid, James Seaton, and W. D. Killen. *History of the Presbyterian Church in Ireland: Comprising the Civil History of the Province of Ulster, from the Accession of James the First.* New ed. 3 vols. Belfast: William Mullan, Donegall Place, 1867.

Richardson, Robert. *Memoirs of Alexander Campbell: Embracing A View of the Origin, Progress and Principles of the Religious Reformation Which He Advocated.* 2 vols. Cincinnati: Standard Publishing Company, 1890.

Richardson, William J. "Alexander Campbell's Conception of Mission." In *Unto the Uttermost: Missions in the Christian Churches/Churches of Christ,* edited by Doug Priest, 95-115. Pasadena: William Carey Library, 1984.

Robert, Dana Lee. *Christian Mission: How Christianity Became a World Religion.* Chichester: Wiley-Blackwell, 2009.

———. "Introduction." In *Converting Colonialism: Visions and Realities in Mission History, 1706-1914,* edited by Dana Lee Robert, 1-20. Studies in the History of Christian Missions. Grand Rapids: Eerdmans, 2008.

Rogers, Richard Lee. "'A Bright and New Constellation': Millennial Narratives and the Origins of American Foreign Missions." In *North American Foreign Missions, 1810-1914: Theology, Theory, and Policy,* edited by Wilbert R. Shenk, 39-60. Studies in the History of Christian Missions. Grand Rapids: Eerdmans, 2004.

Rollmann, Hans. "The Eschatology of the *Declaration and Address*." In *The Quest for Christian Unity, Peace, and Purity in Thomas Campbell's Declaration and Address: Text and Studies*, edited by Thomas H. Olbricht and Hans Rollmann, 341–63. ATLA Monograph Series 46. Lanham: Scarecrow Press, 2000.

Rouse, Ruth. "Voluntary Movement and the Changing Ecumenical Climate." In *A History of the Ecumenical Movement, 1517–1948*, edited by Ruth Rouse and Stephen Charles Neill, 309–52. 3rd ed. Geneva: World Council of Churches, 1986.

———. "William Carey's Pleasing Dream." *International Review of Mission* 38, no. 2 (1949): 181–92.

Roxborough, John. *Thomas Chalmers, Enthusiast for Mission: The Christian Good of Scotland and the Rise of the Missionary Movement*. Rutherford Studies in Historical Theology. Edinburgh: published for Rutherford House by Paternoster Press, 1999.

Schmidt, Leigh Eric. *Holy Fairs: Scotland and the Making of American Revivalism*. 2nd ed. Grand Rapids: Eerdmans, 2001.

Scott, Alfred Russell. "Thomas Campbell's Ministry at Ahorey." *Restoration Quarterly* 29, no. 4 (1987): 229–34.

Sensbach, Jon F. *Rebecca's Revival: Creating Black Christianity in the Atlantic World*. Harvard University Press, 2005.

Shantz, Douglas H. *An Introduction to German Pietism: Protestant Renewal at the Dawn of Modern Europe*. Baltimore: Johns Hopkins University Press, 2013.

Shenk, Wilbert R. *Changing Frontiers of Mission*. American Society of Missiology Series 28. Maryknoll: Orbis Books, 1999.

———. "Introduction." In *North American Foreign Missions, 1810–1914: Theology, Theory, and Policy*, edited by Wilbert R. Shenk, 1–8. Studies in the History of Christian Missions. Grand Rapids: Eerdmans, 2004.

Shurden, Walter B. "The Authority of a Baptist Association." *Baptist History and Heritage* 40, no. 1 (2005): 6–7.

Singh, Brij Raj. "'One Soul, Tho' Not One Soyl'? International Protestantism and Ecumenism at the Beginning of the Eighteenth Century." *Studies in Eighteenth Century Culture* 31 (January 2002): 61–84.

———. *The First Protestant Missionary to India: Bartholomaeus Ziegenbalg, 1683–1719*. New Delhi: Oxford University Press, 1999.

Smith, John Howard. *The Perfect Rule of the Christian Religion: A History of Sandemanianism in the Eighteenth Century*. Albany: State University of New York Press, 2008.

Smith, L. Thomas. "Thomas Campbell's Midlife Crisis: A Biographical Introduction and Historiographical Synthesis." *Stone-Campbell Journal* 14, no. 1 (2011): 3–19.

Schmidt, Martin. "Ecumenical Activity on the Continent of Europe in the Seventeenth and Eighteenth Centuries." In *A History of the Ecumenical Movement, 1517–1948*, edited by Ruth Rouse and Stephen Charles Neill, 73–122. 3rd ed. Geneva: World Council of Churches, 1986.

Smith, Mary Agnes Monroe. "A History of the Mahoning Baptist Association." Master's thesis, West Virginia University, 1943.

Stanley, Brian. "Christian Missions and the Enlightenment: A Reevaluation." In *Christian Missions and the Enlightenment*, edited by Brian Stanley, 1–21. Grand Rapids: Eerdmans, 2001.

———. *The Global Diffusion of Evangelicalism: The Age of Graham and Stott*. Downers Grove: InterVarsity Press, 2004.

———. *The History of the Baptist Missionary Society, 1792–1992*. Edinburgh: T&T Clark, 1992.

Stark, Rodney. *What Americans Really Believe: New Findings from the Baylor Surveys of Religion*. Waco: Baylor University Press, 2008.

Staunton, Michael. *The Voice of the Irish: The Story of Christian Ireland*. Mahwah: HiddenSpring, 2003.

Stewart, David. *The Seceders in Ireland: With Annals of Their Congregations*. Belfast: Presbyterian Historical Society, 1950.

Sweeney, Douglas A. *The American Evangelical Story: A History of the Movement*. Grand Rapids: Baker Academic, 2005.

Sykes, Norman. "Ecumenical Movements in Great Britain in the Seventeenth and Eighteenth Centuries." In *A History of the Ecumenical Movement, 1517–1948*, edited by Ruth Rouse and Stephen Charles Neill, 123–70. 3rd ed. Geneva: World Council of Churches, 1986.

Thomas, Norman E. *Missions and Unity: Lessons from History, 1792–2010*. American Society of Missiology 47. Eugene: Cascade Books, 2010.

Thompson, David M. *Let Sects and Parties Fall: A Short History of the Association of Churches of Christ in Great Britain and Ireland*. Birmingham: Berean Press, 1980.

———. "The Irish Background to Thomas Campbell's *Declaration and Address*." *Journal of the United Reformed Church History Society* 3, no. 6 (1985): 215–25.

———. "The Irish Background to Thomas Campbell's *Declaration and Address*." *Discipliana* 46 (1986): 23–27.

Thompson, Joseph. "The Evangelical Society of Ulster." *The Bulletin of the Presbyterian Historical Society of Ireland*, no. 17 (March 1988): 1–29.

Thuesen, Peter Johannes. *Predestination: The American Career of a Contentious Doctrine*. Oxford: Oxford University Press, 2009.

Tristano, Richard. *The Origins of the Restoration Movement: An Intellectual History*. Atlanta: Glenmary Research Center, 1988. Accessed April 29, 2014. http://www.seenow.net/beavercreek/media/Tristano_Restoration-Movement.pdf.

Turner, Frederick Jackson. "The Significance of the Frontier in American History." In *The Frontier in American History*, 1–38. New York: Henry Holt and Company, 1921.
Tyrrell, Ian. "Reflections on the Transnational Turn in United States History: Theory and Practice." *Journal of Global History* 4, no. 3 (2009): 453–74.
———. *Transnational Nation: United States History in Global Perspective since 1789*. New York: Palgrave Macmillan, 2007.
Van den Berg, Johannes. *Constrained by Jesus' Love: An Inquiry into the Motives of the Missionary Awakening in Great Britain in the Period between 1698 and 1815*. Kampen: J. H. Kok, 1956.
Van der Veer, Peter, ed. *Conversion to Modernities: The Globalization of Christianity*. New York: Routledge, 1996.
Van Dusen, Henry P. *One Great Ground of Hope: Christian Missions and Christian Unity*. Philadelphia: Westminster Press, 1961.
Wakeley, Joseph Beaumont. *Anecdotes of the Rev. George Whitefield, M.A., with Biographical Sketch*. London: Hodder and Stoughton, 1872.
Walls, Andrew F. "The Eighteenth-Century Protestant Missionary Awakening in Its European Context." In *Christian Missions and the Enlightenment*, edited by Brian Stanley, 22–44. Grand Rapids: Eerdmans, 2001.
———. "The Evangelical Revival, the Missionary Movement, and Africa." In *The Missionary Movement in Christian History: Studies in the Transmission of Faith*, 79–101. Maryknoll: Orbis Books, 1996.
———. "Missionary Societies and the Fortunate Subversion of the Church." *Evangelical Quarterly* 88, no. 2 (1988): 141–55.
———. "Missions and Historical Memory: Jonathan Edwards and David Brainerd." In *Jonathan Edwards at Home and Abroad: Historical Memories, Cultural Movements, Global Horizons*, edited by David William Kling and Douglas A. Sweeney, 248–65. Columbia: University of South Carolina Press, 2003.
———. "Romans One and the Modern Missionary Movement." In *The Missionary Movement in Christian History: Studies in the Transmission of Faith*, 55–67. Maryknoll: Orbis Books, 1996.
Wamble, Hugh. "Beginning of Associationalism Among English Baptists." *Review & Expositor* 54, no. 4 (October 1957): 544–59.
Ward, W. R. "Evangelical Awakenings in the North Atlantic World." In *The Cambridge History of Christianity: Volume VII, Enlightenment, Reawakening and Revolution 1660–1815*, edited by Stewart J. Brown and Timothy Tackett, 329–47. Cambridge: Cambridge University Press, 2006.
———. "Enlightenment in Early Moravianism." In *Faith and Faction*, 95–111. London: Epworth Press, 1993.
Weaver, C. Douglas. *In Search of the New Testament Church: The Baptist Story*. Macon: Mercer University Press, 2008.

Webb, Henry. "A History of the Independent Mission Movement of the Disciples of Christ." PhD diss., Southern Baptist Theological Seminary, 1954.

West, Earl Irvin. *The Search for the Ancient Order: A History of the Restoration Movement*. Vol. 1. 4 vols. Nashville: Gospel Advocate Company, 1949.

Williams, David Newell. *Barton Stone: A Spiritual Biography*. St. Louis: Chalice Press, 2000.

———. "The Theology of the Great Revival in the West as Seen Through the Life and Thought of Barton Warren Stone." PhD diss., Vanderbilt University, 1979.

Williams, David Newell, Douglas A. Foster, and Paul M. Blowers, eds. *The Stone-Campbell Movement: A Global History*. St. Louis: Chalice Press, 2013.

Witherow, Thomas. *Historical and Literary Memorials of Presbyterianism in Ireland*. London: William Mullan and Son, 1880.

Wolffe, John. *The Expansion of Evangelicalism: The Age of Wilberforce, More, Chalmers and Finney*. A History of Evangelicalism 2. Downers Grove: InterVarsity Press, 2007.

Wrather, Eva Jean. *Alexander Campbell: Adventurer In Freedom: A Literary Biography*, edited by D. Duane Cummins. Vol. 1. 3 vols. Fort Worth: Texas Christian University Press and the Disciples of Christ Historical Society, 2005.

Wuthnow, Robert. *The Restructuring of American Religion: Society and Faith Since World War II*. Princeton: Princeton University Press, 1988.

Yoder, Don Herbert. "Christian Unity in Nineteenth-Century America." In *A History of the Ecumenical Movement, 1517–1948*, edited by Ruth Rouse and Stephen Charles Neill, 221–62. 3rd ed. Geneva: World Council of Churches, 1986.

www.ingramcontent.com/pod-product-compliance
Lightning Source LLC
Chambersburg PA
CBHW020107020526
44112CB00033B/1082